Self and Identity

Personal, Social, and Symbolic

Self and Identity
Personal, Social, and Symbolic

Edited by

Yoshihisa Kashima
University of Melbourne

Margaret Foddy
Michael J. Platow
La Trobe University

2002

LAWRENCE ERLBAUM ASSOCIATES, PUBLISHERS
Mahwah, New Jersey   London

Lawrence Erlbaum Associates, Inc., Publishers
10 Industrial Avenue
Mahwah, New Jersey 07430

Cover design by Kathryn Houghtaling Lacey

Library of Congress Cataloging-in-Publication Data

Self and identity : Personal, social, and symbolic / edited by Yoshihisa Kashima, Margaret Foddy,
Michael J. Platow.
    p. cm.
   Includes bibliographical references and indexes.
   ISBN 0-8058-3683-7 (cloth : alk. paper) – ISBN 0-8058-3684-5 (pbk. : alk. paper)
   1. Self—Congresses. 2. Self—Social aspects—Congresses. 3. Identity
   (Psychology)—Congresses. 4. Identity (Psychology)—Social aspects—Congresses. I.
   Kashima, Yoshihisa, 1957- II. Foddy, Margaret. III. Platow, Michael J.

BF697 .S4227 2002
155.2—dc21

                                        2001053216

Books published by Lawrence Erlbaum Associates are printed on acid-free paper,
and their bindings are chosen for strength and durability.

Contents

Preface

The phenomenon of selfhood poses dual problems for social psychology. On the one hand, social psychology investigates the phenomenon of self. Humans can conceptualize themselves and construct their self-conceptions because of their symbolic and self-reflective capacity. Once constructed, self-conceptions influence social psychological processes in the future. Humans are self-constitutive beings by virtue of their self-reflexivity. On the other hand, social psychology also provides conceptions of the person, which in part constitute the phenomenon of self. Social psychology as a research enterprise aims to construct theories of the person as a being that is evolutionarily, sociohistorically, and deveopmentally constituted. In this way, social psychology participates in a sociohistorical process by providing conceptions of the person, which may in turn be appropriated by people for the construction of their own self-conceptions. Thus, social psychology is a discipline that both investigates and provides self-conceptions.

At the beginning of the new millennium, the social psychology of self and identity is at a crossroads. Social psychology has seen a great surge of interest in self-processes with the advent of a social-cognitive theory of the self in the last two decades. Equipped with the serial computer metaphor of the mind as a universal symbol processor, it has produced a voluminous literature. At a metatheoretical level, the all powerful central processing unit (CPI), which creates, stores, and manipulates symbols, provided a conceptual device that has enabled social psychologists to investigate the inherently intrapersonal aspect of self-processes, involving memory and inference. At the same time, the CPU may have acted as a metaphor of the asocial self that is always and completely in charge, thus providing a conception of the self as the "totalitarian ego" (as Greenwald, 1980, put it). However, in recent times, a number of metatheoretical and theoretical perspectives of selfhood have emerged that have significantly amended this social-cognitive theory of the self.

This volume outlines the current metatheoretical (Part I) and theoretical (Parts II-IV) contexts of self-research, and points to new directions by collecting chapters written by researchers who are contributing to this newly emerging diversity. Although a reflective soul-searching is not the common mode for social psychology, we believe it important to make explicit the underlying metatheoretical assumption of our research enterprise, which are often implicit and sometimes even hidden. When they remain implicit, research programs may be hampered by unrecognized internal contradictions, which may lead to irreconcilable predictions and expectations, persistent unresolvable puzzles, and paradoxes (e.g., multiple vs. unified self). Further, without explicating assumptions, miscommunication about theory and research is more likely. Finally, when it turns out that we can agree on assumptions, this provides some basis for thinking we may be approaching closer to some kind of truth.

A number of theoretical perspectives of selfhood have recently emerged, significantly revising the image of the self previously dominated by the metaphor of the omnipotent CPU. In agreement with a number of social theorists (e.g., Geertz, 1973; Giddens, 1979; Parsons, 1951), we take a tripartite view of the sociohistorical process, which analytically differentiates personal, social, and symbolic aspects. Although the analytical separation between personal and social processes is customary, the addition of a symbolic aspect is perhaps new in social psychology. In social interaction, there are aspects that are primarily personal to the interactants (Part II), as well as the primarily social ones that transpire between the interactants (Part III). A number of psychological concepts turn on this distinction between the personal and the social: for instance, internal versus external, private versus public, and individual versus social. However, human social interaction is not just any kind of interaction, but meaningful interaction among people (Part IV). Meanings are embedded in public symbols that are shared by people, and transmitted from one generation to the next. It is those symbolic aspects that make human social interaction peculiarly human.

In editing this book, in addition to presenting some new possibilities for theory and research about self and identity, our intention was to raise real and difficult questions. The book arose out of a recent conference on self and identity, which was held at La Trobe University, Melbourne, Australia, with support from the Australian Research Council. Our strategy was to invite speakers with divergent perspectives in the hope that, by bringing together and juxtaposing these views, we might be able to sharpen the contrasts among them, and to make explicit both metatheoretical and theoretical differences. To this end, we provided an earlier version of chapter 1 to the contributors to this volume. As should be evident in the following chapters, they positioned themselves very differently relative to what we took to be the prevailing assumptions of the current literature on self and identity. We highlight these differential positionings in our introductory remarks to each section. Whether their perspectives are reconcilable or irreconcilable remains to be seen. In the end, research on self and identity is an open project.

REFERENCES

Geertz, C. (1973). *The interpretation of cultures.* New York: Basic Books.
Giddens, A. (1979). *Central problems in social theory.* London: Macmillan.
Greenwald, A. G. (1980). The totalitarian ego: Fabrication and revision of personal history. *American Psychologist, 35,* 603-618.
Parsons, T. (1951), *The social system.* London: Routledge.

THEORIES OF THE MIND

Part I addresses two metatheoretical perspectives on the self. One takes the metatheory of serial information processing driven by the central processing Unit (CPU) as a theory of the mind. By contrast, the other is the parallel distributed processing (PDP) metatheory, which regards psychological processes as emerging from interaction among a large number of simple processing units. On the one hand, theories of the mind provide different conceptions of the person, that is, what people and their minds are like. These conceptions of the person can enter into everyday discourse about the self, shaping people's self-conceptions. This is the sense in which social psychology *provides* self-conceptions. On the other hand, theories of the mind provide theoretical frameworks in which to *investigate* self-related phenomena. They both enable and constrain the kind of conceptions of the self that could be developed.

Then, what implications would the CPU and PDP metaphors of the mind have for self-conceptions? Chapter 1 (Foddy and Kashima) provides a background for the book by delineating the core assumptions embedded in what we have called the social cognitive theory of the self, which primarily takes the CPU metaphor of the mind. In this view, the mind that is in control provides a unitary conception of the person. Although this model provides many advantages, it has its own limitations, as discussed in the chapter. In contrast, chapter 2 (Humphreys and Kashima) describes an emerging alternative theory of the mind in the form of connectionism and parallel distributed processing, and discusses its implications for conceptions of the self. The image of the mind presented here is one in which no single entity is in charge, but in which multiple processes continue in parallel. It has strong conceptual affinities with some of the perspectives on the self that are presented in subsequent sections. Although this model may provide some solutions to the puzzles of the unitary self (as discussed in the chapter), it does not deal in a satisfactory way as yet with the issue of control and agency. Its implications for social psychology of self and identity are only beginning to be explored.

Chapter 1

Self and Identity: What Is the Conception of the Person Assumed in the Current Literature?

Margaret Foddy
La Trobe University

Yoshihisa Kashima
University of Melbourne

The topic of self and identity has had its vicissitudes. In the mid-20th century, social psychological research on this topic was almost nonexistent. In fact, in the 1960s, it was declared that the self "looked as dead as a dodo bird" (Pepitone, 1968, p. 347). Nonetheless, in the 1970s, a number of concepts and topics appeared that bore the prefix of "self" in social psychology: self-efficacy, self-monitoring, self-schema, self-consciousness, self-theory, and so on (see Kashima & Yamaguchi, 1999). The 1980s and 1990s saw an explosion of research on self and identity (for recent reviews, see Baumeister, 1998; Tyler, Kramer, & John, 1999). Despite its diversity, the current social psychological research on self and identity has a more or less coherent set of theoretical and methodological assumptions. Rather than reviewing the extensive literature, we present in this chapter what we take to be a set of core assumptions of a research program or research tradition (i.e., Berger & Zelditch, 1993; Lakatos, 1970; Laudan, 1977). Our claim is that this research tradition rests on a set of substantive, if implicit, propositions about what it means to be human, which amount to a particular conception of the person.

This conception of the person is one of an abstract individual, as defined by Lukes (1973, p. 73) as follows:

> Individuals are pictured abstractly as given, with given interests, wants, purposes, needs, etc.; while society and the state are pictured as sets of actual or possible social arrangements which respond more or less adequately to those individuals' requirements. Social and political rules and institutions

are, on this view, regarded collectively as an artifice, a modifiable instrument, a means of fulfilling independently given individual objectives; the means and the ends are distinct. The crucial point about this conception is that the relevant features of individuals determining the ends which social arrangements are held (actually or ideally) to fulfill, whether these features are called instruments, faculties, needs, desires, rights, etc., are assumed as given, independently of a social context. This givenness of fixed and invariant human psychological features leads to an *abstract* [emphasis in the original] conception of the individual.

More than two decades ago, Smith (1978/1991) foresaw that there are three perspectives from which the experience of self and identity may be approached: evolutionary, cultural–historical, and developmental. Indeed, the subsequent literature on self and identity generally followed them. Adding two more to these three, we identify five significant areas for scientific inquiry into self and identity: metatheory of the mind, ontogenesis of the self, self in sociocultural context, self and evolution, and epistemological and methodological issues. We examine core assumptions that characterize the conception of the person underlying the current inquiry into self and identity in each area.

To give a brief outline, first, a human is assumed to be equipped with a mind that is a limited-capacity, universal mechanism of symbol processing and cybernetic control, with the capacity for feeling and desire. Second, from a life-span perspective, self-conceptions are seen to develop through stages not unlike that of general cognitive development, displaying an increase in level of complexity and abstraction, which allow the eventual emergence of an autonomous, self-regulating agent. Third, the resultant self-regulating agent does not operate in a vacuum, but rather is suspended in a web of interpersonal, intergroup, collective and institutional relationships. Fourth, the current social cognitive conception of the person assumes that Darwinian evolutionary processes have affected *Homo sapiens*, a species born with the potential to develop a self-reflective mind. Finally, we turn to a set of methodological assumptions that underlie the theories and findings discussed in the four areas of research on self and identity.

In the end, our claim is this: Despite the current literature's recognition of the social embedding of self and identity, the abstract and independent individual is still a dominant image of the person in much of the social psychological literature of self and identity. Let us see how this is the case.

CORE ASSUMPTION 1: SELF IN THE MIND

There is a model of the mind taken for granted in the current literature on self and identity. It is a mixture of an information processing model based on the serial computer metaphor, and a cybernetic theory of self-

regulation. Nevertheless, the model has gone beyond the typical information processing theory in two significant ways. One is its clear recognition
of the human capacity for self-awareness, and the other is the inclusion of
affect and motivation as integral to human mental processes. Let us explicate these points.

Architecture of the Mind. The architectural core of the mind is assumed to be a *symbol processor*, which creates, manipulates, stores, and re-
trieves various symbols, very much in line with Newell's physical symbol
hypothesis (Newell & Simon, 1990, 1995; see Kihlstrom & Klein, 1994). In
the serial computer metaphor, the symbol processor is often called the
central processing unit (CPU). A personal computer typically has one
CPU, which creates and manipulates symbol tokens; the creation and
transformation of symbol tokens can be conceptualized as a kind of formal
computation based on clearly defined rules (e.g., computer languages).
Without the CPU, no computation occurs. The serial computer metaphor
of the mind regards the creation and transformation of symbols by the
CPU as thought processes.

In addition, the mind is assumed to have a capacity for cybernetic control; that is, it is equipped with a mechanism for self-regulation. This
mechanism is usually assumed to involve the processes of setting an evaluation criterion, observing the current state relative to the criterion, and
computing the discrepancy between the criterion and the current state.
Once a discrepancy is detected between the criterion and the current state,
procedures are executed to decrease the discrepancy (e.g., Carver &
Scheier, 1981; Higgins, 1987). The choice of language to represent the
underlying architecture (*processor, procedures, regulation,* etc.) reveals much
about the nature of the organism assumed.

Despite the diversity in theorizing, the mind is generally assumed to
have several common features. First, its symbol processor is a limited-
capacity processor: Both attention and memory are understood to be relatively limited resources. Second, symbol tokens need to be both available
and accessed to be involved in any psychological activities, although people may or may not be aware of that which is accessed. General cognitive
principles govern availability, and thus accessibility, of symbols. Third, accessed symbol tokens must be in some way relevant to the task at hand in
order for them to have any effects on psychological activities.

This mind acquires symbols or contents from its natural, social and cultural environment, and then executes a set of universal procedures or
processes on those acquired contents. The content–process distinction
roughly corresponds to the distinction between Ryle's (1963) "knowing
that" and "knowing how," or declarative and procedural knowledge, in
the serial computer metaphor of the mind. However, the demarcation line

between process and content is rather unclear and in fact fairly labile. One gains the impression that social cognitive theorists assume the universality of processes, while acknowledging cross-cultural variability of contents, suggesting that content is a fairly arbitrary detail that does not substantially influence process.

Self-Awareness. Nevertheless, one aspect of this mind goes beyond the standard information-processing theory in its clear recognition of the human capacity for self-awareness. Note that the distinction between the self-as-subject and the self-as-object of awareness, the duality of the self that James and Mead identified as the *I* and the *Me* (James, 1890/1950; Mead, 1934), presupposes the capacity that *I* is capable of observing *Me*, a clear recognition of self-awareness. Although the mechanisms enabling humans to achieve this feat are still not well understood, social psychological research is assumed to be able to proceed without waiting for an answer to this question.

The social psychological literature on self and identity began as an inquiry into the Me, the self-as-object, and the mental representation of the self as a network of semantic memory (e.g., Kihlstrom & Cantor, 1984), a prototype (e.g., Kuiper, 1981), or a schema (e.g., Markus, 1977). Nonetheless, as Hermans (1996) noted, the self-as-object in the current social cognitive literature is not a unitary entity, but multifaceted. At the very least, it may consist of multiple attributes, and at most it could be a story (Gergen & Gergen, 1988; Sarbin, 1990) or even a theory (Epstein, 1973). The self-as-object could be visually represented or measured (e.g., Dollinger's autophotographic method: Clancy & Dollinger, 1993; Dollinger, Preston, O'Brien, & DiLalla, 1996; Aron and Aron's circles: Aron, Aron, & Smollan, 1992). Whatever form they may take (semantic memory, prototype, or schema), they are nonetheless all symbols in that they represent (or stand for) the self. Symbolic representations of the self are assumed to be significant contents of the mind.

Affect and Motivation. The mind assumed in social psychological research of self and identity departs from the standard information processing model in its inclusion of affect and motivation. That is, not only does the social cognitive mind process symbols, but it is also capable of having feelings and desires. The underlying model here is a tripartite model of the mind, which has been a long-standing working model for social psychology since the early days of attitude research (e.g., Katz & Stotland, 1959; Rosenberg & Hovland, 1960). Nonetheless, the current literature has gone beyond the classical tripartite model by empirically examining the causal relationships between affect and motivation on the one hand and cognition on the other.

Regarding the effect of cognition on affect, symbolic representations of the self play a major role. A primary example is Higgins's self-discrepancy theory (1987), a theory representative of the work in this area. It views the discrepancies between the representations of actual self on the one hand, and those of ought and ideal self (which are called self guides) on the other, as determinants of different types of affective states such as anxiety and dejection. Affective states for Higgins appear as by-products of the cognitive mechanism's cybernetic control. Presumably, self-discrepancies may be assessed at the time, or the results of a past self-discrepancy assessment may be stored in memory. This causal account of the origin of emotions does not necessarily imply that emotions are under direct cognitive control, but rather that they arise out of self states in relation to self guides.

Affect can influence self-cognitions as well. For example, Sedikides (1995) used Forgas's (1995) affect infusion model (AIM) to hypothesize that the effects of mood should be greater for peripheral self-conceptions than for central self-conceptions. Those characteristics that people were certain that they had were called *central self-conceptions*; characteristics about whose self-descriptiveness they were less certain were called *peripheral self-conceptions*. Consistent with the hypothesis, Sedikides showed that mood congruence effects were stronger for peripheral self-conceptions than for central ones. In particular, judgments about the self became more positive under a positive mood and more negative under a negative mood for those aspects of the self about which the participants were less certain, but this effect was much attenuated for the self-aspects that were central to the participants' senses of themselves.

Motivation and self-cognitions also influence each other. The effects of self-cognitions on motivations are clearly recognized in Higgins's self-discrepancy theory. The discrepancy between the actual self and the ought or ideal self, when activated, can motivate people to decrease the discrepancy. Again within this theoretical framework, motivation is a by-product of self-cognitions. When these discrepancies are accessed, they act as a motivator. The effects of motivation on self-cognitions have been examined as well. For instance, Kunda and Sanitioso (1989) showed that when graduate and undergraduate students were told that either an extravert or introvert was more likely to succeed or fail in two experiments, the students described themselves as more in terms of the characteristic that promoted success or avoided failure. The authors explained this finding in terms of the symbol processor's recruitment of self-relevant cognitions as motivated by a desire for self-enhancement, and these effects in the end produce the motivational effects on self-conceptions. This conclusion holds whether one believes that the self-description was a self-presentation or a self-representation.

Functional Analysis. In the prevailing view, then, self and identity consist of symbols processed by the mind, not importantly different from any other symbols. Both motivation and affect influence our self-conceptions through symbol processing activities. Higgins's (1996) concept of the "self-digest" provides a succinct summary of the current thinking that incorporates many of these elements. The digest

> summarizes a body of information, especially contingency rules and conclusions. A digest serves regulatory functions. The notion of a self-digest is meant to capture the idea that self-knowledge summarizes information about oneself in the world in order to serve self-regulatory functions. The notion of a self-digest, then, is intended to highlight a new conceptualization of the nature of self-knowledge—a summary of what the world is like in relation to oneself. (p. 1063)

As with many other theorists in the social-cognitive tradition, Higgins suggested that the cognitive properties of self-representations are not different from representations of any other objects. Further, the mechanism by which actual selves are perceived and judged in relation to self-guides is not altered by the nature of the events. However, Higgins (1996, p. 1063) insisted that self-knowledge differs in its functional significance—it is the only object in the world that one must regulate in order to survive. To Higgins, the self-digest is a "tool for survival" of the individual organism. The cybernetic metaphor comes through clearly in the self-organizing, self-monitoring person suggested by Higgins's model.

A Hidden Assumption. Most theories of self and identity deal with the nature and with the cognitive, affective, and motivational antecedents and consequences of self-representations. Nevertheless, a question arises quite naturally with regard to these self-representations. That is, who is the constructor of those self-representations? The constructor of a self-representation appears to be able to choose and to alter its symbolic contents. Furthermore, once constructed, there must be a mechanism that selects out a self-representation and deploys it in the process of symbol manipulations. Indeed, this is the question of *the self as subject*, as James put it about a century ago.

The literature seems to provide two possible responses to this question. A first response is to assign the cybernetic self-regulatory mechanism the role of the constructor of self-representations. In this view, one may assume that there is a goal state that requires the mechanism to describe itself. Wherever this goal state comes from, once it is there, the regulatory mechanism will try to reduce the difference between the goal state and the current state of the system. This should result in the construction of a self-representation. Once a self-representation is constructed, another goal state may be placed, which requires that this self-representation be used in a certain way in psychological processes, and so forth. This way, the self-regulatory mechanism becomes the constructor and manipulator of self-representations. However, this answer puts the question only one step back. The question of who or what constructs self-representations is simply replaced by who or what constructs goal states. We need to find an answer elsewhere.

A second response to the question is to say that there is a mechanism that creates and manipulates self-representations. The only contender in the current literature seems to be the central processing unit. The all-powerful mechanism that puts together a self-representation as symbolic constructions and manipulates it while psychological processes continue to proceed seems to be the central processing unit or the CPU of the serial computer metaphor. To the extent that the CPU is a mechanism that is invariant, unaffected by the very symbols that it processes, the conception of the self-as-subject hidden in the current social psychological literature of self and identity is one of the abstract individual, which is at once an autonomous creator and manipulator of the symbolic contents, including the representations of itself.

In summary, the core assumptions of the social cognitive model of self and identity are:

1a. The mind is a universal symbol processor with a cybernetic control system. Symbolic contents are acquired from the mind's environment, but its processes are universally invariant.
1b. The mind is capable of self-awareness.
1c. Although the social cognitive mind acknowledges affect and motivation, the universal symbol processor plays a major role in mediating causal relations between affect and cognition, and motivation and cognition.
1d. An individual's self-cognition increases the probability of survival of the individual.

Implications

How adequate is this model of the mind for further theorizing about self and identity? The idea of motivated cognition has been extended to cognition about the self, with the metaphor of the self as a regulatory tool. Despite the strong cybernetic metaphor, there is a clear assumption of the mind as an abstract and autonomous agent. The purpose of regulation is ostensibly "survival" but may also reflect cultural and social structural influences. As long as these influences are restricted to the content of the self, the model seems adequate. But what if goals (such as self-regulatory goals) and even the process of self-regulation itself are affected by social structural and cultural influences, in an ongoing way (e.g., Rose, 1989; 1996)? Does the focus on the individual as the source of regulation limit our ability to detect other systematic sources of control? And if this central feature of the model of the mind requires modification, what implications will this have for other key features of the model? A related question concerns the object of survival mechanisms: Is it the individual person? Or is it the group, the species, or similar larger unit? Can the current conception of the self deal with this issue?

CORE ASSUMPTION 2: ONTOGENESIS OF THE SELF

We have argued that the social cognitive conception of self as a subject assumes an abstract individual invariant across contexts and unchanged by the very symbols that it processes. In relation to the ontogenetic emergence of the self, too, a similar picture emerges. According to this assumption, the self develops through an interaction of biological maturation and a series of socialization experiences that, while cross-culturally variable, still provide the evoking conditions necessary for the emergence of the sense of an autonomous, continuous, and internalized self. Further, although socialization practices vary widely, they have their effects on the self-concept through a universal set of processes (e.g., providing evidence of consistency of certain kinds of behavior, systematic consensual validation, authoritative feedback about the self, provision of standards, etc.) Thus, the content of the self may vary across cultures, across social class, and across history, but the processes of self-concept formation are seen to be constant. Similarly, socialization experiences produce weaker or stronger degrees of agency, continuity, and distinctiveness, but these constructs are seen to be universally relevant.

Higgins's (1987, 1996) summary of the literature on self-development illustrates the core assumptions of self-development. Higgins suggested that the nature of the child's self-digest (i.e., a summary of the self in relation to the world) changes as a function of changes in its levels of mental representation (1996, p. 1064). Beginning with a simple capacity for learning preconceptual association between events (contingencies of own actions and events, especially responses from others), more complex representations become possible with the emergence of language and symbolic capacity, which allow representation of self and others as distinct "objects." This capacity also depends, in part, on the increasing capacity to simultaneously represent several dimensions and thus several points of view. Increasing ability to represent others, as well as self, forms the basis of anticipation of response contingencies, and of planful, goal-directed action, with reference to the likely responses of others, and the standards held by others. As the child matures, he or she can recognize the possibility of conflicting standards represented by various others, and develops internalized self-standards, which then form the basis for the self-discrepancies that Higgins argued are so central to motivation and affect. A central feature of Higgins's formulation is that representations of self and other become less contextualized, more abstract, and more autonomous, although they build on and remain connected to lower level representations. There is an implicit assumption that more concrete, contextualized forms of response are in some sense "regressive" and occur under stress, fatigue, and so on.

In Higgins's model, different socialization and disciplinary strategies have their impact through their effects on the direction and strength of "regulatory focus," as well as on the child's emerging capacity to represent self and others in increasingly complex and abstract ways. A major source of difference highlighted by Higgins is the relative predominance of socializers' focus on ideal, desired self to be approached (promotion focus), as compared with the "prudent" mode, which emphasizes avoidance of bad outcomes, meeting obligations, and avoidance of danger (prevention focus). Although not mentioned by Higgins, subcultural and cross-cultural differences in socialization practices may produce different distributions of self-digests, with different directions and strengths of self-regulatory focus.

Higgins's (1996) outline of the acquisition of the self, or self-digest, is consistent with earlier developmental psychologists' accounts of self-concept development (e.g., Coopersmith, 1967; Damon & Hart, 1986; Maccoby, 1980; Rosenberg, 1979; Selman, 1980). In these, development of the self is seen to follow the more general sequence of cognitive development. It is characterized by changes from the concrete to the abstract; from the undifferentiated to the differentiated; from single to multiple perspectives; and from a segmented and episodic, to a more integrated sense of the self. Consistent with the cognitive assumptions just outlined, there is a distinction between the self as subject (or agent) and the self as object (Damon & Hart, 1986). Systematic development occurs in both of these (e.g., increase in integration of the content of the self-concept; increase in sense of continuity, distinctiveness, and agency of the self as agent). Self-concept development is seen to rely heavily on language, which provides the possibility of symbolic self-representation. The child begins, then, as a simplified, incomplete, symbol processor.

Studies of cross-cultural differences in social structure and socialization practices suggest differences exist in the extent to which people end up with self-directed, autonomous self-concepts (e.g., Kashima et al., 1995;

Schooler, 1996). An implicit assumption is that it is more "mature" and "better" to be unique, self-governing, and consistent across situations; the developmental literature conveys a strong sense that separation of a self-regulating, consistent self is an important developmental task that must be mastered. This is echoed in theories of moral development, in which the capacity to abstract oneself from particularistic relationships is privileged. One should not find this surprising, given that developmental theorists come from the same cultural and theoretical context as do social cognitive theorists who have conceived the cybernetic metaphor for the self.

The core assumptions concerning the development of the self can be summarized thus:

2a. The self-concept of humans develops in a systematic and uniform sequence of stages, beginning with simple symbolic representations, and ending with an abstract, complex, and stable representation of self as an autonomous agent.

2b. The child's socialization/disciplinary environment facilitates or inhibits developmental changes; not all stages may be reached, and self-concepts will vary in accessibility and coherence.

2c. The nature of the child's relationship to the primary caregivers determines the internal standards and values against which the child judges self, and, consequently, level of esteem and approach to others.

Implications

The developmental assumptions about the self are quite consistent with the cognitive assumptions, including the distinction drawn between universal processes, and content. It remains to be seen whether this approach is adequate to deal with newer conceptualizations of self-development, which stress the importance of dynamic self-organization (Smith & Thelen, 1993; Thelen & Smith, 1994) and highly contextualized social activities (Rogoff, 1990). These latter views of development point to a wider array of outcomes than those envisaged in the linear developmental model. Further, the seemingly clear distinction between universal process and specific content becomes blurred when one considers the emergence of new structures and organizational principles.

Also problematic for the social cognitive view of development is how to conceive of the impact of social structure and culture. Socialization practices are related to social structure, position in the social structure, and culture (Morgan & Schwalbe, 1990; Schooler, 1996), and these in turn produce differences in the self-concept and in personality. It is difficult to think these differences are only minor, but the model of invariant universal development of the self-concept seems rather insensitive to social and cultural differences.

CORE ASSUMPTION 3: SELF IN SOCIAL CONTEXTS

Although the developmental model recognizes the central role of others in the formation of the self-concept, it also presupposes a clear separation of self from others. We argue that the social in the social cognitive inquiry into the self is *social* in a rather limited sense, and the image of the self that emerges out of this literature is still one of the abstract individual. To begin with, it is often assumed that the autonomous self distilled through socialization is represented abstractly, and is described in terms of dispositions (traits, attitudes, values), social identities (including roles, social categories, types), and physical attributes (Deaux, Reid, Mizrahi, & Ethier, 1995; Rosenberg, 1979). Central and important features of the self are held to be more readily accessible, and to exert more influence on behaviour. This is illustrated in research on self-schemas, as well as more sociologically derived studies of role identities.

Markus's highly cited study of self-schemas (Markus, 1977), for example, began with the assumption that people draw generalizations about their central, self-defining characteristics on the basis of regularities they observe in their own behavior. The inferred dispositions then determine information processing about the self, as well as future behavior. She utilized the dispositional continuum "independent-dependent" to provide evidence for the faster accessing of traits by people who rate themselves extremely on a trait, and consider it to be important. Schematic people were also able to recall more instances (tokens) of the attribute. This emphasis on traits is consistent with the overall voluntaristic model of persons with relatively stable characteristics, which they have in some sense "chosen."

Role identity theory (e.g., Stryker, 1987), although placing more emphasis on variability in the self across social settings, also suggests that people organize the self-concept around central or important role identities. Although some roles are ascribed (e.g., female), and others adopted, people choose to embrace some roles more completely than others (Turner, 1988). Roles higher in the person's hierarchy exert more influence over behavior. Once committed to a role identity, it acts as a cybernetic control system. The person strives to approximate role expectations and internalized identity standards, feels distress at discrepancies, and so on. Although role identity theory has not been systematically integrated with more cognitive approaches to the social self, it appears to share many assumptions with it.

It is clearly the case that this image of the autonomous, stable self epitomized by abstract and stable summary terms such as personality traits in role identities may be significantly offset by a widely accepted view of the social self that has been present since the writing of William James. It is the view that we have many "social selves," reflecting the differences in responses made to us by others who encounter us in a variety of social contexts, each of which may evoke from us a different range of behaviors, competencies, attitudes, and affect. In a similar vein, Higgins's self-discrepancy theory postulates that other individuals can be incorporated into self-cognitions as the provider of perspectives. That is, actual, ought, and ideal selves can be assessed from various viewpoints. These selves may be seen from the viewpoint of oneself, but may also reflect significant others' viewpoints. It should not be too surprising that Baumeister's recent review chapter on the self organizes the literature on the impact of social context under the heading "interpersonal being," with the self described as "essentially an interpersonal tool" (Baumeister, 1998, p. 22).

A further assumption of the social cognitive tradition is that perception of others and perception of self follow the same principles, as in various treatments of attribution principles (e.g., Bem, 1972). Others are characterized in terms of their stable traits, although there is an assumption that greater simplification occurs in the perception of others, except those others with whom one has extensive interaction (e.g., Andersen, Reznik, & Manzella, 1996). The exception occurs with others who are particularly close and significant. Some researchers have suggested ways of describing individuals in relation to others in terms of the degree of overlap of their self-concepts (e.g., Aron et al., 1992). Others have suggested that significant role others are included as part of, or extensions of, the self (e.g., Lancaster & Foddy, 1988; Rosenberg, 1979). It is also noteworthy that recent self researchers have emphasized that the social aspect of the self may be constructed not only in relation to other individuals, but also in relation to collectives. Social identity includes the self's social group memberships. Recent social cognitive approaches have been adopted to examine the symbolic representation of the self as a member of the group (Brewer & Gardner, 1996; Deaux et al., 1995; Reid & Deaux, 1996; Smith, 1978/1991; Trafimow, Triandis, & Goto, 1991). From this perspective, others, broadly conceptualized as individuals or groups, may be absorbed symbolically into the self.

Thus, the social context of a self is often framed in terms of self–other interpersonal relationships or self–group relationships, and the significance of the social is acknowledged. Still, more often than not, the image of the unitary, abstract, and autonomous self asserts itself in various forms. To put it differently, those "others" are more like the backdrop against which one's self-story is told, rather than an integral part of a thoroughly socialized and contextualized self. In fact, it may be the image of the autonomous self that seems to occupy more of the research attention in the area of the self in social context. For instance, in a recent survey of the literature, Baumeister (1998) devoted several pages to the question, "How are self views affected by others?"; a longer section detailed research on self-presentation, or "How are others' views of self influenced by self?" It is symptomatic of the image of the autonomous self that it is in charge and in control of the social contexts.

In theoretical and empirical terms, how does the image of the unitary, abstract, and autonomous self appear in the current literature of self and identity? First of all, while it is acknowledged that others are an essential source of self-knowledge and self-affirmation throughout life, this social influence is often seen to be regulated by the self (Sedikides & Skowronski; 1995). In particular, others are seen to provide confirmation and correction for this self that is projected. Where possible, people selectively interact with others who support the emergent self. Swann's (1987) work on identity negotiation and self-verification highlights this view of the self. Although superficially different in emphasis, Taylor and Brown (1988) also argued that a range of social cognitive biases serves to sustain a view of self as an internally directed agent who acts upon the social world to produce goal-related outcomes (see also Brown, 1998).

Furthermore, once formed, the self is often seen to strive to maintain a stable, and usually positive, set of abstract characteristics. The autonomous, abstract, stable self-representation provides a mechanism for organizing responses to others. This implies that a person will be alert to evidence of stable internal dispositions in the form of consistency across situations, across time, and across interaction partners. Granted, many traits that describe the self can only exist in social interaction with one or more others (e.g., cooperativeness, altruism, competitiveness, and nurturance are all traits that have no meaning outside the social context). Nevertheless, individuals are supposed to "possess" traits; this means they will express their traits across time, contexts, and interaction partners, if the term is to have any meaning at all.

Even if there may be some diverse aspects of the self that may arise from diverse social relationships, there still is an assumption that a continuous self exists that can integrate this diversity. As summarized by Knowles and Sibicky (1990), various explanatory metaphors have been offered to explain how unity emerges from multiple selves (e.g., the self-theory; the computer or information processor; the story plot; etc.). This type of theoretical construction is in line with the image of the unitary, abstract, and autonomous self in two ways. First, the unity provided by an integrative framework in itself portrays the self as a unified construct. Despite the apparent diversity, there is a deep structure that unifies, or so it is argued. Second, there is an assumed mental agent that constructs the unifying framework out of diversity.

Not much attention is given in the social cognitive perspective, to the broader question of the *source* of the array of traits and identities available to be incorporated into a given self. Culture and social structure determine in part the range of roles and relationships one has available, and those that receive the highest evaluation. These in turn influence the pattern of behaviors a given individual will exhibit, providing the informational basis for the inference of individual characteristics. Thus, a person excluded from any positions of authority is unlikely to develop a self-representation as powerful, authoritative, and so on. However, the model of the person as an autonomous agent in charge of his or her fate tends to move such external factors into the background. Class, gender, race, and religion, for example, may be recognized as ingredients (or contents) of an identity, but it is not part of the social cognitive theorists' mission to explain how these social structural variables condition and constrain the self. Perhaps these are left out as part of the distal, macro social structure, and are considered to belong to the intellectual and academic territory of sociology.

It is interesting to note, however, that at least some sociologists share the model of the autonomous self outlined earlier. For example, in a recent *Annual Review of Sociology* article, Schooler (1996) stated:

> Social-structural conditions associated with industrialization are linked to an increase in individuals' being open to new experience, rejecting traditional authority, and taking a rational, ambitious, and orderly approach to both work and human problems. . . . Self-directed work increases intellectual functioning and self-directed orientations. (p. 323)

Here, too, the autonomous self is seen as a desirable endpoint, the emergence of which is facilitated or hindered by the existing economic and social environment.

The core assumptions of the model of the social may be summarized thus:

3a. The model of the self in social contexts portrays a motivated cognitive miser. The individual depends on others for feedback about the self. However, once formed, the self relies on others to confirm a stable, and usually positive, set of characteristics.

3b. The individual actively chooses the attributes and identities that make up his or her self-concept.

3c. Despite the many facets of self that arise from varying relationships with others, there is an assumption that a continuous self exists that can integrate this diversity.

3d. The principles of social perception are same for perception of self and others, and incorporate universal rules for attribution of internal dispositions, responsibility, and blame.

3e. The self encounters the social largely through interpersonal relationships with specific significant others, although the nature of these interactions is influenced by role-related norms and expectations.

Implications

Because we are talking about psychology, it is not surprising that when the social nature of the self is theorized, only the proximal context of the social environment is considered. Despite increased awareness of the importance of large groups and shared category membership on an individual's behavior and self-perceptions (Brewer & Gardner, 1996; Oakes, Turner, & Haslam, 1994), the dominant image of the self-as-social is still one of the individuals in relation to other individuals. Consistent with the image of the autonomous self, individuals are viewed as largely able to regulate and to choose their social personae; failure to do so is linked to inadequacy and lack of adjustment. For example, uncertainty about the self and susceptibility to variable life events is linked to low self-esteem (Campbell & Lavallee, 1993).

There is also little consideration of the wider social structure in which people conduct their lives, and the potential influence this has on the selves available to the person. How limiting is the lack of attention to distal factors? Should these be left to other disciplines? If macro social structures are to be included into the discussion about self and identity, how should those social structures be conceptualized? Will their inclusion lead to major changes in the social cognitive model of the self? Similar questions may be asked about how cultural variation exerts deep as well as superficial influence on the structure and content of the self. Of particular interest in the last decade is the potential influence of social structures created through the technology of the internet. If social structures form selves, and if new global structures emerge through information technology, will "new selves" emerge?

CORE ASSUMPTION 4: SELF AND EVOLUTION

Homo sapiens is a species equipped with a mind capable of self-awareness and self-representation. This capacity for reflective self-awareness is a product of evolution. Evolutionary pressure came from early human ancestors' move from the forest area to savanna, bipedal walking posture, tool making and hunting, and a concomitant enlargement of brain size, resulting in the enhanced mental capacity of our species. The other evolutionary pressure derived from the particular sociality of our species—that is, humans live in bands or groups. This living condition tends toward social complexity, which may give rise to the condition in which a well-developed symbolic capability is highly likely to increase reproductive fitness (Sedikides & Skowronski, 1997).

All in all, greater brain capacity and social complexity enabled and facilitated the survival of the human capacities for reflective self-awareness and symbol manipulation. A result is what Sedikides and Skowronski (1997) called the *symbolic self*, that is, a symbolic construction of the self, a phenomenon that appears to be unique to our species. By symbolic, Sedikides and Skowronski (1997) mainly meant language-based representations; however, this may be more broadly interpreted to include other symbolic forms, such as pictures and nonverbal behaviors. Sedikides and Skowronski (1997) suggested that ecological and social conditions of early humans are highly mutually constitutive of each other, and are closely related to the evolution of the symbolic self.

In summary, the evolutionary assumption is:

4a. The capacity for reflective self-awareness is a product of evolution. It was dependent on increased brain size, and a high degree of social complexity, both of which contributed to the emergence of symbolic representation in general.

Implications

Although ecological and social conditions may have given rise to the condition in which symbolically capable organisms are reproductively successful, once the symbolic apparatus—that is, culture—is there, could the symbolic cultural process itself have participated in the coevolutionary process (e.g., Cole, 1996; Durham, 1991; Geertz, 1973)? In other words, when a first human symbolic capacity produced a symbolic environment in a human group, this symbolic environment may have provided a stable environment to which the very symbolic capacity that gave rise to it may have continued to adapt. As Deacon (1997) argued, language and the brain that uses language may have influenced each other in the process of coevolution. Could it be the case that culture and the symbolic brain too have coevolved as mutually constitutive components? Are there, therefore, any evolutionary constraints on the symbolic self?

CORE ASSUMPTION 5: EPISTEMOLOGICAL
AND METHODOLOGICAL ISSUES

With some exceptions, theorists in the social cognitive tradition of self and identity adopt a realist approach to science. That is, they assume that there is a "truth of the matter" with reference to self-cognition, as there is to cognition in general. Abstract theory is valued inasmuch as it successfully summarizes, or models, general principles underlying observable behavior. Abstract theory that can subsume a wide range of phenomena is particularly valued, and thus, theories of cognition that are also adequate to deal with the range of phenomena related to self-cognition are regarded as worthy of development.

As in mainstream psychology, there is a preference for the experiment and controlled observation as the means for testing hypotheses derived from abstract theory. The self-concept becomes a legitimate topic for scientific inquiry to the extent that it is conceptualized as similar to any other cognitive concept. The information-processing model, or model of the self as symbol processor, lends itself to systematic study, using the techniques of cognitive psychology. As Ericsson and Simon (1985) noted, these techniques include the analysis of verbal reports, which can be used to test models of cognitive process.

The use of the abstract theory testing experiment in social psychology (Greenwood, 1989) has been accompanied by a relative lack of concern with particulars of social settings and social identities. This is a coherent approach, given the assumption that there are general and abstract processes involved in self-formation and regulation. An example of this is the study of self-schemas (Markus, 1977). These schemas are conceived as sets of general traits (e.g., independent, honest, female, sports-loving) that are thought to characterize a given person and to be important to the person. It should not matter for the general predictions from self-schema theory whether the traits were creative, empathetic, masculine, or work obsessed. The general predictions that behavior will be directed by self-schemas, that well-established self-schemas should be resistant to change, and so on should not vary with the content of the schema. Even the major development of the cross-cultural comparison of self-schemas (Markus & Kitayama, 1991), seems to embrace the assumption that self-schemas in all cultures could described along abstract dimensions, albeit with the addition of the idea that the important dimensions might be different in different social relationships.

The epistemological commitment to the generality and abstractness of principles governing human (social) behavior is widely shared in the discipline, and is a major basis for the claim that psychology is a science. However, this assumption is not often explicated, and there is often poor understanding of the relationship between general theory, and the specific experimental situations devised to test implications of the theory. For example, the assumption that there will be self-schemas "of some sort" in every culture takes for granted the idea that selves will be characterized by abstract trait dimensions, and that people will actively construct these dimensions, act on them, recognize them, and resist any attempts to contradict them. Similarly, there is an assumption that the person's self-concept is entirely contained within his or her mind, not distributed among others. This means that the individual can be relied on to report or reflect the structure and content of his or her self.

There are two issues here. One is a tendency to believe that there is only one theory that is or will be adequate to explanation of the development of the self, and that modern conceptions of the social cognitive self are getting close to this adequate account. The other is the tendency to assume that, even if selves appear different at different times and different cultures, there is some important similarity in the underlying processes of development and execution that can be identified. It may well turn out that these assumptions are justified. However, it is important to identify them as assumptions.

Implications

There have been many criticisms of the scientific/experimental approach to the study of social psychology (e.g., Gergen, 1973; Harre, 1973; Manicas, 1987). It is not our intention to engage in this debate, nor do we wish to deny the achievements that have resulted from the application of the experimental method. Rather, we wish to raise a question, now common in modern philosophy of science (e.g., Chalmers, 1999; Hacking, 1999, Laudan, 1990), about unquestioning realism concerning our theories of phenomena, including human social behavior. Given the range of competing theories for any given phenomenon in social psychology, it is surprising that there is not wider acceptance of the view that theory guides observation, and that theory is underdetermined by facts (Hesse, 1985). Yet in psychology, the assumption that unbiased observations and experiments will yield true general principles of nature (abandoned in most philosophical quarters) is still held by many.

Note that these features of naive realism make theorists of the self less alert to the importance of the influence of their particular theory on the observations they think relevant or even possible. More importantly, because this view denies the importance of theory in observation, it makes invisible, or at least less obvious, the range of social and cultural influences on the theorist. In this sense, the theorist is abstracted from his or her sociocultural context, and is regarded as an autonomous epistemic agent, just as the self that is theorized is an autonomous, abstract agent that constructs and manages, and yet to a large extent is untouched by, its sociocultural environment. If this characterization is correct, to what extent are the conceptions of the self theorized and the conception of the theorist epistemologically presumed, in fact, mutually constituted?

CONCLUDING COMMENTS

To state the conclusion concisely, the person portrayed in the current social psychological literature of self and identity is an abstract individual equipped with a fixed set of abilities and needs (e.g., self-enhancement, self-verification). Obviously, this person is not a rational "economic man" of classical economics, but it is a person endowed with a mind unaffected by the symbols that it processes. The symbols are merely the throughput of the social cognitive mind. Despite the centrality of the symbolic, the social cognitive mind stands apart from it. Cultural and historical variations in self processes are explained in terms of the symbolic content, which the social cognitive person processes with no fundamental change to the processor. The person does enter into a variety of social relationships with other individuals and collectives. To this extent, this image of the person is one of a social being. However, this sociality is still abstracted from concrete social activities embedded in the social institutional structure of the society. The person is conceptualized as a biological being as well. It is widely accepted that people, with their capacity for symbolic self-awareness, are a result of evolutionary processes. Yet human evolution is seen to be unaffected by the symbolic environment that humans themselves have constructed. The conception of the person embedded in the social psychological literature of self and identity is of an individual abstracted from its social structural and symbolic context. Finally, we also noted that naive realist epistemology and methodology dominate scientific investigation of self and identity. In this conception, the role played by a theorist's theory in the evaluation of and search for facts is often downplayed, portraying the theorist as an autonomous abstract epistemic agent largely unaffected by sociocultural contexts.

　　Ironically, the ontological commitments to the unitary, autonomous, and abstract agent that is regarded as the self and the epistemological commitments may have in part arisen from the same sociocultural background. As is well known, the framework of scientific investigation that social psychologists adopted developed out of the Enlightenment period in 18th-century Western Europe (for a brief outline, see Kashima, 2000). The person in this tradition was conceptualized as fundamentally constituted by the universal natural law, which governs everything in nature including human nature. Reason, which was then regarded as a human embodiment of this universal natural law, was therefore a human disposition that is abstracted from and untouched by sociocultural specificities. It is true that this Enlightenment vision gave rise to the current conception of human rights as inalienable properties of an individual person, and provided a significant theoretical backbone to the institution of democracy. It may also be true that this Enlightenment conception of the person provided a basis both for the conception of the theorist as an autonomous abstract epistemic agent and for the conception of the self as an autonomous abstract agent.

Obviously, acknowledging the sociocultural basis of the abstract conception of the person embedded in the theories and methodology of social psychological investigation into self and identity does not make either the theory or the method wrong or problematic in and of itself. What is wrong or problematic is to deny the very sociocultural embeddedness of the social psychological research of self and identity itself. The awareness of this makes it possible for researchers to put under reflective scrutiny the connection between the sociocultural context and their theories and research. After all, research on self and identity is a systematic investigation of people's self-reflective processes; researchers too can subject themselves to the same process of self-reflection. The awareness of the sociocultural embeddedness of our own research may not enable us to transcend our sociocultural context entirely, but may be a first step toward going beyond it.

REFERENCES

Andersen, S. M., Reznik, I., & Manzella, L. M. (1996). Eliciting facial affect, motivation and expectancies in transference: Significant-other representations in social relations. *Journal of Personality and Social Psychology, 71*, 1108–1129.

Aron, A., Aron, E. N., & Smollan, D. (1992). Inclusion of other in the self scale and the structure of interpersonal closeness. *Journal of Personality and Social Psychology, 63*, 596–612.

Baumeister, R. F. (1998). The self. In D. T. Gilber, S. T. Fiske, & G. Lindzey (Eds.), *The handbook of social psychology* (Vol. 47, pp. 506–516). Boston, MA: McGraw-Hill.

Bem, D. (1972). Self-perception theory. In L. Berkowitz (Ed.), *Advances in Experimental Social Psychology, 6*, 1–62.

Berger, J., & Zelditch, M. (1993). Orienting strategies and theory growth. In J. Berger & M. Zelditch (Eds.), *Theoretical research programs: Studies in the growth of theory* (pp. 3–19). Stanford, CA: Stanford University Press.

Brewer, M. B., & Gardner, W. (1996). Who is this "We"? Levels of collective identity and self representations. *Journal of Personality and Social Psychology, 71*, 83–93.

Brown, J. (1998). *The self.* Boston: McGraw-Hill.

Bruner, J. (1990). *Acts of meaning.* Cambridge, MA: Harvard University Press.

Campbell, J., & Lavallee, L. F. (1993). Who am I? The role of self-concept confusion in understanding the behavior of people with low self-esteem. In R. F. Baumeister (Ed.), *Self-esteem: The puzzle of low self-regard* (pp. 3–20). New York: Plenum Press.

Carver, C. S., & Scheier, M. F. (1981). *Attention and self-regulation: A control theory approach to human behaviour.* New York: Springer-Verlag.

Chalmers, A. (1999). *What is this thing called science?* (3rd ed.). Brisbane: University of Queensland Press.

Cole, M. (1996). *Cultural psychology: A once and future discipline.* Cambridge, MA: Harvard University Press.

Coopersmith, S. (1967). *The antecedents of self esteem.* San Francisco: Freeman.

Damon, W., & Hart, D. (1986). Stability and change in children's self-understanding. *Social Cognition, 4,* 102–118.

Deacon, T. W. (1997). *The symbolic species.* New York: Norton.

Deaux, K., Reid, A., Mizrahi, K., & Ethier, K. A. (1995). Parameters of social identity. *Journal of Personality and Social Psychology, 68,* 280–291.

Dollinger, S. J., Preston, L. A., O'Brien, S. P., & DiLalla, D. L. (1996). Individuality and relatedness of the self: An autophotographic study. *Journal of Personality and Social Psychology, 71,* 1268–1278.

Durham, W. H. (1991). *Coevolution: Genes, culture and human diversity.* Stanford, CA: Stanford University Press.

Epstein, S. (1973). The self-concept revisited: Or a theory of a theory. *American Psychologist, 28,* 404–416.

Ericsson, K. A., & Simon, H. A. (1985). *Protocol analysis: Verbal reports as data.* Cambridge, MA.: MIT Press.

Forgas, J. P. (1995). Mood and judgment: The affect infusion model. *Psychological Bulletin, 117,* 39–66.

Geertz, C. (1973). *The interpretation of cultures.* New York: Basic Books.

Gergen, K. (1973). Social psychology as history. *Journal of Personality and Social Psychology, 26,* 309–320.

Gergen, K., & Gergen, M. (1988). Narrative and the self as relationship. *Advances in Experimental Social Psychology, 21,* 17–56.

Greenwood, J. D. (1989). *Explanation and experiment in social psychological science.* New York: Springer-Verlag.

Hacking, I. (1999). *The social construction of what?* Cambridge, MA: Harvard University Press.

Harre, R. (1973). *The explanation of social behaviour.* Oxford, UK: Basil Blackwell.

Hermans, H. (1996). Voicing the self: Information processing to dialogical interchange. *Psychological Bulletin, 119,* 31–50.

Hesse, M. (1985). *Revolutions and reconstructions in the philosophy of science.* Brighton, England: Harvester.

Higgins, E. T. (1987). Self-discrepancy: A theory relating self and affect. *Psychological Review, 94,* 319–340.

Higgins, E. T. (1989). Continuities and discontinuities in self-regulatory and self-evaluative processes: A developmental theory relating self and affect. *Journal of Personality, 57,* 407–444.

Higgins, E. T. (1996). The self digest: Self-knowledge serving self-regulatory functions. *Journal of Personality and Social Psychology, 71,* 1062–1083.

James, W. (1950). *The Principles of Psychology.* New York: Dover. (Original work published 1890)

Kashima, Y. (2000). Conceptions of culture and person for psychology. *Journal of Cross-Cultural Psychology, 31,* 14–32.

Kashima, Y., & Yamaguchi, S. (1999). Introduction to the special issue on self. *Asian Journal of Social Psychology, 2,* 283–287.

Kashima, Y., Yamaguchi, S., Kim, U., Choi, S.-C., Gelfand, M.J., & Yuki, M. (1995). Culture, gender, and self: A perspective from individualism-collectivism research. *Journal of Personality and Social Psychology, 69*, 925–937.

Katz, D., & Stotland, E. (1959). A preliminary statement to a theory of attitude structure and chanage. In S. Koch (Ed.), *Psychology: A study of a science* (Vol. 3, pp. 423–475). New York: McGraw-Hill.

Kihlstrom, J. F., & Cantor, N. (1984). Mental representations of the self. *Advances in Experimental Social Psychology, 17*, 1–47.

Kihlstrom, J. F. & Klein, S. B. (1994). The self as a knowledge structure. In R. S. Wyer & T. K. Srull (Eds.), *Handbook of social cognition* (Vol. 1; 2nd ed., pp. 153–208). Hillsdale, NJ: Lawrence Erlbaum Associates.

Knowles, E. S., & Sibicky, M. E. (1990). Continuity and diversity in the stream of selves. *Personality and Social Psychology Bulletin, 16*, 676–687.

Kuiper, N. A. (1981). Convergent evidence for the self as prototype: The "inverted-U RT effect" for self and other judgments. *Personality and Social Psychology Bulletin, 7*, 438–443.

Kunda, Z., & Sanitioso, R. (1989). Motivated changes in the self-concept. *Journal of Experimental Social Psychology, 25*, 272–285.

Lakatos, I. (1970). Falsification and the methodology of scientific research programmes. In I. Lakatos & A. Musgrave (Eds.), *Criticism and the growth of knowledge*. Cambridge: Cambridge University Press.

Lancaster, S., & Foddy, M. (1988). Self-extensions: A conceptualisation. *Journal for the Theory of Social Behaviour, 18*, 77–94.

Laudan, L. (1977). *Progress and its problems: Toward a theory of scientific growth*. Berkeley: University of California Press.

Laudan, L. (1990). *Science and relativism: Some key controversies in the philosophy of science*. Chicago: University of Chicago Press.

Lukes, S. (1973). *Individualism*. Oxford, UK: Basil Blackwell.

Maccoby, E. E. (1980). *Social development: Psychological growth and the parent–child relationship*. New York: Harcourt, Brace, Jovanovich.

Manicas, P. (1987). *A history and philosophy of the social sciences*. Oxford, UK: Basil Blackwell.

Markus, H. R. (1977). Self-schemata and processing information about the self. *Journal of Personality and Social Psychology, 35*, 63–78.

Markus, H., & Kitayama, S. (1991). Culture and the self: Implications for cognition, emotion, and motivation. *Psychological Review, 98*, 224–253.

Mead, G. H. (1934). *Mind, self, and society*. Chicago: University of Chicago Press.

Morgan, D. L., & Schwalbe, M. L. (1990). Mind and self in society: Linking social structure and social cognition. *Social Psychology Quarterly, 53*, 148–164.

Newell, A., & Simon, H. A. (1990). Computer science as empirical enquiry: Symbols and search. In M. A. Boden (Ed.), *The philosophy of artificial intelligence* (pp. 105–132). Oxford: Oxford University Press.

Newell, A., & Simon, H. (1995). GPS, a program that simulates human thought. In E. A. Feigenbaum & J. Feldman (Eds.), *Computers and thought* (pp. 279–293). Cambridge, MA: MIT Press.

Pepitone, A. (1968). An experimental analysis of self-dynamics. In C. Gordon & K. Gergen (Eds.), *The self in social interaction* (p. 347). New York: Wiley.

Reid, A., & Deaux, K. (1996). Relationship between social and personal identities: Segregation or integration? *Journal of Personality and Social Psychology, 71*, 1084–1091.

Rogoff, B. (1990). *Apprenticeship in thinking: Cognitive development in social context*. New York: Oxford University Press.

Rose, N. (1989). Individualizing psychology. In J. Shotter & K. J. Gergen (Eds.), *Texts of Identity* (pp. 119–132). London: Sage Publications.

Rose, N. (1996). *Inventing our selves*. Cambridge: Cambridge University Press.

Rosenberg, M. (1979). *Conceiving the self.* New York: Basic Books.

Rosenberg, M. J., & Hovland, C. I. (1960). Cognitive, affective and behavioral components of attitudes. In C. I. Hovland & M. J. Rosenberg (Eds.), *Attitude organization and change: An analysis of consitency among attitude components* (pp. 1–14). New Haven, CT: Yale University Press.

Ryle, G. (1963). *The concept of mind.* Hammondsworth, Middlesex: Penguin.

Sarbin, T. R. (1990). The narrative quality of action. *Theoretical and Philosophical Psychology, 10,* 49–65.

Schooler, C. (1996). Cultural and social-structural explanations of cross-national psychological differences. *Annual Review of Sociology, 22,* 323–349.

Sedikides, C. (1995). Central and peripheral self-conceptions are differentially influenced by mood: Tests of the differential sensitivity hypothesis. *Journal of Personality and Social Psychology, 69,* 759–777.

Sedikides, C., & Skowronski, J. J. (1995). Sources of self-knowledge: On the perceived primacy of self-reflection. *Journal of Social and Clinical Psychology, 14,* 244–270.

Sedikides, C., & Skowronski, J. J. (1997). The symbolic self in evolutionary context. *Personality and Social Psychology Review, 1,* 80–102.

Selman, R. L. (1980). *The growth of interpersonal understanding.* New York: Academic Press.

Smith, L. B., & Thelen, E. (1993). *A dynamic systems approach to development: Applications.* Cambridge, MA: MIT Press.

Smith, M. B. (1991). Perspectives on selfhood. In M. B. Smith (Ed.), *Values, self & society: Toward a humanist social psychology* (pp. 19–35). New Brunswick, NJ: Transaction Publishers. (Original work published 1978)

Stryker, S. (1987). *Identitiy theory: Developments and extensions.* In K. Yardley & T. Honess (Eds.), *Self and identity* (pp. 89–103). New York: Wiley.

Swann, W. B. (1987). Identity negotiation: Where two roads meet. *Journal of Personality and Social Psychology, 53,* 1038–1051.

Taylor, S. E., & Brown, J. D. (1988). Illusion and well-being: A social psychological perspective on mental health. *Psychological Bulletin, 103,* 193–210.

Thelen, E., & Smith, L. B. (1994). *A dynamic systems approach to the development of cognition and action.* Cambridge, MA: MIT Press.

Trafimow, D., Triandis, H., & Goto, S. G. (1991). Some tests of the distinction between private self and collective self. *Journal of Personality and Social Psychology, 60,* 649–655.

Turner, R. H. (1988). Personality in society: Social psychology's contribution to sociology. *Social Psychology Quarterly, 51,* 1–10.

Tyler, T. R., Kramer, R. M. & John, O. P. (1999). *The psychology of the social self.* Mahwah, NJ: Lawrence Erlbaum Associates.

Chapter 2

Connectionism and Self: Distributed Representational Systems and Their Implications for Self and Identity

Michael S. Humphreys
University of Queensland

Yoshihisa Kashima
University of Melbourne

Connectionism is sometimes described as a class of theories of cognition that are neurologically inspired. This description has some merit, although there are many differences between the actions of real neurons and the actions of the abstract units in our connectionist models. Nevertheless, the idea that cognition emerges from the interactions of a very large number of simple processing units is appealing not only because of the neurological link, but because this approach seems capable of explaining some of the key aspects of human memory in a simple and straightforward manner. In connectionist-inspired thinking about cognition, many phenomena are seen to arise relatively directly from the memory system with little need for additional processes. In this chapter, we review some of the basic ideas about composite memories and show how they promote this new view of human memory and cognition. We then extend these ideas to selected aspects of the self and identity research. The idea is to show that new ideas about the self can emerge from connectionist thinking and that some of the traditional dilemmas or paradoxes may not appear as problematical when viewed from a connectionist perspective.

Traditionally, the general image of human memory involved the separate storage of memories and a sequential search process to access them. Memories of different concepts are stored at "different places," and those storage locations may be connected to each other. To access these memories, a person would use a control mechanism of some sort to search through these locations one by one in a sequential fashion. These ideas have been around for several years, and most researchers, including a number of social psychologists, might find them intuitive. In contrast, the connectionist-inspired image of human memory takes the view that memories are not stored in separate places, but stored at "the same place" in a distributed fashion, and accessed by direct pattern matching. This distributed representational assumption typically consists of two major ideas: Memories are distributed patterns of activation over a large number of cognitive processing units and memories are superimposed on each other. We will call this *composite memory storage*. To access such composite memories, a person is assumed to use pattern matching, which permits parallel access to the stored memories.

Although distributed representational systems have recently become well known in social psychology (Kashima, Woolcock, & Kashima, 2000; Smith, 1996; Smith & DeCoster, 1998; cf. Read, Venman, & Miller, 1996), the ideas of composite memory and parallel access are relatively new. In this chapter, we explicate them enough to permit explorations (and largely speculations) about issues pertinent to self and identity from this perspective. As we show, a result of this exploration is a remarkable congruity of the connectionist perspective with classical insights of William James and George Herbert Mead. We use a particular class of models of human memory, which we have been developing in our research programs, to explain the basic ideas related to composite memory storage and parallel access of memory. Granted that the points discussed here do not generalize to all connectionist inspired models of human cognition (e.g., Smith & DeCoster, 1998; see Kashima et al., 2000, for a brief discussion on this). Nevertheless, we hope this brief exposition is sufficient for illustrative purposes, and serves to provide a new metaphor for thinking about the self and identity in social psychology.

A DISTRIBUTED REPRESENTATIONAL SYSTEM

The use of vectors, matrices, and tensor products has been explored by several authors for their potential to illuminate aspects of human memory (Anderson, 1973; Humphreys, Bain, & Pike, 1989; Pike, 1984). Although they are inadequate in some ways and we are still very far from having a comprehensive theory, these mathematical formalisms provide a good starting point in trying to understand storage and access in composite memories. Our strategy here is to start with the simplest model (vector memory) to discuss some of the most fundamental processes, and to show that more complex models are required to describe human memory. Those readers who are familiar with distributed connectionist systems may wish to go directly to a section on *Self*.

Vector Memory

One of the simplest memories that have some psychological interest is a vector memory. In such a memory model, a concept can be understood as being represented by a pattern of activation over a set of processing units. Mathematically, a concept is represented as a vector, a set of ordered numbers, where a number indicates the level of activation of a processing unit. We represent a vector by lower case letters in bold face such as **a** and **b**. In this formalism, storage operation is vector addition the result of which is also a vector (hence the name, *vector memory*). The memory access operation is the dot or inner product between a probe vector and the memory vector. Thus, **a** would represent a vector, and a_i would represent the ith element in the vector **a**. Vector addition is the element by element sum of two vectors so **a** + **b** would be $(a_1 + b_1, a_2 + b_2, \ldots, a_n + b_n)$, where n is the number of elements in each vector. The dot product of two vectors is the sum of the element by element cross products of the vector elements, so **a** · **b** is $a_1 \times b_1 + a_2 \times b_2 + \cdots a_n \times b_n$. In social psychology, Fiedler's (1996) BIAS model uses this formalism.

Recognition Memory.   To see how this works, it is best to use a simple recognition memory experiment for illustration. Suppose that the items in a study list are *A*, *B*, and *C*, and participants are to recognize later on whether an item was in the list. Perhaps this is analogous to the social situation in which we see someone and try to decide whether we have met the person before. The memory for this list can be represented as the vector addition of the corresponding vectors (**v** = **a** + **b** + **c**). When participants are to recognize whether an item (i.e., probe item) appeared in the study list, the representation of the probe item is matched to the memory. This operation is described as the computation of the dot product between the vector representing the probe item and the memory vector. The result is what we call a *matching strength*, which can be interpreted as indicating the strength of the subjective feeling of knowing. It is assumed that people use this "feeling" to decide whether a probe item is old or new. If the probe is old (e.g., *B*), then **b** · **v** = **b** · **b** + **b** · **a** + **b** · **c**. In other words, the probe vector matches its own representation in memory (i.e., **b** · **b**) plus the representations of the other items in the list (i.e., **b** · **a** and **b** · **c**). If the probe is new (e.g., *D*) then **d** · **v** = **d** · **a** + **d** · **b** + **d** · **c**. On average, **b** · **v** is expected to be greater than **d** · **v**. This is because under reasonable mathematical assumptions the dot product of an item with itself (e.g., **b** · **b**) is greater than the dot product between two unrelated items (e.g., **b** · **a**, **d** · **a**). Therefore, the probe item that is in fact old (i.e., *B*) is more likely to be recognized as old than the probe item that is in fact new (i.e., *D*). The appendix on recognition memory gives further details.

The vector memory model captures the intuitive ideas that at least some recognition memory is graded, and that apart from some appreciation of the strength of "feeling of knowing," there is no conscious knowledge of the evidence on which the decision of "Yes, I can recognize this as an old item" is being made. That is, the individual may be able to report that there is weak evidence in favor of the item being old, somewhat stronger evidence, or still stronger evidence, but not be able to describe the contents of the information. Dennis and Humphreys (2001) referred to this type of decision process as subsymbolic and contrasted it with a symbolic decision process where the decision is based on categorical information ("I was making pleasantness judgments about the words in the study list and I remember making a judgment about this word. Therefore, it must be old").[1]

The Problem With a Vector Memory: "Recognition in Context." Now imagine the situation where we see someone and we have to decide whether we have met this person at school or at work. This is the case of recognition in context. Although a vector memory has some psychologically interesting properties, it has problems with recognition of an item in a specific context, that is, differentiating the memories of the same item in different contexts. Perhaps this is somewhat counterintuitive. It is often assumed that context could be included in a vector memory by adding the vector representing the context X (i.e., $\mathbf{x}$) to the item vector (i.e., $\mathbf{a} + \mathbf{x}$). However, this does not work. To see this, again in a recognition memory experiment, assume that items A and B have been studied in context X and items C and D in context Y. The memory that includes these two study lists is, according to vector memory,

$$\mathbf{v} = (\mathbf{a} + \mathbf{x}) + (\mathbf{b} + \mathbf{x}) + (\mathbf{c} + \mathbf{y}) + (\mathbf{d} + \mathbf{y}) \qquad (1)$$

Participants may be asked to say if A occurred in context X or in context Y. They may decide by first determining whether A occurred in X, second determining whether A occurred in Y, and then finally comparing the two resultant matching strengths. The two matching strengths are described mathematically as follows:

---

[1]The vector model also has the property that the noise comes from the match between the probe item and the nontarget items in the list. This item noise property also holds when context is included (Humphreys, Bain, & Pike, 1989). In contrast, Dennis and Humphreys (2001) presented a model for recognition where the noise comes from the previous contexts in which an item (their model was restricted to already well known words) has been encountered not from the other items in the list. However, the Dennis and Humphreys (2001) model still used a subsymbolic decision process where subjects could make generally accurate decisions even though they might be largely unaware of the contents of memory.

$$(a + x) \cdot v = (a + x) \cdot (a + x) + (a + x) \cdot$$
$$(b + x) + (a + x) \cdot (c + y) + (a + x) \cdot (d + y)$$
$$(a + y) \cdot v = (a + y) \cdot (a + x) + (a + y) \cdot$$
$$(b + x) + (a + y) \cdot (c + y) + (a + y) \cdot (d + y) \qquad (2)$$

It turns out, on average, that these matching strengths are identical (see Appendix on Recognition in Context for a mathematical discussion). Thus, the system cannot tell whether A occurred in context X or Y. This is because the system "knows" that A occurred and that X and Y occurred twice each, but it does not "know" that A occurred with X. Without additional processes, context that is added onto a vector representation would simply increase the matching strengths of old and new items by the same amount. The result is no net increase in discrimination between the two contexts (Humphreys, Bain, & Pike, 1989; Humphreys, Pike, Bain, Tehan, 1989; Murnane & Phelps, 1993).

In order to use context to determine in which setting an item occurred, a binding that links the item and context must be stored in memory. In the separate storage and sequential search model of human memory, in which items are stored in unique locations (e.g., Flexser & Tulving, 1978), we can add the item and context vectors and store the composite vector in a unique location. In such a system, matching a probe vector (the sum of the item and context vectors) against each memory location and then basing the decision on the single strongest match will also provide information about the joint occurrence of item and context. In a way, the location of memory storage provides the information about the item–context binding. However, with a distributed composite memory, another solution must be found. The solution proposed by Humphreys, Bain, and Pike (1989) was to store a context-to-item association in matrix memory.

Matrix Memory

In the matrix memory model, a binding of two concepts (represented by two vectors **a** and **b**) is mathematically modeled by forming the matrix (represented by a capital letter in bold) or outer product of a vector (**a**) with another vector (**b**). In social psychology, Kashima and Kerekes (1994) used it to model person impression formation, in which a person is associated with an impression formed of the person. We use the multiplication symbol with a circle around it ($\otimes$) for the outer product. So, the resultant memory, $\mathbf{M} = \mathbf{a} \otimes \mathbf{b}$, is an n by n matrix where n is the number of elements in each vector. The entry of this matrix in the ith row and jth column is the product of the ith element of vector **a** and the jth element of vector **b** ($a_i b_j$).

Recall Memory.   The matrix operation is useful in clarifying the difference between recognition and recall. In recognition, our intuition is that
there is a vague "feeling of knowing" as we suggested before; in recall, by
contrast, we retrieve a contentful item in our consciousness. So instead of
simply recognizing a person as someone we have met before, we may have
to recall who this person's friend was. Again, let us use a simple memory
experiment for illustration. Suppose that a study list consists of the pairs
AB and *DC* (we refer to the first item in each pair as the *cue* and the second
as the *target*). The memory for the study list is a matrix where each element is the sum of the corresponding elements in the two matrices:

$$\mathbf{M} = \mathbf{a} \otimes \mathbf{b} + \mathbf{c} \otimes \mathbf{d} \tag{3}$$

Note that the entry in the ith row and jth column of $\mathbf{M}$ equals $a_i b_j + c_i d_j$.
Further, suppose that participants are asked to recall an item associated
with a cue. This recall process is modeled by the following mathematical
operation, in which the memory $\mathbf{M}$ is premultiplied by the vector representing that cue:

$$\mathbf{aM} = \mathbf{a}(\mathbf{a} \otimes \mathbf{b}) + \mathbf{a}(\mathbf{c} \otimes \mathbf{d}) = (\mathbf{a} \cdot \mathbf{a})\mathbf{b} + (\mathbf{a} \cdot \mathbf{c})\mathbf{d} \tag{4}$$

The memory retrieved here can be understood as a blending of two items,
$\mathbf{b}$ and $\mathbf{d}$.

Note that, in this example, the output of the retrieval process is a
weighted sum of the two vectors, $\mathbf{b}$ and $\mathbf{d}$, which represent two possible targets, *B* and *D*. Also recall that the dot products such as $\mathbf{a} \cdot \mathbf{a}$ can be interpreted as a measure of similarity. The vector corresponding to the correct
target, $\mathbf{b}$, is weighted by the similarity of the retrieval cue to itself, $\mathbf{a} \cdot \mathbf{a}$,
whereas the vector corresponding to the incorrect target, $\mathbf{d}$, is weighted by
the similarity between the retrieval cue and an unrelated cue, $\mathbf{a} \cdot \mathbf{c}$.
Roughly speaking, the matching term like $\mathbf{a} \cdot \mathbf{a}$ is greater than the mismatching term like $\mathbf{a} \cdot \mathbf{c}$. The result is a noisy output, which blends the representations of the two list targets, but one in which the correct target receives a heavier weighting than the incorrect target. In fact, in a very
special case where $\mathbf{a} \cdot \mathbf{a}$ is 1, and $\mathbf{a} \cdot \mathbf{c}$ is 0, the resultant memory is $\mathbf{b}$, which
is the correct item.

Although this memory system can "recall" in principle, in order to
make a specific prediction, a mechanism for response selection is necessary. For this purpose, Chappell and Humphreys (1994) added an auto-
associative memory to the tensor product model. Autoassociative memories are essentially an association of an item to itself. Such a memory can
remove noise by producing the vector with the largest weight in the output. In the terminology of nonlinear dynamics, this vector can be inter-

preted as an attractor of a dynamical system. However, this mechanism does not always produce a single item. That is, it may fail to converge to an attractor, and instead it can result in a state where every processing unit in memory is activated or a state where no elements are activated. Chappell and Humphreys (1994) interpreted these states as a situation where the production of a response was blocked by some response competition (see Humphreys, Tehan, O'Shea, & Boland, 2000, for empirical support). Autoassociators also produce categorical behavior. One set of similar input patterns is mapped onto the same stable internal representation, whereas a different set is mapped onto a different internal representation. Patterns that are mapped onto the same internal representation are said to *fall into the same basin of attraction*, and the stability of the internal representations is referred to as the *depth of the energy minimum*.

"Recognition in Context" Revisited. The same mathematical formalism, matrix structure, can be used to model the recognition of an item in a specific context, the process with which the vector model had problems. This is accomplished by binding a context to an item, thus constructing a contextualized item representation. In the example we used, items A and B were studied in context X, and items C and D were studied in context Y. In this case, the items A and B are bound to context X and the items C and D with context Y as follows:

$$\mathbf{M} = \mathbf{x} \otimes \mathbf{a} + \mathbf{x} \otimes \mathbf{b} + \mathbf{y} \otimes \mathbf{c} + \mathbf{y} \otimes \mathbf{d} \qquad (5)$$

Again, people may decide whether A occurred in context X or in context Y by first determining whether A occurred in X, second determining whether A occurred in Y, and then finally comparing the two resultant feelings of knowing. However, the probe and memory representations are different in matrix memory. In trying to see whether A occurred in context X, the vector representing the relevant context ($\mathbf{x}$) is used as a retrieval cue and the output of this retreival process is then matched against the vector representing the item A. A similar process may be followed in trying to see whether A occurred in context Y. The results are two matching strengths represented as follows:

$$\begin{aligned}
(\mathbf{xM}) \cdot \mathbf{a} &= (\mathbf{x} \cdot \mathbf{x})(\mathbf{a} \cdot \mathbf{a}) + (\mathbf{x} \cdot \mathbf{x})(\mathbf{a} \cdot \mathbf{b}) \\
&\quad + (\mathbf{x} \cdot \mathbf{y})(\mathbf{a} \cdot \mathbf{c}) + (\mathbf{x} \cdot \mathbf{y})(\mathbf{a} \cdot \mathbf{d}) \\
(\mathbf{yM}) \cdot \mathbf{a} &= (\mathbf{y} \cdot \mathbf{x})(\mathbf{a} \cdot \mathbf{a}) + (\mathbf{y} \cdot \mathbf{x})(\mathbf{a} \cdot \mathbf{b}) + (\mathbf{y} \cdot \mathbf{y}) \\
&\quad (\mathbf{a} \cdot \mathbf{c}) + (\mathbf{y} \cdot \mathbf{y})(\mathbf{a} \cdot \mathbf{d})
\end{aligned} \qquad (6)$$

It turns out that the matching strength for the item retrieved with the correct context, $(\mathbf{xM}) \cdot \mathbf{a}$, is greater than the matching strength with the wrong context, $(\mathbf{yM}) \cdot \mathbf{a}$. This is because the matching terms $\mathbf{x} \cdot \mathbf{x}$ and $\mathbf{a} \cdot \mathbf{a}$ are generally greater than the mismatching terms like $\mathbf{y} \cdot \mathbf{x}$ and $\mathbf{a} \cdot \mathbf{b}$ (see

Recognition in Context in Appendix for a more precise discussion). This way, the matrix memory model can solve the vector memory's problem with recognition in context.

Tensor Product Memory

Although a matrix memory can bind two items together, it is inadequate for binding three items. That is, we often remember that a person A and another person B are friends (a binding of two items), but also remember that they are friends at school (i.e., a binding of A and B in context X). To be sure, we can easily remember that a president may be paired with his wife in a family context, but that he may be paired with another person in a different context! To create such three-way bindings, Humphreys, Bain, and Pike (1989; also see Wiles & Humphreys, 1993) introduced a tensor product memory. Tensor is a mathematical formalism that generalizes the concepts of vector and matrix. A tensor of rank 1 is a vector, a tensor of rank 2 is a matrix, and a tensor of rank 3 is a generalization of the concept of a matrix to three dimensions. With tensors, the mathematical operations we have encountered before (i.e., outer product, inner product, and the premultiplication of a tensor by a tensor of a lower rank) are straightforward generalizations of the same operations with vectors and matrices. Again, in the following discussion, we use $\otimes$ for the outer product, $\cdot$ for the inner (dot) product, and the placing of a tensor of a lower rank in front of a tensor of a higher rank as premultiplication.

In traditional memory experiments, such a three-way binding is required for pair recognition and cued recall, where the items used are the same in two different contexts but the pairings are changed. For instance, the same items (e.g., A, B, C) are studied in two different contexts X and Y, but an item (e.g., A) is paired with another item (e.g., B) in context X but it is paired with a different item (e.g., F) in context Y, and participants are to recognize whether a pairing AB occurred in a particular context X or to recall what was paired with an item (A) in a particular context (X). In the following example, assume that the pairings AB, CD, and EF have been studied in context X and AF, CB, and ED in context Y, and participants are asked to recall the target that went with a cue in the specified context. The three-way binding involving the context X, the cue A, and the target B is modeled as the outer product of the corresponding vectors ($\mathbf{x} \otimes \mathbf{a} \otimes \mathbf{b}$). Note that the elements in this tensor product have the form $x_i a_j b_l$ where x_i is the ith element of the vector $\mathbf{x}$, a_j is the jth element of the vector $\mathbf{a}$, and $\mathbf{b}_l$ is the lth element of the vector $\mathbf{b}$. In this example, the memory for all the items learned in contexts X and Y is as follows:

$$\mathbf{T} = \mathbf{x} \otimes \mathbf{a} \otimes \mathbf{b} + \mathbf{x} \otimes \mathbf{c} \otimes \mathbf{d} + \mathbf{x} \otimes \mathbf{e} \otimes \mathbf{f} + \mathbf{y} \\ \otimes \mathbf{a} \otimes \mathbf{f} + \mathbf{y} \otimes \mathbf{c} \otimes \mathbf{b} + \mathbf{y} \otimes \mathbf{e} \otimes \mathbf{d} \qquad (7)$$

What would participants retrieve if they are required to remember what went with item *A* in context *X*? According to the tensor memory formalism, this operation is modeled as the premultiplication of the memory tensor by the tensor formed from the context vector **x** and the cue vector **a** as follows:

$$(\mathbf{x} \otimes \mathbf{a})T = [(\mathbf{x} \cdot \mathbf{x})(\mathbf{a} \cdot \mathbf{a}) + (\mathbf{x} \cdot \mathbf{y})(\mathbf{a} \cdot \mathbf{c})]\mathbf{b}$$
$$+ \, [(\mathbf{x} \cdot \mathbf{x})(\mathbf{a} \cdot \mathbf{c}) + (\mathbf{x} \cdot \mathbf{y})(\mathbf{a} \cdot \mathbf{e})]\mathbf{d}$$
$$+ \, [(\mathbf{x} \cdot \mathbf{x})(\mathbf{a} \cdot \mathbf{e}) + (\mathbf{x} \cdot \mathbf{y})(\mathbf{a} \cdot \mathbf{a})]\mathbf{f} \qquad (8)$$

Again, the retrieved representation has the form of a weighted composite of items. It can be readily seen that the weight on the correct vector **b**, the vector representing the target that occurred with *A* in context *X*, is larger than the weights on the other two vectors. This occurs because one of the terms of this weight is the inner product of the context matching itself $(\mathbf{x} \cdot \mathbf{x})$ and of the cue matching itself $(\mathbf{a} \cdot \mathbf{a})$. All of the other terms have at least one mismatch. Therefore, the correct item *B* is retrieved to the cue *A*, although it is blended with memory traces of other items such as *D* and *F*. Nonetheless, in a very special case where all the mismatches are zero and a match is one, the retrieved vector turns out to be **b** in Equation 8, which is the correct item. Thus, a memory using a tensor of rank 3 can in principle distinguish between pairs learned in different contexts.

The use of context that involves the computation of the outer product of the context and cue was called by Humphreys, Bain, and Pike (1989) the *interactive* use of context. However, context does not have to be used in this fashion. It is also possible to use context in the way we described for the vector memory model (Equation 2), where context and item vectors were added together. Humphreys, Bain, and Pike (1989) referred to this as the *additive* use of context. The difference between the two ways of using context can potentially influence a variety of memory performances. In fact, the ability to use context additively or interactively turned out to be one of the most important properties of these memories. In total, the cue used to access memory can be a vector representing a single item, a vector sum representing an item plus context, or a tensor representing an item in context. Different ways in which cues are used play an important role in human memory, and this class of memory model captures this cue-based variability in human memory performance.

Evidence for Distributed Storage

If memories are in fact distributed patterns of activation, and if two or more memories are superimposed, then shouldn't we observe memories that are blends of the constituent memories (Metcalfe, 1990)? Although we can certainly observe blends of memories with larger semantic units such as sentences, paragraphs, and stories (e.g., Bartlett, 1932), when words are used as stimuli, it has been difficult to produce evidence for blended memories (Metcalfe, 1990). It is possible to explain this by assuming that a word has a sparse representation, that is, a word is represented by a pattern of activation in which only few units are activated. However, is there other empirical evidence for the idea that even words have distributed representations?

In fact, evidence is emerging that supports the distributed representational assumption (Humphreys, Burt, & Lawrence, in press; Tehan & Humphreys, 1998). For example, Tehan and Humphreys (1989) had subjects study two lists of four words. After the first list was presented, they were either asked to recall it or to forget it, and the second list was immediately presented. Following the second list, a cue was presented and subjects were asked to recall a related word from the second list. On some trials, there was an interfering word in List 1. For example, the target in List 2 might be *cat*, the cue *ANIMAL*, and the interfering word in List 1 *dog*. A substantial amount of interference was observed in this experiment when the cue was presented at a 2-sec delay. That is, a number of people produced *dog*, which was an incorrect item, when they should have produced *cat*. This suggests that the representations of the two lists are superimposed on each other.

Interestingly, very little interference was observed (i.e., they remembered *cat* correctly) when the cue, *ANIMAL*, was presented immediately after the second list. The immunity to interference here may be due to the presence of a transient phonemic code, which should be largely absent on the delayed test. In other words, the subjects may have felt that *dog* did not sound right, but *cat* did. This hypothesis provided an opportunity to test further the assumption of distributed, superimposed memory representations. The superimposition assumption suggests that memories for items in the second list should be simultaneously activated when participants are told to remember a word from the second list. If the phonemic information present in the words in the second list was compatible with the pronunciation of *dog*, it would increase the interfering effects. In the first test of this proposal, Tehan and Humphreys presented a rhyme of the interfering word (e.g., *log*) in the second list along with the target word. On an immediate test, this manipulation significantly increased the probability that the interfering word, *dog*, would intrude. In another test, they presented the phonemes of the interfering word in three different words of the second list (e.g., *dart*, *mop*, and *fig*). They found a significant increase in the probability that the interfering word would intrude. Unless we assume that the phonemic cues are represented in a distributed fashion, this latter finding is difficult to explain. There is now fairly good evidence that memories do consist of patterns of superimposed activation patterns, but that with words we are only likely to observe blended memories in rather exceptional circumstances.

Properties of the Tensor Product Model

There are two properties of the tensor product model that are of special relevance to the social psychology of self and identity. First, the tensor product memory provides an easy way to handle the temporal continuity and discontinuity of memories of the present in relation to the memories of the past. On one level, memories of the present seem to continue seamlessly from the past; there appears to be no drastic discontinuity. So even if we learn new information in the current context, this new experience does not wipe out preexisting memories. Yet, on another level, there seems to be a discontinuity of the memories of the present from the past memories. When required, we can separate the memories of the present from those of the past to some extent. Clearly, however, the separation is imperfect, and memories of the present are influenced by the preexisting memories and the new experience alters the memories of the past to a small extent. In other words, there is a mixture of the past and the present in memory, but despite the mutual influence between the two, there is a possibility of separating them. This flexibility of merging and separating of the past and the present seems to be a characteristic of human memory.

Although the continuity of memories from the past to the present may seem like an obvious property of human memory, some connectionist theories have a problem with this property. They tend to predict that when new information is encountered, it causes a "catastrophic forgetting" of preexisting memories (McCloskey & Cohen, 1989) under some circumstances. The tensor product model does not have this problem, and preserves the preexisting memories though the new experience may alter them to some extent. One property of the tensor memory model (and vector and matrix memory models as its special cases) is that current information is simply added onto preexisting information without eliminating or suppressing the preexisting information. As a result, the preexisting memories influence memories of the present (i.e., continuity of the past into the present) as a natural consequence of the memory process.[2]

The flexible merging and separation of the past and the present in memory is accomplished by the tensor memory model by a flexible use of

---

[2]A very large amount of research on nonsense syllables showed that they were not really nonsense. In addition, there have been many demonstrations that prior learning intrudes into or influences a current memory, especially after a brief retention interval (Bartlett, 1932; Hebb, 1961; Miller & Selfridge, 1950). More generally, nobody has been able to identify a pure short-term memory task or a pure episodic memory task.

context representation. When a memory is formed about the present context, this contextualized, episodic representation is added onto the preexisting, background memory. With such a memory if context is used as an interactive retrieval cue, the episodic memories are largely, although not entirely, isolated from the background memories. This makes for the separation and isolation of the present from the past. However, if context is not used as a cue the influence of the background in memories predominates in memories, clearly preserving the continuity of the past into the present. To put it differently, contexts are used in the tensor product model to provide the categorization of temporality, or to punctuate the flow of experience, to separate one time period from others. Kashima et al. (2000; also see Kashima & Kerekes, 1994) used this property to explain a variety of time–dependent phenomena in impression formation experiments in social psychology (e.g., order effects such as primacy and recency effects).

Another property of the tensor memory that needs highlighting here is the possibility to produce a generalized memory. This property of the tensor memory allows a large number of memories about specific episodes to be collapsed across different contexts, to generate something akin to a prototype of a concept from a large number of instances of the concept (i.e., the central tendency of the past memories; see the section on Generalized Memory in Appendix). Although a number of other connectionist models have this ability, a crucial point is how this is done by different models. Some connectionist models extract the central tendency by suppressing information that is weak or information that is not shared by a large number of instances. Such a process is certainly appropriate when the weak information can be regarded as "noise" that should be suppressed. By contrast, the tensor product model preserves the weak and isolated information, but information that is common across a number of memories comes out as a strong response by virtue of its sharedness. More generally, the human ability to remember a huge range of isolated facts and incidents is suggestive of a system where weak information is not suppressed.

Humphreys, Bain, and Pike (1989) used this property to propose a theory of the relationship between episodic and semantic memory. That is, an episodic memory emerges when an item is bound to a particular context, and retrieved with the context as a cue, whereas a semantic memory is a memory collapsed across all contexts. Using a similar mechanism, Kashima et al. (2000) modeled the process by which impressions of a social group are formed on the basis of the information about individual members of the group. In their analysis, when memories about the social group are collapsed across different individual members, there emerges a prototype-like impression, which approximately averages all the information about the individual members. However, this model was also capable of preserving the information associated with an individual member of the group.

What Else Do We Need?

As Humphreys and his colleagues argued, a provision for three-way bindings is a minimum requirement for a model of human memory (Humphreys, Bain, & Pike, 1989; Humphreys, Wiles, & Bain, 1993; Humphreys, Wiles, & Dennis, 1994). The tensor memory model's capacity to support a three-way binding makes it an attractive model. Yet the tensor memory model as developed so far cannot explain some human memory phenomena by itself. One example comes from Rubin and Wallace (1989). They examined how subjects combined information from a semantic cue and a rhyming cue to retrieve a target word. For example, "What mythical being rhymes with ost?" Their subjects only produced *ghost* 1% of the time when either a semantic or rhyming cue was used by itself. However, 100% of their subjects produced it as a response when both cues were used at the same time. Another example may come from social psychological experiments in which partially contradictory concepts such as *Harvard educated* and *carpenter* are combined (e.g., Hastie, Schroeder, & Weber, 1990; Kunda, Miller, & Claire, 1990). When participants were asked to list the attributes of either the constituents or their combinations, they would list emergent attributes for the combination that were not listed for the constituents. In these examples, two retrieval cues are used to access memories, and generate a response that is not generated by either cue alone. Such phenomena point to a degree of creativity and generativity in human memory.

There are several explanations for such creativity. Kunda et al. (1990) proposed that subjects employed causal reasoning. Thus the concept of *nonmaterialistic* might be used in an explanation as to why a Harvard-educated person might be a carpenter. This proposal, however, does not explain where the concept of *nonmaterialistic* comes from in the first place and especially why at times it emerges quickly and seemingly effortlessly into consciousness. Smith and DeCoster (1998) proposed a connectionist model that can explain how an emergent concept can be activated. They trained their model on three sets of items. One set had elements of the form *ABC* (e.g., *Harvard educated*), the second *DEF* (e.g., *carpenter*), and the third *CFG*, which includes the concept *G* of *nonmaterialistic* as its part. They then presented the model with patterns of the form *ABDE* and observed that not only were the concepts *C* and *F* activated, but so was the concept *G*. This connectionist model in essence infers that *G* goes with *AB* and *DE* even though *G* had never been associated with them before. A potential problem with the Smith and DeCoster (1998) approach is that it simply adds information to the concept without suppressing any of the existing information. As Humphreys et al. (1993) argued, there are times when the memory system must suppress (weaken) existing concepts. They coined the term *intersection process* to refer to any process using two cues that enhanced the probability of recalling a target that was separately associated with each of the cues, and weakened any target that was only associated with one of the cues. For example, *rich* and *materialistic* may be strongly linked with *Harvard educated* and only weakly linked or not at all linked with *carpenter*. Under these circumstances it is possible (probable) that someone's concept of a person who is both *Harvard educated* and a *carpenter* will not include or include only weakly the concept of *rich and materialistic*. The point here is that in the memory literature, memory access processes that weaken as well as enhance are being seriously proposed. It would be appropriate to consider whether such processes may also have applications in social psychology.

What Are the General Properties of Human Memory?

It is certainly possible to build a very powerful memory model around the hypotheses of distributed storage and parallel access. These hypotheses suggest that (a) memories are represented by patterns of activation over a number of processing units, (b) they are superimposed on each other, (c) cues provide parallel access to memories, and (d) the same memory system can be cued in a variety of ways to produce different outcomes. There is no compelling need to postulate sequential search processes. Furthermore, the sequential search processes that are required or that we introspect about may be searches through *cues*, rather than searches through *memories*. For example, most of us will report that when blocked on a person's first name we may try to generate names to see if a generated name will jog our memory.

The memory models that rely on distributed storage and parallel access can explain a number of human cognitive phenomena as natural consequences of the memory process. For instance, they can explain in a straightforward manner the differences between recognition and recall, the existence of bizarre memory errors such as a merging of two distinct episodes, and the responsiveness to the environment, especially to its statistical regularities (see Kashima et al., 2000). In particular, we highlighted two of the tensor product model's properties. First was its capacity to handle the temporal continuity and discontinuity of memories. The human memory system permits a series of events to be substantially isolated from the previous series of events. At the same time, it permits a near seamless integration of current memories (memories from the recent past) and long-held memories. Second was the capacity to focus on a memory for the particular (Where did you park your car this morning?) or a memory for the general (Where do you generally park your car?), as well as the intermingling of memories for both the particular and general. Finally, the human memory system has elements of creativity in that what is retrieved to two, or possibly more, cues does not have to have been explicitly bound, as a unit, with all of the cues. That is, two cues can serve to retrieve a novel response using only pairwise information without the need to assume that the two cues and the response have co-occurred as a triplet.

SELF

What is the image of the self that emerges from the connectionist-inspired theories of the mind? Indeed, this question can be considered at two different levels. At one level, connectionism can be seen as providing a theoretical framework in which to investigate people's self processes. Understood this way, the original question becomes "How can selfhood, or people's experience of the self, be understood when viewed from a connectionist perspective?" However, at another level, connectionism may be seen as providing a metaphor for people in their reflective projects of considering what their selves are. Foddy and Kashima (this volume, chap. 1) suggest that the serial computer metaphor of the mind, and the central processing unit (CPU) in particular, may serve as a concrete metaphor for the notion of the abstract individual as a unitary and universal entity that is in control, and that stands unaffected by its sociohistorical contingencies. If their analysis has merit, it is very well to ask a parallel question, "What does connectionism serve as a metaphor for?" That is, what is the image of the self that connectionism may provide when people try to think of themselves in terms of connectionism?

Connectionism presents an image of the mind as comprised of interconnected limited-capacity processing units, which reminds us of something like a brain. In three ways, this seems to depart from the CPU metaphor. First, there is not just one, but many processors that collectively participate in the emergence of cognition and memory. This multiplicity may easily be translated into multiple selves, multiple voices, and multiple controllers in a person's mind. Second, connectionism seems to permit greater ambiguity and fluidity in its portrayal of the mind. When a concept is represented as a pattern of activation, rather than one clear location in the representational space, a concept seems not only to have a fuzzy boundary, but also to permit some merging of concepts, blurring of a category boundary, and perhaps a more dissipated and fused sense of self. Finally, the image of the brain, however flawed and much more simplified and abstracted in connectionism than in the real one, appears to ground the disembodied and abstract CPU to the body and its wetware.

What Are the General Properties of Selfhood
From a Connectionism Perspective?

As we show, this image of the person as having multiple, ambiguous, and embodied (or brainy) selves is not the kind of selfhood connectionism always anticipates. In speculating on the question "How can selfhood be understood?" when viewed from a connectionist perspective, especially from the perspective of the distributed storage and parallel access model outlined earlier, it is best to make explicit the assumptions for our speculation as clearly as possible. Our assumption is essentially an empiricist one (e.g., Locke, 1690/1975). We start with the assumption that a person's concept of him- or herself has been acquired over a considerable period of time and has been influenced by many different incidents in his or her life. These life episodes are interpreted by the person within the capacity and concepts accessible to the person at the time, and are stored in memory (also see Kashima et al., 2000). We also assume that those interpreted and stored self-related episodes can be retrieved to such queries as "Who am I?" (Kuhn & McPartland, 1954) or in order to evaluate a description as "Me" or "Not me" (Markus, 1977). Finally, we assume that whatever is retrieved by these questions can be matched against other concepts such as our concepts of others, or can be combined with other concepts, to be used as a cue for further memory retrieval. It is assumed that through these processes, that is, the constructing of cues and accessing of memory, we come to have an understanding of what our own selves are.

The general contour of selfhood that emerges here is remarkably congruent with the one sketched out by George Herbert Mead (1934). In Mead's analysis, human social conduct is meaningful (or functions as a "significant symbol," as he put it) to the extent that it invokes a response in others with whom one interacts, but also invokes a similar response in one's own experience. In other words, a social action needs to be interpreted in a similar way by the actor and his or her audiences. Mead argued that this comes about as a result of a human capacity to "take the role of others," or to empathize. As one acts in a certain way to others, it invokes responses in those others; those responses are then "internalized" in one's own experience. According to Mead, these internalized responses by others to one's action can affect one's course of action. In anticipating what others might do (this is what internalized responses permit, namely, anticipation of others' reactions), one may inhibit the action one has just initiated, or change the next action in some way. Mead insisted that this is the time when a self emerges. To Mead, a self is primarily an emergent property of self-regulation of social action.

An idealized sequence of mental events that Mead considered can be characterized as follows.

1. An actor initiates an action directed to others.
2. A cluster of responses emerges in reaction to the initiated action, which are internalized responses learned from others in the actor's social environment.
3. The actor then changes the action in reaction to the responses in step 2.

In this sequence, a self emerges in two forms. Mead called "Me" the responses emerged in step 2, and "I" the actor's reaction to the step 2 responses. A self then emerges in the interaction between the "Me" (step 2 responses) and the "I" (step 3 response). In this scheme, "Me" is the totality of others' responses that the actor has encountered in his or her social environment up to the point of initiating the action, or what Mead called the "generalized other." In contrast, "I" is a reaction to the generalized other, an expression of agency, a leap into the future, which may contain an element of uncertainty and perhaps creativity. The response attributed to the "I" in step 3 then is further directed to the others with whom the actor has been interacting.

Without going further into the details of Mead's theory of mind, self, and society, Mead's selfhood can be approximately translated into the distributed storage and parallel access model of human memory. Here, only a verbal description is provided although a more formal treatment is possible. Assuming that an actor's representation of an interaction episode includes a three-way binding of actor, action, and recipient, that is, who did what to whom, the three steps outlined earlier can be thought of as follows:

1'. A retrieval cue is constructed by combining the actor representation and the action representation, and used to access memory.
2'. Representations of others' responses that the actor has encountered in the past are retrieved en masse, and they act as a retrieval cue perhaps by itself or in combination with the representation of the actor.
3'. A response that is retrieved from step 2 operation is then enacted as a new action.

In fact, steps 2' and 3' are similar to what Kashima and Lewis (2000) theorized in their model of behavior generation, that is, how people generate options of their action in social contexts.

This reconceptualization of Mead provides a novel interpretation of his concepts. First, Mead's "Me" as a generalized other can be simply understood as a kind of "generalized memory" in which all memory traces that are retrieved by the cue in step 1' are collapsed across. As we noted earlier, one of the properties of the tensor product model and other distributed connectionist models is to generate a prototype as a natural consequence of retrieval operation. In this sense, "Me" can be thought of as a prototype of others' responses to an actor's step 1 action in the past. Nevertheless, it is also important to note that, according to the tensor product model, specific responses of specific others or in specific contexts can also be retrieved. Whether a general or a specific notion is retrieved largely depends on the manner in which retrieval cues are constructed.

In addition, this reconceptualization gives a new interpretation to Mead's speculation about the correspondence between the unity of community and the unity of self. According to Mead, when a community in which the actor lives is unified and organized, then "Me" is unified; when the community is divided in opinion, "Me" is also likely divided. Analogously, if the actor's similar actions induce similar reactions from others, the retrieved memory is likely to have a clear single response. In contrast, if the actor's similar actions are met by a number of diverse reactions by others in the past interaction episodes, the retrieved composite memory (Equations 4 and 8) should contain a diverse array of responses, resulting in a highly noisy and ambiguous representation. Would this give a sense of divided self or multiple selves? This may indeed be the case. It is when the retrieved responses have a clear center of gravity (or roughly interpreted as an attractor in the autoassociative network; note the section earlier on autoassociator) that "Me" may be experienced and interpreted as unified. We elaborate on this point later.

Second, Mead's "I" as a reaction to "Me" can be interpreted as a response retrieved when memory is cued by the representations of others' actions. Mead's conception of "I" is clearly agentic and in a way asocial:

> [A] novel reply to the social situation involved in the organized set of attitudes constitutes the "I" as over against the "me." The "me" is a conventional, habitual individual. . . . It has to have those habits, those responses which everybody has; otherwise the individual could not be a member of the community. But an individual is constantly reacting to such an organized community in the way of expressing himself . . . The attitudes involved are gathered from the group, but the individual in whom they are organized has the opportunity of giving them an expression which perhaps has never taken place before. (Mead, 1934, pp. 197–198)

In Mead's conception, "I" functions as a source of innovation, uncertainty, and unsocialized agency.

Despite Mead's insistence on the individual agency of "I," the current conception of memory implies that although "I" may be a novel response as Mead suggested, it may in fact be a voice appropriated from other agents in the social environment. Hermans (this volume, chap. 4) suggests that, borrowing Bakhtin's dialogic conception of discourse, others' voices (or actions more generally) may be appropriated as one's own in the construction of one's self-narrative. Onorato and Turner (this volume, chap. 7) also suggest that one may appropriate one's group's normative response as one's own in the process of self-categorization. The current formulation is consistent with these proposals. To the extent that the retrieval cues are similar to the representation of others and the representation of one's ingroup, what may be retrieved is those actions that were associated (or bound together) with the others and the ingroup in memory. Whatever is retrieved, one is unlikely to question the authenticity of the response, assuming that the retrieved action is one's own.

Nevertheless, there still is a possibility that what is retrieved in the current memory model is a novel response that has never been associated with other people or ingroups. This is because of the creative element in human memory we noted earlier. When a variety of cues are combined to access memory, what is retrieved may be novel, and to this extent "I" may be "uncertain" (Mead, 1934, p. 176) or "movement into the future" (p. 177). Still, the almost unbounded agency accorded Mead's "I" is significantly curtailed within the current formulation of human memory as a distributed storage and parallel access system.

William James's Paradox of Self Revisited

One of the paradoxes of self that William James (1890/1950) so vividly described is the problem of the unitary self versus multiple selves. As he put it, a person "has as many social selves as there are distinct *groups* of persons about whose opinion he [sic] cares. He generally shows a different side of himself to each of these different groups" (p. 294; emphasis in the original). And yet, one experiences an "unbrokenness in the stream of selves" (p. 335), and one says, "Here's the same old self again" (p. 334) when one awakens. Knowles and Sibicky (1990) dubbed it a "one-in-many-selves" paradox. This age-old question of personal identity has exercised a number of philosophers since the empiricist philosopher John Locke (1690/1975). This paradox seems to consist of two interlinked but separable aspects: one on the contextual multiplicity of social selves, and the other on the temporal continuity of personal identity. We believe the current connectionist formulation sheds some light on both issues.

Unity and Contextual Multiplicity of Self. To simplify the task of speculating on various memory access operations and their likely consequences on selfhood, let us imagine that an individual is asking him- or herself "Who am I?" or an equivalent question in a language. In fact, if the language used is not English (say, Japanese), the issue becomes more complicated as there may be multiple first-person singular pronouns, whereas there is only one pronoun "I" in English (see Kashima, Kashima, & Aldridge, 2001, on this point). Recall that one of the properties of the tensor product model is its capacity to retrieve both generalized and specific memories by using different retrieval cues. If we assume that a first-person pronoun provides a cue for retrieving memories that are regarded by the individual as relevant to his or her own self, at times self would appear unified (unitary self) and at times it would appear fragmented (multiple selves), depending on the variability of information associated with the retrieval cue, and how the retrieval cue is used.

The self could appear unified when a generalized memory is retrieved to the cue of "Who am I?" collapsing across different contexts and different group memberships. When there is strong commonality among what the individual does and thinks across different contexts, what is retrieved likely has a clear central tendency, resulting in a sense of the unitary self. Nevertheless, even in this case, there are several reasons why what is retrieved to the cue of a first-person pronoun would vary and therefore there appear to be multiple selves. First of all, if there are multiple first-person pronouns (as in Japanese), each first-person pronoun may retrieve different information (for some empirical evidence, see Leuers & Sonoda, 1999). Even if there is only one first-person pronoun, this retrieval cue may combine additively with such factors as mood state and background context (e.g., work, home, school, etc.), producing some variation in what is retrieved. Furthermore, when the cue is combined interactively with another cue (e.g., context such as work and home) to retrieve more context-specific information, the change in what is retrieved could be dramatic (cf. Cousins, 1989). These momentary fluctuations in self-understanding resemble James's (1890/1950) description of the self as a stream of consciousness. These fluctuations could be even greater if there is large variability in what the individual does and thinks across different contexts (possibly due to social demands or otherwise). What is retrieved to the cue of "Who am I" then may have a central tendency, but variability around it could be considerable. Here, an activation pattern may change almost continuously and more greatly as a function of additional cues such as mood and background context. Here, a fluid sense of self may emerge, underlining the multiplicity of selves, rather than their unity.

So far, we have considered the possibility of accessing memory with different cues. It is also possible to speculate what may emerge when an autoassociator is used after accessing memory. Under this circumstance, the self could appear unified when what is retrieved has a clear central tendency with a wide and deep basin of attraction (see the discussion of autoassociators). This is the case in which there is some commonality among what the individual does and thinks across different contexts. The autoassociator is likely to produce a stable pattern of activation, generating the sense of unitary self. Alternatively, under some circumstances, it is possible that there are multiple basins of attraction, and therefore multiple attractors for different selves. This is the case in which what is bound with the cue of "I" may be radically different and distributed with multiple modes. This condition may indeed produce a sense of multiple stable selves, almost resembling multiple personalities.

Temporal Continuity and Discontinuity of Self.   Our belief in the continuity of personal identity over time is unshakeable. However, when an empiricist, skeptical stance is taken with Locke and James, the belief becomes surprisingly difficult to substantiate with certainty. In the end, what enables us to say "Here's the old self again" when we wake up? James's (1890/1950) answer was the resemblance of what we remember today to what we think we remembered yesterday, or the similarity in what is retrieved over time. Indeed, this is basically what the current connectionist formulation suggests. Recall that the tensor product model is flexible in handling temporal continuity and discontinuity of memory. To recapitulate, the model suggests that time, or a continuous flow of events, may be punctuated in some form, and temporal contexts may be constructed to be bound with one's experience. So the temporal context of "yesterday" and the temporal context of "today" are bound with yesterday's and today's experiences, respectively, and stored in memory. To the extent that the representations of the temporal contexts are not completely independent of each other, and only imperfectly dissociated from each other, the cues "Who am I today?" and "Who was I yesterday?" should retrieve similar memory contents.

There are at least four reasons for this speculation. First, the self-concept of an adult is based on a considerable amount of prior experience and will change only slowly with new experience. This is especially true if we think of the retrieved memory content as a linear composite of prior experiences without there being any suppression of these prior experiences, as postulated by the tensor product model. Second, it is likely that one set of experiences that has gone into the self-concept cannot be completely isolated from other sets. That is, there is an inevitable similarity between temporally contiguous events as interpreted by the individual. Third, there is one thing that does remain constant in the different time periods in which we retrieve our self-concept—that is, the cue (Who am I?) that we use (e.g., Benveniste, 1971). Even if there are multiple first-person singular pronouns, it is most likely that the same set of pronouns is used over time (unless there is a radical language shift overnight!). Finally, there are other people, social institutions, and culture that keep reminding the individual that he or she is the same person today as the one he or she was yesterday. Once the temporal continuity of one's personal identity is taken for granted, this would provide a basis for encoding today's self as similarly to yesterday's self, which then reinforces the difficulty in completely separating one time period from another. In other words, the memory system in conjunction with one's belief in the temporal continuity of self may further strengthen the belief in temporal continuity of the self (e.g., Nelson, 1997).

Nonetheless, this does not mean that one's autobiographical memory should be seamlessly continuous. In fact, Bruner (1994) suggested that people's self-narratives are often marked by landmark events (e.g., marriage, divorce, move), and that there is a degree of discontinuity from one self beforehand and another self afterward. This phenomenon can be explained within the current framework again in terms of temporal punctuation of the life course. One is likely to punctuate time at the point of a landmark event, before and after the event, and these may be fairly differently encoded in memory. In trying to retrieve memories by using the cue of "Before" and "After" interactively with "I," one is likely to bring up different experiences that are associated with these different time periods. The discontinuity in self-narratives may be more a product of reconstructive memory processes than a consequence of straight memory retrieval; however, the current model at least provides a plausible mechanism for it.

CONNECTIONISM AND SELF: A FUTURE?

In this chapter, we attempted to provide a simple introduction to a class of memory models that assume distributed storage and parallel access, and to explore implications of this type of theories of mind for investigating the process of self and identity. In particular, we showed how connectionist approaches provide dynamic pictures of self-processes that are largely congruent with classical insights offered by William James and George Herbert Mead. Most importantly, the current formulation offers a way of resolving the paradox of unitary self and multiple selves. What appears to be a unitary self or multiple selves could emerge depending on how memory is cued and what kind of information is stored in memory. Also, the subjective sense of continuity of personal identity could result despite some feelings of punctuation of one's life course associated with landmark life events such as marriage and career moves. In all, a connectionist perspective provides a conceptual framework in which the old paradox loses its power and dissipates into banality.

During the period of writing this chapter, several papers appeared that discussed implications of models for self and identity. Some use what is known as a localist connectionist model (Smith, Coats, & Walling, 1999) in which self is regarded as a single, localized node, and others made use of a distributed connectionist model of a different variety (Kashima & Kashima, 1999) and a new variety that extends connectionism to a more socialized version by linking multiple connectionist models (Kashima et al., 2001). There is also an application of a cellular automata (Nowak, Vallacher, Tesser, & Borkowski, 2000), which is a mathematical model that is closely related to distributed connectionist models in its spirit. All these research activities suggest that explorations of connectionist theories of mind and ideas represented by them are only beginning now, and likely to continue. It is nonetheless important to recognize that what is significant in this new metaphor of the mind is not necessarily its mathematical formalisms, but its capacity to shed light on some of the old puzzles and paradoxes, and to move the field forward by presenting new possibilities and to intellectual horizons.

REFERENCES

Anderson, J. A. (1973). A theory for the recognition of items from short memorized lists. *Psychological Review, 86,* 417–438.

Banks, W. P. (1970). Signal detection theory and human memory. *Psychological Bulletin, 74,* 81–99.

Bartlett, F. C. (1932). *Remembering.* Cambridge, UK: Cambridge University Press.

Benveniste, E. (1971). *Problems in general linguistics* (M. E. Meek, Trans.). Coral Gables, FL: University of Miami Press. (Original work published 1966)

Bruner, J. (1994). The "remembered" self. In U. Neisser & R. Fivush (Eds.), *The remembering self: construction and accuracy in the self-narrative* (pp. 41–54). Cambridge, UK: Cambridge University Press.

Chappell, M., & Humphreys, M. S. (1994). An auto-associative neural network for sparse representations: Analysis and application to models of recognition and cued recall. *Psychological Review, 101,* 103–128.

Cousins, S. D. (1989). Culture and self-perception in Japan and the United States. *Journal of Personality and Social Psychology, 56,* 124–131.

Dennis, S., & Humphreys, M. S. (2001). A context noise model of episodic recognition memory. *Psychological Review, 108,* 452–478.

Fiedler, K. (1996). Explaining and simulating judgment biases as an aggregation phenomenon in probabilistic, multiple-cue environments. *Psychological Review, 103,* 193–214.

Flexser, A. V., & Tulving, E. (1978). Retrieval independence in recognition and recall. *Psychological Review, 85,* 153–171.

Halford, G. S., Wilson, W. H., & Phillips, S. (1998). Processing capacity defined by relational complexity: Implications for comparative, developmental, and cognitive psychology. *Behavioral and Brain Sciences, 21,* 803–864.

Hastie, R., Schroeder, C., & Weber, R. (1990). Creating complex social conjunction categories from simple categories. *Bulletin of the Psychonomic Society, 28,* 242–247.

Hebb, D. O. (1961). Distinctive features of learning in the higher animal. In A. Fessard, R. W. Gerard, J. Konorski, & J. F. Delafresnaye (Ed.), *Brain mechanisms in learning: A symposium* (pp. 32–54). Oxford: Blackwell.

Humphreys, M. S., Bain, J. D., & Pike, R. (1989). Different ways to cue a coherent memory system: A theory for episodic, semantic and procedural tasks. *Psychological Review, 96,* 208–233.

Humphreys, M. S., Pike, R., Bain, J. D., & Tehan, G. (1989). Global matching: A comparison of the SAM, Minerva II, Matrix and TODAM models. *Journal of Mathematical Psychology, 33,* 36–67.

Humphreys, M. S., Tehan, G., O'Shea, A., & Boland, S. W. (2000). Target similarity effects: Support for the parallel distributed processing assumptions. *Memory & Cognition, 28,* 798–811.

Humphreys, M. S., Wiles, J., & Bain, J. D. (1993). Memory retrieval with two cues: Think of intersecting sets. In D. E. Meyer & S. Kornblum (Eds.), *Attention and Performance XIV: Synergies in Experimental Psychology, Artificial Intelligence, and Cognitive Neuropsychology—A Silver Jubilee* (pp. 489–508) Cambridge, MA: MIT Press.

Humphreys, M. S., Burt, J. S., & Lawrence S. (in press). Expecting dirt but saying dart: The creation of a blend memory. *Psychonomic Bulletin & Review.*

Humphreys, M. S., Wiles, J., & Dennis, S. (1994). Toward a theory of human memory: Data structures and access processes. *Behavioral and Brain Sciences, 17,* 655–692.

James, W. (1950). *The principles of psychology.* New York: Dover. (Original work published 1890)

Kashima, Y., & Kashima, E. S. (1999). Culture, connectionism, and the self. In J. Adamopoulos & Y. Kashima (Eds.), *Social behavior in cultural contexts* (pp. 77–94). London: Sage.

Kashima, Y., & Kerekes, A. R. Z. (1994). A distribution memory model of averaging phenomena in person impression formation. *Journal of Experimental Social Psychology, 30,* 407–455.

Kashima, Y., Kashima, E., & Aldridge, J. (2001). Towards cultural dynamics of self-conceptions. In C. Sedikides & M. B. Brewer (Eds.), *Individual self, relational self, and collective self: Partners, opponents, or strangers* (pp. 277–298). Philadelphia, PA: Psychology Press.

Kashima, Y., & Lewis, V. (2000). Where does the behavior come from in attitude–behavior relations? Toward a connectionist model of behavior generation. In D. J. Terry & M. A. Hogg (Eds.), *Attitudes, behavior, and social context: The role of norms and group membership* (pp. 115–133). Mahwah, NJ: Lawrence Erlbaum Associates.

Kashima, Y., Woolcock, J., & Kashima, E. S. (2000). Group impressions as dynamic configurations. *Psychological Review, 107,* 914–942.

Knowles, E. S., & Sibicky, M. E. (1990). Continuity and diversity in the stream of selves: Metaphorical resolutions of William James's one-in-many-selves paradox. *Personality and Social Psychology Bulletin, 16,* 676–687.

Kuhn, M. H., & McPartland, T. S. (1954). An empirical investigation of self-attitudes. *American Sociological Review, 19,* 68–76.

Kunda, Z., Miller, D. T., & Claire, T. (1990). Combining social concepts: The role of causal reasoning. *Cognitive Science, 14,* 551–577.

Leuers, T. R. S., & Sonoda, N. (1999). Independent self bias. In T. Sugiman, M. Karasawa, J. H. Liu, & C. Ward (Eds.), *Progress in asian social psychology* (Vol. 3, pp. 87–104). Seoul, Korea: Kyoyook-Kwhak-Sa Publishing.

Locke, J. (1975). *An essay concerning human understanding.* Oxford, UK: Clarendon Press. (Original published 1690)

Markus, H. (1977). Self-schemata and processing information about the self. *Journal of Personality and Social Psychology, 35,* 63–78.

McCloskey, M., & Cohen, N. J. (1989). catastrophic interference in connectionist networks: The sequential learning problem. In G. H. Bower (Ed.), *The psychology of learning and motivation* (Vol. 24, pp. 109–164). New York: Academic Press.

Mead, G. H. (1934). *Mind, self, and society.* Chicago: University of Chicago Press.

Metcalfe, J. (1990). Composite holographic associative recall model (CHARM) and blended memories in eyewitness testimony. *Journal of Experimental Psychology: General, 119,* 145–160.

Miller, G. A., & Selfridge, J. A. (1950). Verbal context and the recall of meaningful material. *American Journal of Psychology, 63,* 176–185.

Murnane, K., & Phelps, M. P. (1993). A global activation approach to the effect of changes in environmental context on recognition. *Journal of Experimental Psychology: Learning, Memory, and Cognition, 19,* 882–894.

Nelson, K. (1993). The psychological and social origins of autobiographical memory. *Psychological Science, 4,* 7–14.

Nowak, A., Vallacher, R. R., Tesser, A., & Borkowski, W. (2000). Society of self: The emergence of collective properties in self-structure. *Psychological Review, 107,* 39–61.

Pike, R. (1984). A comparison of convolution and matrix distributed memory systems. *Psychological Review, 91,* 281–294.

Read, S. J., Venman, E. J., & Miller, L. C. (1996). Connectionism, parallel constraint satisfaction processes, and gestalt principles: (Re)introducing cognitive dynamics to social psychology. *Personality and Social Psychological Review, 1,* 26–53.

Rubin, D. C., & Wallace, W. T. (1989). Rhyme and reason: Analysis of dual retrieval cues. *Journal of Experimental Psychology: Learning, Memory, and Cognition, 15,* 698–709.

Smith, E. R. (1996). What do connectionism and social psychology offer each other? *Journal of Personality and Social Psychology, 70,* 893–912.

Smith, E. R., Coats, S., & Walling, D. (1999). Overlapping mental representations of self, ingroup, and partner. *Personality and Social Psychology Bulletin, 25,* 873–882.

Smith, E. R., & DeCoster, J. (1998). Knowledge acquisition, accessibility, and use in person perception and stereotyping: Simulation with a recurrent connectionist network. *Journal of Personality and Social Psychology, 74,* 21–35.

Tehan, G., & Humphreys, M. S. (1998). Creating proactive interference in immediate recall: Building a dog from a dart, a mop, and a fig. *Memory & Cognition, 26,* 477–489.

Wiles, J., & Humphreys, M. S. (1993). Using artificial neural networks to model implicit and explicit memory. In P. Graf & M. Masson (Eds.), *Implicit memory: New directions in cognition, development, and neuropsychology* (pp. 141–166). Hillsdale, NJ: Lawrence Erlbaum Associates

Wiles, J., Humphreys, M. S., Bain, J. D., & Dennis, S. (1991). Direct memory access using two cues: Finding the intersection of sets in a connectionist model. In R. P. Lippman, J. E. Moody, & D. S. Touretzky (Eds.), *Advances in neural information processing systems 3* (pp. 635–641). San Mateo, CA: Morgan Kaufmann.

APPENDIX

Recognition Memory

Let α equal the average value of the dot product of an item with itself and β equal the average value of the dot product between two randomly chosen items (this can be thought of as the average similarity between two items). The match of an old probe with the memory vector will on average be $\alpha + (k - 1)\beta$ and the average match of a new item will be $k\beta$, where k is the number of items in the list. We refer to the dot product between the vector representing a probe item and the memory vector as the matching strength of the probe item. By setting certain conditions on the vector elements (e.g., they are randomly and independently chosen), we can compute the average matching strength and variance associated with these matching strengths, which follows directly from the representational and memory access assumptions. Thus, the vector model maps directly onto the signal detection analysis of recognition memory (Banks, 1970). That is, the appropriate decision rule for an organism or machine utilizing a vector memory is to set a criterion so that the appropriate response is *yes* if the matching strength exceeds the criterion and *no* if it does not. In addition, the distance between the average matching strengths of old and new items when scaled by the standard deviation of the new item matching strength is the appropriate measure of sensitivity.

Recognition in Context

Suppose that A and B occurred in context X, and C and D occurred in context Y. The task is to determine whether A occurred in context X or in context Y. The following shows that this can be achieved by the matrix model, but not by the vector model.

Within the vector memory formalism, the memory is $\mathbf{v} = (\mathbf{a} + \mathbf{x}) + (\mathbf{b} + \mathbf{x}) + (\mathbf{c} + \mathbf{y}) + (\mathbf{d} + \mathbf{y})$ (Equation 1 in text). The process of trying to see if A occurred in context X or in context Y may be described as follows. The probe is $(\mathbf{a} + \mathbf{x})$, which is then matched against the memory vector $\mathbf{v}$. Similarly, participants may try to see whether A occurred in context Y (the probe then is $\mathbf{a} + \mathbf{y}$).

$$
\begin{aligned}
(\mathbf{a} + \mathbf{x}) \cdot \mathbf{v} &= (\mathbf{a} + \mathbf{x}) \cdot (\mathbf{a} + \mathbf{x}) + (\mathbf{a} + \mathbf{x}) \cdot (\mathbf{b} + \mathbf{x}) \\
&\quad + (\mathbf{a} + \mathbf{x}) \cdot (\mathbf{c} + \mathbf{y}) + (\mathbf{a} + \mathbf{x}) \cdot (\mathbf{d} + \mathbf{y}) \\
&= (\mathbf{a} \cdot \mathbf{a} + \mathbf{x} \cdot \mathbf{x} + 2\mathbf{a} \cdot \mathbf{x}) + \\
&\quad (\mathbf{a} \cdot \mathbf{b} + \mathbf{x} \cdot \mathbf{x} + \mathbf{a} \cdot \mathbf{x} + \mathbf{b} \cdot \mathbf{x}) \\
&\quad + (\mathbf{a} \cdot \mathbf{c} + \mathbf{x} \cdot \mathbf{y} + \mathbf{a} \cdot \mathbf{y} + \mathbf{c} \cdot \mathbf{x}) \\
&\quad + (\mathbf{a} \cdot \mathbf{d} + \mathbf{x} \cdot \mathbf{y} + \mathbf{a} \cdot \mathbf{x} + \mathbf{d} \cdot \mathbf{y})
\end{aligned} \tag{1}
$$

$$
\begin{aligned}
(\mathbf{a} + \mathbf{y}) \cdot \mathbf{v} &= (\mathbf{a} + \mathbf{y}) \cdot (\mathbf{a} + \mathbf{x}) + (\mathbf{a} + \mathbf{y}) \cdot (\mathbf{b} + \mathbf{x}) \\
&\quad + (\mathbf{a} + \mathbf{y}) \cdot (\mathbf{c} + \mathbf{x}) + (\mathbf{a} + \mathbf{y}) \cdot (\mathbf{d} + \mathbf{y}) \\
&= (\mathbf{a} \cdot \mathbf{a} + \mathbf{y} \cdot \mathbf{x} + 2\mathbf{a} \cdot \mathbf{x}) \\
&\quad + (\mathbf{a} \cdot \mathbf{b} + \mathbf{x} \cdot \mathbf{x} + \mathbf{a} \cdot \mathbf{x} + \mathbf{b} \cdot \mathbf{x}) \\
&\quad + (\mathbf{a} \cdot \mathbf{c} + \mathbf{x} \cdot \mathbf{y} + \mathbf{a} \cdot \mathbf{y} + \mathbf{c} \cdot \mathbf{x}) \\
&\quad + (\mathbf{a} \cdot \mathbf{d} + \mathbf{y} \cdot \mathbf{y} + \mathbf{a} \cdot \mathbf{y} + \mathbf{d} \cdot \mathbf{y})
\end{aligned} \tag{A2}
$$

Let α equal the average value of the dot product of an item with itself (e.g., $\mathbf{a} \cdot \mathbf{a}$) and β equal the average value of the dot product between two randomly chosen items (e.g., $\mathbf{a} \cdot \mathbf{b}$; this can be thought of as the average similarity between two items). Also assuming that, on average, $\mathbf{x} \cdot \mathbf{x} = \mathbf{y} \cdot \mathbf{y}$

$= \gamma$, that $\mathbf{x} \cdot \mathbf{y} = \mathbf{y} \cdot \mathbf{x} = \delta$, and that $\mathbf{a} \cdot \mathbf{x} = \mathbf{a} \cdot \mathbf{y} = \mathbf{b} \cdot \mathbf{x} = \mathbf{b} \cdot \mathbf{y} = \mathbf{c} \cdot \mathbf{x} = \mathbf{c} \cdot \mathbf{y} = \mathbf{d} \cdot \mathbf{x} = \mathbf{d} \cdot \mathbf{y} = \pi$, the expected value of both Equations A1 and A2 equals $\alpha + 4\beta + 2\gamma + 2\delta + 8\pi$. Therefore, the vector model cannot determine whether A occurred in context X or in context Y. Therefore, the vector representation does not allow for a differentiation between the two recognition probes.

By contrast, within the matrix memory formalism, the memory representation is $\mathbf{M} = \mathbf{x} \otimes \mathbf{a} + \mathbf{x} \otimes \mathbf{b} + \mathbf{y} \otimes \mathbf{c} + \mathbf{y} \otimes \mathbf{d}$ (Equation 3 in text). The process of trying to see if A occurred in context X or in context Y may be described as follows. First, context X is used to retrieve memory content, and then the output is matched by item A. Similarly, participants may try to see whether A occurred in context Y. The resultant matching strengths are as follows:

$$
\begin{aligned}
(\mathbf{xM}) \cdot \mathbf{a} &= \mathbf{x}(\mathbf{x} \otimes \mathbf{a}) \cdot \mathbf{a} + \mathbf{x}(\mathbf{x} \otimes \mathbf{b}) \cdot \mathbf{a} + \mathbf{x}(\mathbf{y} \otimes \mathbf{c}) \cdot \mathbf{a} \\
&\quad + \mathbf{x}(\mathbf{y} \otimes \mathbf{d}) \cdot \mathbf{a} \\
&= (\mathbf{x} \cdot \mathbf{x})(\mathbf{a} \cdot \mathbf{a}) + (\mathbf{x} \cdot \mathbf{x})(\mathbf{a} \cdot \mathbf{b}) + (\mathbf{x} \cdot \mathbf{y})(\mathbf{a} \cdot \mathbf{c}) \\
&\quad + (\mathbf{x} \cdot \mathbf{y})(\mathbf{a} \cdot \mathbf{d})
\end{aligned} \tag{A3}
$$

$$
\begin{aligned}
(\mathbf{yM}) \cdot \mathbf{a} &= \mathbf{y}(\mathbf{x} \otimes \mathbf{a}) \cdot \mathbf{a} + \mathbf{y}(\mathbf{x} \otimes \mathbf{b}) \cdot \mathbf{a} + \mathbf{y}(\mathbf{x} \otimes \mathbf{c}) \cdot \mathbf{a} \\
&\quad + \mathbf{y}(\mathbf{x} \otimes \mathbf{d}) \cdot \mathbf{a} \\
&= (\mathbf{y} \cdot \mathbf{x})(\mathbf{a} \cdot \mathbf{a}) + (\mathbf{y} \cdot \mathbf{x})(\mathbf{a} \cdot \mathbf{b}) \\
&\quad + (\mathbf{y} \cdot \mathbf{y})(\mathbf{a} \cdot \mathbf{c}) + (\mathbf{y} \cdot \mathbf{y})(\mathbf{a} \cdot \mathbf{d})
\end{aligned} \tag{A4}
$$

Under the same assumptions as before, there is one term where the context at test matches the context at study and the test item matches the study item (expected value $\gamma\alpha$), a second term where the contexts match but the items do not (expected value $\gamma\beta$), plus two terms where neither the context nor the item matches (expected value $\delta\beta$). Thus the overall expected value when an item is tested in the correct context (Equation A3) is $\gamma\alpha + \gamma\beta + 2\delta\beta$ and the value when it is tested out of context (Equation A4) is $2\gamma\beta + 2\delta\beta$. Because the average similarity of a context to itself is greater than the average similarity between two different contexts ($\gamma > \delta$) and the average similarity of an item to itself is greater than the average similarity of two different items ($\alpha > \beta$), the matching strength when an item is tested in the correct context, $(\mathbf{xM}) \cdot \mathbf{a}$ (Equation A3), is on average greater than the matching strength with the wrong context $(\mathbf{yM}) \cdot \mathbf{a}$ (Equation A4). Therefore, it is possible within the matrix memory model to determine whether an item was studied in context X or Y.

Cued Recall in Tensor Memory

This shows the derivation of Equation 8 in the text.

$$
\begin{aligned}
(\mathbf{x} \otimes \mathbf{a}) \cdot \mathbf{T} = {} & (\mathbf{x} \otimes \mathbf{a})(\mathbf{x} \otimes \mathbf{a} \otimes \mathbf{b}) + (\mathbf{x} \otimes \mathbf{a}) \cdot (\mathbf{x} \otimes \mathbf{c} \otimes \mathbf{d}) \\
& + (\mathbf{x} \otimes \mathbf{a})(\mathbf{x} \otimes \mathbf{e} \otimes \mathbf{f}) \\
& + (\mathbf{x} \otimes \mathbf{a})(\mathbf{y} \otimes \mathbf{a} \otimes \mathbf{f}) + (\mathbf{x} \otimes \mathbf{a}) \cdot (\mathbf{y} \otimes \mathbf{c} \otimes \mathbf{b}) \\
& + (\mathbf{x} \otimes \mathbf{a})(\mathbf{y} \otimes \mathbf{e} \otimes \mathbf{d}) \\
= {} & (\mathbf{x} \cdot \mathbf{x})(\mathbf{a} \cdot \mathbf{a})\mathbf{b} + (\mathbf{x} \cdot \mathbf{x})(\mathbf{a} \cdot \mathbf{c})\mathbf{d} \\
& + (\mathbf{x} \cdot \mathbf{x})(\mathbf{a} \cdot \mathbf{e})\mathbf{f} + (\mathbf{x} \cdot \mathbf{y})(\mathbf{a} \cdot \mathbf{a})\mathbf{f} \\
& + (\mathbf{x} \cdot \mathbf{y})(\mathbf{a} \cdot \mathbf{c})\mathbf{b} + (\mathbf{x} \cdot \mathbf{y})(\mathbf{a} \cdot \mathbf{e})\mathbf{d} \\
= {} & [(\mathbf{x} \cdot \mathbf{x})(\mathbf{a} \cdot \mathbf{a}) + (\mathbf{x} \cdot \mathbf{y})(\mathbf{a} \cdot \mathbf{c})]\mathbf{b} \\
& + [(\mathbf{x} \cdot \mathbf{x})(\mathbf{a} \cdot \mathbf{c}) + (\mathbf{x} \cdot \mathbf{y})(\mathbf{a} \cdot \mathbf{e})]\mathbf{d} \\
& + [(\mathbf{x} \cdot \mathbf{x})(\mathbf{a} \cdot \mathbf{e}) + (\mathbf{x} \cdot \mathbf{y})(\mathbf{a} \cdot \mathbf{a})]\mathbf{f} \qquad (8)
\end{aligned}
$$

Generalized Memory

To see how "generalized memory" can be created mathematically, assume that the vector elements have been randomly and independently drawn from a normal distribution with a mean of $1/\sqrt{n}$, where n is the number of elements in the vector. Also define a fixed vector $\mathbf{r}$ where all of its elements equal $1/\sqrt{n}$. The vector $\mathbf{r}$ has the property that the expected value between it and any other vector is 1.0. If we premultiply the tensor memory by a context vector $\mathbf{x}$ and the fixed vector $\mathbf{r}$ $(\mathbf{x} \otimes \mathbf{r})$ the result is a composite of all of the items that occurred in that context. Similarly, if we premultiply by $\mathbf{r}$ and a cue $\mathbf{a}$ $(\mathbf{r} \otimes \mathbf{a})$ the result is a composite of all of the items that have been associated with that cue. For a somewhat different but related analysis, see Kashima et al. (2000). Graeme Halford and his associates (Halford, Wilson, & Phillips, 1998) also used this property in a model of analogies. In this model they stored argument–relationship–argument triples. They could then collapse over the relationship dimension to obtain the set of items that are related in any fashion to a cue or over one of the argument dimensions to obtain the set of relationships that a cue enters into.

PERSONAL PROCESSES

Part II highlights personal perspectives on selfhood. They point to two different directions in which personal perspectives on selfhood can go beyond the omnipotent central processing unit (CPU). In chapter 3, Twenge and Baumeister make a significant amendment to the totalitarian ego metaphor of the self while generally endorsing the social cognitive perspective on the self. They present their recent work investigating the property of the control process as a limited-capacity, self-regulatory mechanism that is much less powerful than that envisaged as the CPU. The metaphor that they propose, the control mechanism as "muscle," brings in a reference to the embodied self, a concept that is somewhat incompatible with the disembodied control mechanism implied by the computer metaphor of the mind.

In contrast, in chapter 4, Hermans makes a move to complement the social cognitive model of the self by taking a narrative psychological view. He gives an overview of his theory of self, which dissolves the unitary totalitarian ego into multivoiced, dialogical self-narratives. In his view, the personal self consists of stories that are constructed in interaction with multiple others, and woven into diverse, sometimes consistent and sometimes inconsistent, narratively structured streams of thoughts. The image of self portrayed here is more compatible with the

PDP metaphor of the mind than the CPU metaphor. Social psychologists may be largely unfamiliar with the perspective represented by Hermans, but his careful unwinding of the paradox of unitary versus multiple selves warrants further attention.

Chapter 3

Self-Control: A Limited
Yet Renewable Resource

Jean M. Twenge
San Diego State University

Roy F. Baumeister
Case Western Reserve University

If people always acted in a deliberate, logical manner, many of the world's problems would disappear. Dieters would never overeat, angry people would never strike out in rage, and teenagers would never become addicted to drugs. Yet all of these things can and do happen when people lose the ability to *self-regulate* (a term we use interchangeably with *self-control*, both of which we define as the human capacity to alter or override one's natural responses, including thoughts, emotions, and actions). But why and how does self-control break down? Given the ill effects of self-control failures, one might think that human self-control would be relatively strong and enduring. In general, self-control behaviors maximize people's long-term best interests (Barkley, 1997; Kanfer & Karoly, 1972; Mischel, 1996). Yet any dieter will tell you that resisting a piece of chocolate cake often requires more resources than most of us possess. This chapter explores why self-control breakdowns occur (including the all-too-common breakdown over chocolate), and how self-regulatory resources can be restored.

Self-regulation is an essential part of most general theories of the self. Higgins (1996) argued that self-regulation is a master function that organizes many other activities and processes. One of us (Baumeister, 1998) proposed that the self has three basic functions. The first is basic self-awareness, which leads to outcomes such as self-esteem, self-perception, and self-knowledge. The second involves interpersonal processes such as self-regulation. The third is the executive function, which oversees external acts such as choice, volition, and initiative, as well as the internal process of self-regulation. Two of these aspects involve self-regulation in some form. Here, we are mainly concerned with the executive function of the self, which makes most choices relevant to self-control and self-regulation.

IMPORTANCE OF SELF-REGULATION

It is difficult to exaggerate the benefits of self-control. At their base, many modern social problems are caused by self-regulation failures (see Baumeister, Heatherton, & Tice, 1994, for a review). Addiction, alcohol abuse, drug abuse, and other forms of dependency involve regulating one's substance use. Problems in regulating eating are very common, running the gamut from anorexia nervosa to overeating and dieting failures. People's inability to regulate their spending and saving results in innumerable bankruptcies, gambling debts, and excessive credit card use—actions that may benefit the lucky few who own casinos and credit card companies, but disasters for most individuals involved. Considerable mental and physical distress results from the breakdown of sexual self-control, including unwanted pregnancy, AIDS and other venereal diseases, marital problems caused by infidelity, and the general embarrassment of realizing one's mistakes after a night of inebriation. Violent and criminal behavior may often be traced to the failure to regulate aggressive impulses; in fact, Gottfredson and Hirschi (1990) argued that deficient self-control is the most important theoretical key in understanding criminality. (Criminals may rarely exclaim "A failure in self-regulation made me do it!" but it seems true nonetheless.) Underachievement in school and work is often linked to poor self-regulation, such as the failure to persist in the face of difficulties and that ever-present lure of procrastination (a temptation that may be as difficult to resist as chocolate). Self-regulation is also crucial to good health. Medical research suggests that we would all live longer if we only performed the three seemingly simple tasks of eating right, exercising regularly, and refraining from smoking. Yet even on these life-and-death decisions, many people find themselves falling far short of their goals—figuratively (and sometimes literally) sitting on the couch all evening, smoking a cigarette and eating an entire bag of potato chips.

The exercise of self-control can prevent all of these negative outcomes. In general, successful self-regulation includes four basic types of activities. First, self-regulation often involves managing and controlling emotions. For example, control over feelings of anger and frustration can prevent violent outbursts. Self-regulation also encompasses control over one's mental processes, such as the ability to concentrate and to persist on tasks. If a child is going to be successful in school, for example, she must learn this skill eventually; the frustrating math problems must be completed, and the tedious 18th-century essay read, despite the natural desire to give up and watch TV instead. Impulse control is another important aspect of self-regulation. The most obvious example of the problems of self-regulation failure in this sphere is addiction to drugs or alcohol. Impulses to overeat must also be controlled, lest the entire box of cookies disappear or the chocolate cake mysteriously evaporate. Last, self-regulation involves setting and reaching goals. To achieve in life, we must often work toward a long-term goal at the expense of short-term ones; the lack of instant gratification makes self-control necessary for this type of goal-setting. For example, going to graduate school might be described as a half-decade-long exercise in delayed gratification. But if a student is going to receive a degree, shorter term temptations such as a significant salary must be resisted.

INDIVIDUAL DIFFERENCES AND THE PREDICTIVE POWER OF SELF-REGULATION

The benefits of self-control are perhaps most evident in studies of individual differences in self-control, although most of these findings are correlational and the causal impact of self-control is thus not proven in them. Still, it is quite apparent that a high level of self-control is associated with success across many different types of activities. Tangney and Baumeister (2000) found that high scores on their trait measure of self-control were associated with superior task performance in the form of better grades in college; with better mental and emotional health, as indicated by a broad measure of pathological symptoms; with better interpersonal functioning, as indicated by better relationships, stronger family cohesion, more secure attachments to others, and better skills at managing interpersonal relations; and with healthier emotional patterns, including less anger and better management of anger when it does arise.

The relationships among trait self-control and these measures of adjustment were all linear rather than curvilinear (Tangney & Baumeister, 2000). These patterns are contrary to the hypothesis that excessive self-control is liked to obsessive-compulsive symptoms and other mental health problems; apparently, high self-control carries many more benefits than detriments.

Previous work also demonstrated the importance of high self-control. In several classic studies, Mischel and his colleagues measured children's ability to delay gratification (e.g., by telling them that they could have two marshmallows later if they refrained from eating one marshmallow right away). Children who were able to delay gratification later grew up to be more successful in school and work and were better liked both by their peers and by authority figures (Mischel, Shoda, & Peake, 1988; Shoda, Mischel, & Peake, 1990). In another study, students who were chronic pro-crastinators (and thus failed to self-regulate their time effectively) suffered greater stress and health problems than other students. Procrastinators also made lower grades in college (Tice & Baumeister, 1997). Dutch ado-lescents who scored higher on the trait self-control scale tended to avoid delinquent actions such as petty theft, vandalism, and fighting; they also had better relationships with their parents (Engels, Den Exter Blokland, & Baumeister, & Finkenauer, 2000). Thus people with high self-control reap many rewards for themselves and others. Given the effects on work per-formance and crime, high trait self-control also seems to create benefits for society at large.

It is interesting to compare self-control with self-esteem. Parents, schools, and even statewide commissions (e.g., the California Task Force) have at-tempted to raise and cultivate high levels of self-esteem in children and ado-lescents. Yet most research suggests that self-esteem produces few direct ben-efits or desirable consequences. Correlations between individual self-esteem and most outcomes are weak, and the direction of causation may run from the "outcomes" to self-esteem rather than self-esteem producing the out-comes. As a nation, it might benefit us to cultivate high levels of self-control rather than high levels of self-esteem.

SELF-CONTROL AS A LIMITED RESOURCE

Resisting temptation and maintaining self-control are easier at some times than at others. If we have had to restrain ourselves from yelling at our boss all day, the smoking on the potato-chip-laden couch scenario becomes much more likely. Recent work suggests that this is true because we have a limited amount of self-control, often colloquially referred to as "will-power" (see Mischel, 1996). Apparently, the mental resource of self-control operates much like our physical resource of muscles: it becomes weak and finally fails after constant use (Muraven & Baumeister, 2000). People have only a limited amount of self-control, so only a finite number of depleting behaviors may be performed. There is thus an aftereffect of self-control as well: It takes a certain amount of time and/or replenish-ment before the reserve of self-control is filled once again.

Before the recent research was performed, however, the strength model was not the only plausible theory of self-regulation. If self-control relies on a cognitive schema, then the first act of self-control would prime the schema, thereby facilitating the second act, and so on. Thus the net ef-fect would be improvements in self-control over consecutive tasks. If self-control is primarily a skill, there would be little change from one trials to the next, because skill remains fairly stable between trials (although it gradually improves with practice).

However, recent research suggests that self-control becomes depleted over consecutive tasks (Baumeister, Bratslavksy, Muraven & Tice, 1998; Muraven, Tice, & Baumeister, 1998). In one vivid illustration of this effect, participants in the crucial condition sat at a table displaying tempting chocolates and cookies. They had skipped a meal, but the experimenter asked them not to eat the tasty chocolate but instead to consume at least two radishes from another bowl. Later, these participants were asked to work on a series of unsolvable geometric tracing puzzles; they gave up on the puzzles significantly more rapidly than participants in the two control conditions (one control group was allowed to eat the chocolate, whereas the other was not exposed to any food at all). In another experiment, depletion was manipulated by asking participants to list their thoughts; those in the experimental group were told that they could think about anything they wanted to except a white bear (this thought-suppression procedure was adapted from Wegner, Schneider, Carter, & White, 1987). After the thought-listing task, the experimental group had a more difficult time refraining from smiling and laughing in response to a comedy video (the same type of emotional suppression used as an independent variable in the previous study). Another thought-suppression study showed that those in the experimental condition gave up sooner on unsolvable anagrams (Muraven et al., 1998).

Controlling emotions also depletes self-control. Participants in the experimental condition were asked not to show or feel any emotions while watching a humorous or sad video; the members of the control group were allowed to express their emotions freely (Baumeister et. al., 1998). When asked to work on unsolvable anagrams, the members of the experimental group once again gave up sooner than those in the control group. A reversed order also produced significant results (Muraven et al., 1998).

Recent research has demonstrated that controlling one's emotions also impairs the encoding of information, another important duty of the executive function. Richards and Gross (2000) asked a group of participants to supress their emotions while watching an upsetting video. These participants did not remember as much about the details of the video as those who were simply instructed to watch and react naturally. This effect also occured in self-reports of real-world behavior: People who supressed their emotions also reported poor memory for those situations. These results are important because they show that self-control depletes more than one's supply of willpower; cognitive resources are also affected. Although emotion regulation is often beneficial, it has the side effect of drawing our attention away from useful details of situations. We control our feelings at the expense of rich and accurate memories.

Making choices also seems to require a crucial resource that erodes self-control. In one experiment (Baumeister et al., 1998), some participants were given a choice about making a counterattitudinal speech (arguing that the university should raise tuition, never a popular opinion among undergraduates). Other participants were told that they had no choice about which speech to make (presumably because the experimenter already had enough people making the attitude-consistent speech). Those who made a choice about giving the speech gave up sooner on the unsolvable tracing puzzles, compared to two control groups (one given no choice about which speech its members would make, and another that did not prepare to make a speech). Somewhat surprisingly, people who had chosen to perform a pro-attitudinal behavior—in this case, to make a speech favoring low tuition rates—showed the same degree of depletion as those who chose the counterattitudinal behavior. Thus, depletion resulted from the act of choice, regardless of the behavior that was chosen.

The reverse effect also occurred: When self-control was depleted, people avoided making choices. Participants were depleted by overriding their natural response in a verbal task. They were first taught an easy task: crossing out all instances of the letter "e" in a page of text. Then they were told to perform a similar task with additional rules, such as not crossing out any "e" that was adjacent to or two letters removed from another vowel. These rules required people to override (repeatedly) their newly acquired habit of crossing out every "e"; this overriding likely depleted self-control. In contrast, control participants solved three-digit multiplication problems, which are difficult and mentally taxing but do not involve self-regulation (because one follows well-learned procedures rather than having to override incipient responses). After the initial task, passivity was measured. People were shown a film of a boring video (of a blank wall!) and were given control over how long they would sit and watch it. Continuing to see the movie was passive whereas quitting was active: They were told that the movie would continue until they pressed the button in front of them. The participants who overrode their natural response in the verbal task were more likely to passively watch the video of the blank wall without making the active choice to stop watching it. Thus, in this case, being depleted by another task caused people to avoid making active choices, even when that choice would be beneficial (as avoiding watching a video of a wall must be).

Even making choices between objects seems to be depleting (Twenge, Tice, Schmeichel, & Baumeister, 2001). Participants in the crucial condition spent more than a half-hour making dyadic choices between consumer products (e.g., Do you prefer the green t-shirt or the blue t-shirt? Do you prefer the vanilla-scented candle or the pine-scented candle?). They believed that these choices were self-relevant, because they thought they would receive a gift at the end of the study based on their product choices. The control group either reported how often they had used certain products or wrote down their opinions about advertisements. Participants were then asked to drink a bad-tasting but healthy beverage (Kool-Aid made with vinegar) and told they would receive some money for each ounce they drank. The horribly bad-tasting drink was presented in one-ounce paper cups, so drinking each ounce required a separate action. This served as the measure of self-regulation, because forcing oneself to drink a bad-tasting beverage requires self-control. Those who had just made the long series of choices were able to drink less vinegar Kool-Aid than those in the nonchoices control condition, showing that making choices can deplete our reserves of self-control. A third study replicated the effect using a cold pressor task; participants who had just made choices held their hand and lower arm in a tank of ice water for significantly less time than those in the control condition. Although the individual choices were relatively easy and minor, they apparently accumulated to produce a fatigue effect on the self. Depleted by those choices, participants were unable to make themselves drink as much vinegar Kool-Aid (or hold their hand as long in ice water) as participants in the control condition.

SELF-CONTROL IN REAL-LIFE SETTINGS

Feelings of self-control are also influential outside the laboratory. In a recent study, a group of students provided weekly reports of their personal and academic stresses, sleep habits, and health problems, as well as their current feelings of self-control (Twenge, Muraven, Harter, & Tice, 2001). Students who had experienced personal problems, obtained little sleep, endured health problems, and/or described high levels of stress all reported a lower state of self-control. Thus many negative experiences in everyday life tend to diminish our feelings of self-control and make it harder for us to self-regulate.

Life experiences can also influence self-control measured in the laboratory. Vohs and Heatherton (2000) found that chronic dieters displayed less self-control after being tempted. When tempted with fattening snacks placed within arm's reach, dieters ate more ice cream during a subsequent taste test compared to a low-temptation group in which the snacks were placed across the room. Thus dieters who had to exercise self-control (to resist eating the snacks at arm's reach) were less able to restrain themselves from eating ice cream later. This effect did not occur for nondieters. This effect is especially interesting because one might expect that dieters had practiced self-control regarding food and would thus be better at controlling their responses even under high-temptation conditions. However, it seems that the constant self-control required to maintain a diet depletes the self's resources so much that a small act of self-control leads to a failure in self-regulation. This occurred even when the measure of ego depletion (Vohs & Heatherton, 2000, Study 2) or first act of self-control was not related to food (Study 3). This follows the general model of self-control as a limited resource; because dieters must inhibit their natural responses toward food all the time, they apparently go through life with noticably lower levels of self-control than nondieters. Resisting eating potato chips every hour of every day makes other self-control breakdowns more likely.

Previous work on a variety of topics also suggests that the strength model of self-regulation is correct. Coping with stress generally requires people to override or stop emotions, thoughts, and impulses; it also requires strict regulation of attention (Muraven & Baumeister, 2000). Research shows that exposure to stress often leads to deficits in self-control. For example, Glass, Singer, and Friedman (1969) subjected people to unpredictable noise versus regular, predictable noise. Those exposed to the unpredictable noise performed less well on tasks requiring frustration tolerance. In another study, high school students who had been stressed by overcrowding in a small room gave up faster on unsolvable puzzles (Sherrod, 1974). [Based on these results, some people have hypothesized that it is better to take important exams in conditions that minimize crowding (e.g., large rooms, fewer people)]. Other studies have shown that self-control suffers after exposure to other stresses, including bad odors (shown, appropriately, by Rotton, 1983), electric shock, and even being the object of discrimination (Glass & Singer, 1972). The element of control seems to be important here: In most of these studies, self-control deficits were reduced when participants believed that they had some control over the stressful situation (Muraven & Baumeister, 2000).

THE CONSERVATION OF SELF-CONTROL

The results of these experiments suggest that self-control is a limited resource. People who resisted eating chocolate for a mere 5 min showed a subsequent self-control deficit of nearly two standard deviations (Baumeister et al., 1998). The ego depletion experiments may thus suggest that the self has a very small reserve of energy and self-control. However, these findings may support another explanation: People could be actively conserving their supply of mental energy. If this is true, resisting chocolate (for example) does not deplete all or most of the self's resources; it simply depletes enough that people try to conserve the energy that remains. This conservation theory also fits well with the analogy to muscular activity. For example, experienced athletes often conserve their energy so they will be able to surge ahead at the end of a race. Even inexperienced athletes will begin conserving their energy once their muscles begin to fatigue, because they know that continued intense exertion will "empty the tank" and leave them without enough energy to finish the race. In a team sport, athletes tired from a long game might seek economy of movement and might even avoid chasing balls that they judge to be poor prospects for success (whereas a fresh athlete might try for every shot).

People might conserve their self-control or mental energy in the same way; like a fatigued muscle, the depleted self begins to conserve resources in order to ensure that some energy is left for other tasks, expected or unexpected. For example, a tired office worker might let her self-control slip on a relatively unimportant task (e.g., not eating the chocolate bar in her purse) so she has enough energy left to commute home, make dinner, or make an urgent decision in an emergency. We know that depleting all of our self-control leaves us vulnerable. This question invokes a version of the ongoing debate about self-control failure: Does it occur because irresistible impulses overwhelm the person, or does it arise when people indulge themselves or otherwise permit their control to lapse? Baumeister et al. (1994) concluded from an extensive review of the literature on self-control failure that some degree of acquiescence is the norm. Relatively few instances of self-control failure involve truly irresistible impulses.

This conservation hypothesis receives support from Muraven's (1998) studies. In one study, participants were first depleted by an initial self-control task. However, the participants were able to exert self-control on a second task when they were offered substantial amounts of money for doing well (they were offered up to 25 cents an ounce for drinking the previously mentioned vile-tasting vinegar Kool-Aid; one participant who drank 40 ounces was thus awarded $10). When they were offered only 1 cent per ounce, however, depleted participants (perhaps wisely) decided not to exert their self-control and drank fewer ounces of vinegar Kool-Aid compared to a control group. Thus participants were able to exert self-control when the task was made important. If the first task had truly used all of the participants' self-control, the money would make no difference, because the self would have no energy left to use. When the task is important enough, however, people will use some of their remaining reserves of self-control.

Another study from Muraven (1998) provides converging evidence. As in the other studies, participants first performed two consecutive acts requiring self-control. In a change from the other studies, some participants were led to anticipate performing a third self-control task. They received this information immediately before the second task. These participants gave up significantly faster on the second task (the cold pressor, involving holding one's had in ice water), presumably because they were conserving their resources in order to perform the third task.

Research on other topics also suggests that people conserve their self-control and energy. For example, vigilance deteriorates steadily over repeated trials (e.g., Parasuraman, 1984). However, the deterioration of vigilance stops and even typically reverses when the participant knows that the study is almost over. To many researchers, this pattern is merely an annoying bit of error variance, and they try to eliminate it by removing the participant's wristwatch and not letting him or her know when the experiment is nearing its end. Nevertheless, these results suggest that the decline in vigilance is caused by depletion and conservation: The participant conserves resources for the long, demanding task, but when the participant knows the study is almost over, he or she feels free to expend more of the remaining self-control.

These studies suggest that the self's reserve of energy and control is limited, but not extremely so. When energy is depleted, the process of evaluation and conservation begins. Apparently, we evaluate each task for importance and then decide if it is worth further depletion of our resources. If it is not, we conserve our resources for future tasks. We must sometimes make these decisions without complete information, because we never know when we might be required to resist an urge, make a challenging decision, or act in an emergency. We probably conserve at least some of our self-control for such situations.

THE REPLENISHMENT OF SELF-CONTROL

If self-control can be depleted, can it also be replenished? If we could never replenish our reserves of self-control, we would continually be ego depleted and unable to function at everyday tasks such as school, work, and resisting chocolate chip cookies. Self-control must be restored somehow. One possible candidate is rest in general, and sleep in particular. Rested people generally have better self-control. Self-control tends to diminish as the day wears on and we have gone longer without sleep: Diets are broken more often in the evening, impulsive crimes occur more often at night, and relapses into drug or alcohol addiction are more common in the evening and nighttime hours (Baumeister et al., 1994). In a longitudinal study, students who got an adequate amount of sleep reported greater state self-control in a weekly questionnaire (Twenge et al., 2001). The actual number of hours slept was not correlated with state self-control. Only self-perceived adequacy of sleep amount correlated with the questionnaire measure of self-control.

Positive emotions also help to replenish the self's store of energy and control. Tice, Dale, and Baumeister (2000) performed several studies to test the effects of positive emotions on depleted self-control. As in many of the previous experiments, participants engaged in two consecutive acts of self-control. Some participants, however, experienced an induction of positive or negative mood in between the two tasks. Participants in the positive mood group showed less ego depletion on the second task. Thus it seems that experiencing positive emotions can offset deficits in self-control.

Meditation may also help allay the effects of ego depletion. Smith (2000) had some participants perform a brief meditation exercise in between two self-control tasks. These participants performed better on the second task than those who only sat quietly without meditating.

INCREASING SELF-CONTROL STRENGTH

Another important question is whether self-control can be improved and strengthened. Some correlational evidence suggests that it can. If self-control truly operates like a muscle (Muraven & Baumeister, 2000), then its performance should improve with continued use and practice. For example, people who have broken their addiction to alcohol are subsequently more successful at conquering the addiction to smoking nicotine (Breslau, Peterson, Schultz, Andreski, & Chilcoat, 1996; Zimmerman, Warheit, Ulbrich, & Auth, 1990). Thus, overcoming one addiction may build the skills and strength necessary to overcome another. This pattern even appears within the same addiction: for example, people who quit smoking generally do so only after multiple attempts (Schachter, 1982). This may occur because they somehow get better at quitting smoking, just as muscular performance improves with continued exercise.

Experimental longitudinal research has also been promising. In a study designed to test the idea that self-control can improve with practice, students performed various self-control drills over a period of 2 weeks (including improving posture, regulating moods, or keeping a diary of what they ate). When tested later in the laboratory, these participants were able to squeeze a handgrip longer than a control group of participants who had not practiced the regimen of self-control (Muraven, Baumeister, & Tice, 1999). Because squeezing a handgrip requires self-regulation, these results suggest that self-control can improve with continued practice, much like a muscle.

A muscle can gain strength either in terms of power (for maximum exertion) or stamina (resistance to fatigue). In the longitudinal study, the improvements in self-control conformed to the stamina pattern rather than increased power. At the second laboratory session, people who had been exercising self-control were less affected by a depletion manipulation, but their initial level of self-control did not differ from the control group or from their own baseline 2 weeks earlier. These results tentatively suggest that the first benefit of exercising self-control is a greater capacity to resist the debilitating effects of ego depletion.

Although the results combined from all experimental groups showed an overall benefit of exercising self-control, the results were not consistent across type of exercise. The posture exercise produced the largest gain in self-control. In contrast, participants given the affect regulation exercise performed no differently than the no-exercise control group. Thus, if one seeks to improve self-control, the exercise of trying to regulate one's feelings is not promising. Possibly this is because people often regulate their emotions anyway. Alternatively, it may be because affect regulation typically relies on indirect strategies (e.g., distracting oneself, or seeking pleasure) rather than direct control, so the person fails to use and hence fails to exercise the "muscle," that is, the self's capacity for control.

CONCLUSION

The human ability to regulate oneself and alter a person's own responses is one of the most powerful and adaptive capacities that people have, and it is probably responsible for the immense diversity and flexibility of human behavior. Many other species live out their lives largely at the mercy of their own instinctive promptings and the stimulus environment, but human beings can resist the pressures and temptations of the immediate setting, as well as overcome their own normal or natural impulses. This capacity enables people to conform their behavior to long-term goals, moral ideals, and rational guidelines. Sure enough, high self-control is associated with a wealth of positive outcomes, including better task performance, better interpersonal relationships, and better mental and emotional health.

Evidence suggests that self-control operates on the basis of a limited resource, akin to strength or energy. Acts of self-control deplete this resource, and people are then motivated to conserve what remains, so after an act of self-control the capacity to regulate the self further is temporarily reduced. The same energy resource is used for decision-making and other acts of volition, and so making many or difficult decisions can also impair self-control (as the private lives of some politicians and executives suggest!). Because this resource is limited, people cannot use it constantly, and it becomes essential for people to live much of their lives by habits, routines, rules, and other means of avoiding having to exert volition.

Although the human capacity for self-control is limited, it seems far in excess of what most other creatures on the planet have. The capacity for self-control is one of the most distinctively human traits. It is probably also one of the crucial reasons that the human self has evolved to take the form that it currently has. Understanding how the self regulates itself may hold important and fascinating insights into the very nature of human selfhood.

REFERENCES

Barkley, R. A. (1997). *ADHD and the nature of self-control.* New York: Guilford Press.

Baumeister, R. F. (1998). The self. In D. T. Gilbert, S. T. Fiske, & G. Lindzey (Eds.), *Handbook of social psychology* (4th ed., pp. 680–740). New York: McGraw-Hill.

Baumeister, R. F., Bratslavsky, E., Muraven, M., & Tice, D. M. (1998). Ego depletion: Is the active self a limited resource? *Journal of Personality and Social Psychology, 74,* 1252–1265.

Baumeister, R. F., Heatherton, T. F., & Tice, D. M. (1994). *Losing control: How and why people fail at self-regulation.* San Diego, CA: Academic Press.

Breslau, N., Peterson, E., Schultz, L., Andreski, P., & Chilcoat, H. (1996). Are smokers with alcohol disorders less likely to quit? *American Journal of Public Health, 86,* 985–990.

Engels, R. C., Den Exter Blokland, A., Baumeister, R. F., & Finkenauer, C. (2000). *Parenting practices, self-control, and delinquency in adolescence.* Unpublished manuscript, Utrecht University, Utrecht, the Netherlands.

Glass, D. C., & Singer, J. E. (1972). *Urban stress: Experiments on noise and social stressors.* New York: Academic Press.

Glass, D. C., Singer, J. E., & Friedman, L. N. (1969). Psychic cost of adaptation to an environmental stressor. *Journal of Personality and Social Psychology, 12,* 200–210.

Gottfredson, M. R., & Hirschi, T. (1990). *A general theory of crime.* Stanford, CA: Stanford University Press.

Higgins, E. T. (1996). The "self digest": Self-knowledge serving self-regulatory functions. *Journal of Personality and Social Psychology, 71,* 1062–1083.

Kanfer, F. H., & Karoly, P. (1972). Self-control: A behavioristic excursion into the lion's den. *Behavioral Therapy, 3,* 398–416.

Mischel, W. (1996). From good intentions to willpower. In P. Gollwitzer & J. Bargh (Eds.), *The psychology of action* (pp. 197–218). New York: Guilford Press.

Mischel, W., Shoda, Y., & Peake, P. K. (1988). The nature of adolescent competencies predicted by preschool delay of gratification. *Journal of Personality and Social Psychology, 54,* 687–696.

Muraven, M. (1998). *Mechanisms of self-control failure: Motivation and limited resources.* Doctoral dissertation, Case Western Reserve University, Cleveland, OH.

Muraven, M., & Baumeister, R. F. (2000). Self-regulation and depletion of limited resources: Does self-control resemble a muscle? *Psychological Bulletin, 126,* 247–259.

Muraven, M., Baumeister, B. F., & Tice, D. M. (1999). Longitudinal improvement of self-regulation through practice: Building self-control strength through repeated exercise. *Journal of Social Psychology, 139,* 446–457.

Muraven, M., Tice, D. M., & Baumeister, R. F. (1998). Self-control as limited resource: Regulatory depletion patterns. *Journal of Personality and Social Psychology, 74,* 774–789.

Parasuraman, R. (1984). Sustained attention in detection and discrimination. In R. Parasuraman & D. R. Davies (Eds.), *Varieties of attention* (pp. 243–271). Orlando, FL: Academic Press.

Richards, J. M., & Gross, J. J. (2000). Emotion regulation and memory: The cognitive costs of keeping one's cool. *Journal of Personality and Social Psychology, 79,* 410–424.

Rotton, J. (1983). Affective and cognitive consequences of malodorous pollution. *Basic and Applied Social Psychology, 4,* 171–191.

Schachter, S. (1982). Recidivism and self-cure of smoking and obesity. *American Psychologist, 37,* 436–444.

Sherrod, D. R. (1974). Crowding, perceived control, and behavioral after-effects. *Journal of Applied Social Psychology, 4,* 171–186.

Shoda, Y., Mischel, W., & Peake, P. K. (1990). Predicting adolescent cognitive and self-regulatory competencies from preschool delay of gratification: Identifying diagnostic conditions. *Psychology, 26,* 978–986.

Smith, R. (2000). *Meditation and the replenishment of the capacity for self-regulation.* Doctoral dissertation, Case Western Reserve University, Cleveland, OH.

Tangney, J. P., & Baumeister, R. F. (2000) *High self-control predicts good adjustment, less pathology, better grades, and interpersonal success.* Unpublished manuscript, George Mason University, Fairfax VA.

Tice, D. M., & Baumeister, R. F. (1997). Longitudinal study of procrastination, performance, stress, and health: The costs and benefits of dawdling. *Psychological Science, 8,* 454–458.

Tice, D. M., Dale, K., & Baumeister, R. F. (2001). *Positive affect and ego depletion.* Unpublished manuscript.

Twenge, J. M., Tice, D. M., Schmeichel, B. J., & Baumeister, R. F. (2001). *Decision fatigue: Making multiple personal decisions depletes the self's resources.* Unpublished manuscript.

Twenge, J. M., Muraven, M., Harter, A., & Tice, D. M. (2001). *Measuring state self-control: Reliability, validity, and correlations with physical and psychological stress.* Unpublished manuscript.

Vohs, K. D., & Heatherton, T. F. (2000). Self-regulatory failure: A resource-depletion approach. *Psychological Science, 11,* 249–254.

Wegner, D. M., Schneider, D. J., Carter, S. R., & White, T. L. (1987). Paradoxical effects of thought suppression. *Journal of Personality and Social Psychology, 53,* 5–13.

Zimmerman, R. S., Warheit, G. J., Ulbrich, P. M., & Auth, J. B. (1990). The relationship between alcohol use and attempts and success at smoking cessation. *Addictive Behaviors, 15,* 197–207.

Chapter 4

The Dialogical Self:
One Person, Different Stories

Hubert J. M. Hermans
University of Nijmegen

In its most concise form, the *dialogical self* can be defined as a dynamic multiplicity of *I*-positions in an imaginal landscape. A most typical example that may illustrate the dialogical self is an author who submits a manuscript to a scientific journal. As part of the review procedure, he or she receives three helpful but critical comments, with the possibility of resubmitting the paper. The author, eager to see the paper in print, faces a challenging situation that entails new and even confusing information and some new problems to resolve. These problems can only be solved if the author takes the positions of the reviewers into account in relation to his or her own position. That is, the author has to move to and fro among the several reviewers to check them on consistencies and inconsistencies. Moreover, the author moves between the reviewers and his or her original position as represented by the old manuscript. In making these movements the author is imagining what the reviewers want to say, even between the lines, what their backgrounds are, and even tries to guess who they are. At first all these positions may sound like a "cacophony of voices," but after several rounds of intensive dialogical interchange a new structure begins to emerge. In the course of this process the author may arrive at a point of juxtaposition, where the several views are simultaneously present, thus permitting some overview and new, sometimes suddenly emerging, relationships between the diversity of insights. Finally, a new structure emerges that may differ considerably from the original one. The author may decide to write a thoroughly revised manuscript, in which the information of all reviewers is incorporated. The original position of the author, as materialized in the first manuscript, may be significantly altered as a result of the intensive interchange. The new manuscript is the result of a process in which the original position of the author, the opposing positions of the reviewers, and the repositioning of the author are part of a highly open, dynamic, multivoiced dialogical self (Hermans, 1996a).

The reviewer example illustrates the workings of a dialogical process that is certainly not restricted to intellectual accomplishments. Rather, it is an example of a more general process in the everyday life of most people. It works in similar ways when parents are confronted with the disagreeing voices of their children or when people in their working environment are challenged by voices that tell them about technological innovations that may change their traditional ways of organizing their jobs and even their thinking. It is also reflected when we hear about the views, practices, and lifestyles of people from different cultures, which, at first sight, we may not understand but which change the views we have about ourselves and the world. All these examples illustrate the working of a self that is, to borrow a term from Bruner (1986), "distributed"—that is, it is not unified and centralized but rather heterogeneous and decentralized. What does this heterogeneity and decentralization mean? In order to answer this question, a brief journey through the history of the psychology of the self is required.

FROM JAMES'S *I* TO DOSTOYEVSKY'S POLYPHONIC NOVEL

In James's (1890) view, the *I* is equated with the self-as-knower and is characterized by three features: continuity, distinctness, and volition (see also Damon & Hart, 1982). The continuity of the self-as-knower is reflected in a sense of personal identity, that is, a sense of sameness across time. A feeling of distinctness from others, or individuality, also derives from the subjective nature of the self-as-knower. A sense of personal volition is expressed by the continuous appropriation and rejection of thoughts by which the self-as-knower manifests itself as an active processor of experience. The *Me* is identified by James as the self-as-known and is composed of the empirical elements considered as belonging to oneself. Because James was aware that there is a gradual transition between *Me* and *mine*, he concluded that the empirical self is composed of all that the person can call his or her own, "not only his body and his psychic powers, but his clothes and his house, his wife and children, his ancestors and friends, his reputation and works, his lands and horses, and yacht and bank-account" (p. 291). Note that for James, people and things in the environment belong to the self, as far as they are felt as "mine." This means that not only *my mother* belongs to the self but even *my enemy*. In this way, James paved the way for later theoretical developments in which contrasts, oppositions, and negotiations are part of a distributed, multivoiced self.

Drawing on James's *I–Me* distinction, Sarbin (1986) supposed that people, in the process of self-reflection, order their experiences in a storylike fashion. His thesis was that James, Mead, Freud, and others emphasized the distinction between the *I* and the *Me* and their equivalents in other Anglo-European languages precisely because of the narrative nature of the self. The uttered pronoun *I* stands for the author, whereas the *Me* represents the actor or narrative figure. In this configuration, moreover, the *I* can imaginatively construct a story with the *Me* as the protagonist. Such narrative construction is possible because the self as author can imagine the future and reconstruct the past.

The conception of *I* as author and *Me* as actor can be pursued further by considering the self as being organized not by one *I*-position, but by *several* interrelated *I*-positions (Hermans, Kempen, & Van Loon, 1992). In this view, which is inspired by Bakhtin, the self consists of more than one author or narrator.

Characters as Authors

In his book *Problems of Dostoevsky's Poetics* (1929/1973), the Russian literary scholar Mikhail Bakhtin argued that Dostoyevsky—a brilliant innovator in the realm of literary form—created a peculiar type of artistic thought, the polyphonic novel. Central to Bakhtin's thesis is the idea that in Dostoyevsky's works there is not a single author at work—Dostoyevsky himself— but *several* authors or thinkers—characters such as Raskolnikov, Myshkin, Stavrogin, Ivan Karamazov, and the Grand Inquisitor. Instead of being obedient slaves of the one author, Dostoyevsky, each of these heroes is ideologically authoritative and independent and uses his own voice to ventilate his view and philosophy. Each hero is perceived as the author of his own ideology, and not as the object of Dostoyevsky's finalizing artistic vision. There is not a multitude of characters and fates within a unified objective world, organized by Dostoyevsky's individual consciousness, but a plurality of consciousnesses and worlds. In Bakhtin's (1929/1973) terms, "The plurality of independent unmerged voices and consciousnesses and the genuine polyphony of full-valued voices are in fact characteristics of Dostoevsky's novels" (p. 4). As in a polyphonic musical work, multiple voices accompany and oppose one another in a dialogical way. For Bakhtin, agreement and disagreement are, like question and answer, basic dialogical forms.

The notion of dialogue enabled Dostoyevsky to express a character's inner world and articulate a character's personality. As soon as a neutral utterance is attributed to a particular character, dialogical relations may spontaneously occur between this utterance and the utterances of another character. For example, in Dostoyevsky's novel *The Double,* the second hero (the double) was introduced as a personification of the interior voice of the first hero (Golyadkin). In this way the interior voice is externalized, and a dialogue between two independent parties is allowed to develop, where each character—as an independent author—can tell a story about himself. As a result of a process of exchange, the stories are not only differentiated and contrasted but also further developed.

Logical Versus Dialogical Relationships

The metaphor of the polyphonic novel can only properly be understood if a distinction is made between logical and dialogical relations (see also Vasil'eva, 1988). Consider the phrases "Life is good" and "Life is good." These phrases are connected by the logical relationship of *identity,* because they are the same statement. However, from a dialogical perspective they are different because they come from the mouths of two people who are differentially located. They may be seen as two sequential remarks from two communicating subjects, who entertain a relationship of *agreement.* Although the two phrases are identical from a logical point of view, they are different as utterances: The first is a statement, the second a confirmation. Similarly, the phrases "Life is good" and "Life is not good" can be analyzed. According to the traditional rules of logic, one is the *negation* of the other. There is no dialogical relation between them because, in Bakhtin's terms, there are no interacting people supposed uttering the phrases. However, when the two phrases are considered utterances of two different speaking subjects, a dialogical relation will evolve—that is, a relationship of *disagreement* (Vasil'eva, 1988).

In Bakhtin's view, personal meanings (e.g., ideas, thoughts, memories) can only become dialogical when they are embodied. They are embodied when there is a "voice" that creates utterances that can be meaningfully related to the utterances of another voice. Only when an idea or thought is endowed with a voice and is expressed as emanating from a personal *position* do dialogical relations emerge (Vasil'eva, 1988). Note that Bakhtin's emphasis on embodiment, voice, and position is consonant with the notion of narrative as organized in time and space (Bruner, 1986; Sarbin, 1986).

The urge to see all things as being coexistent—as if side by side in space and time—led Dostoyevsky to dramatize the inner contradictions and stages of development of a single person as two characters in conversation. On the basis of this principle, characters are allowed to converse with their doubles, with the devil (Ivan and the Devil), with their alter egos (Ivan and

Smerdyakov), and with caricatures of themselves (Raskolnikov and Svidrigailov). This device explains the frequent appearance of paired heroes in Dostoyevsky's novels. He made two persons out of every contradiction within an individual in order to dramatize such contradictions. This multiplicity of voices in dialogical opposition to each other constitutes the polyphonic quality of Dostoyevsky's novels.

In summary, the dialogical self, inspired by the metaphor of the polyphonic novel, expands on the original narrative conception of the *I* as an author and the *Me* as an actor. In Sarbin's (1986) view, a single author is assumed to tell a story about himself or herself as an actor, whereas the dialogical self goes one step further: Each individual lives in a multiplicity of worlds, with each world having its own author, who may tell a story relatively independently of the authors of the other worlds. It is assumed, moreover, that the multiple authors may enter into dialogical relationships with each other, thus creating a highly dynamic and complex organization of the self. (For comprehensive review of the notion of voice and dialogue in contemporary psychology and modern novelistic literature see Hermans and Kempen [1993].)

THE OTHER IN THE *I*

How can the dialogical self as a composite of relatively independent voices be compatible with the commonsense experience that we are "one I" that is unified in itself? Part of the problem is in the observation that we use the word *I*, or the equivalents in other Anglo-European languages, indiscriminately for a wide variety of states of mind, which, despite their differences, contrasts, and contradictions, are thought as being subsumed by a centralized ego. Certainly, cultural factors, closely related to linguistic practices, play an important part in supporting the idea that there exists a centralized ego separate from its environment. This Cartesian supposition is so deeply entrenched in our self-definition that we adhere to it as self-evident. It may be helpful to look at the linguistic practices in other cultures for which the centralized ego is not that obvious. Wekker (1994), for example, discussed the Sranon Tongo, the language of Afro-Surinam people, who adhere to the African-American Winti religion. Adherents of this religion believe in supernatural forces, and in their ancestors in particular, who are supposed to play an influential role in the daily affairs of their living offspring. The language of this group contains different words expressing different modalities of the word *I*:

Mi	I
Mi kra	My soul, I

A misi (f'mi)	My feminine part
A masra (f'mi)	My masculine part
Mi misi nanga mi masra	My feminine and masculine part
Mi dyodyo	My divine parents
Mi skin	My body, I
Mi geest	My spirit, I

These examples suggest that a wide variety of voices is directly associated with the word *I*, including not only singular but also plural voices, not only spiritual but also corporeal ones, and not only internal but also external ones. In this language, *I* is not to be understood as an isolated, sovereign subject, essential in itself, and having an existence apart from the flux of person-situation interactions. Rather, *I* is conceived of as a multiplicity and as a relationship. The *I* is believed to be part of a relationship at the same time being able to shift from one relationship to another, which implies a change in the experiencing *I* itself. The parents in Winti religion are not simply outside the individual, they are "here" and "there" at the same time and are experienced as simultaneously inside and outside. As Holquist (1990) would have it, a relation between two bodies occupying simultaneous but different space is assumed. It should be emphasized that such experience is certainly not foreign to what we are used to in so-called Western culture. There are moments in which I feel that I'm acting like my father, experiencing my father simultaneously outside and inside myself. In a particular situation I just feel like him, as if he is me and I am him. In other words, what is explicitly present in Sranon Tongo is implicitly working in any other language (see also Caughey, 1984, for the deep commonality between the experiences of people from Western and non-Western cultures).

SPACE IN THE SELF

Another part of the problem posed by the conception of the unified self is in the Cartesian dualism and its aftermath. Cartesian dualism is not to be conceived as an abstract philosophical issue to be discussed in sophisticated treatises; it is still part of the implicit assumptions in our daily lives. One of these assumptions concerns the oversimplified opposition between "self" and "other." In an elucidating paper, Straus (1958) argued that Descartes's *Cogito* implies not only a dualism between mind and body but also a dissociation between self and other. When lay people and social scientists talk, often too easily, about the "outside world," the question can be posed: To what does the word "outside" refer? In Cartesian terms it means that the world (*res extensa*) is supposed to have an existence outside of consciousness (*res cogitans*) and that, reciprocally, consciousness is outside of the world. In Straus's view, the Cartesian dichotomy thus separates not only mind from body, but also one individual from another individual. In the realm of consciousness this means that each person is alone with him- or herself. Certainly, Descartes does not deny, or even seriously doubt, the existence of the so-called outside world. However, he insists that it is never *directly* accessible to us. The existence of the world is no more than probable; it must be proved. However, as Straus reasoned, the fact that proof is needed emphasizes the distance between self and other with the implication that the prelogical sphere of the immediate experience of reality is eliminated. In opposition to the Cartesian view, Straus (1958) concluded: "In sensory experience I always experience myself *and* the world at the same time, not myself directly and the Other by inference, not myself before the Other, not myself without the *Other*, nor the *Other* without myself" (p. 148). In agreement with Straus, it can be concluded that the other person and the space in which the other person finds himself are not simply outside the self but also in the self (see also Fogel, 1993, for the opposition between a dialogical and a Cartesian view of the self).

In agreement with the anti-Cartesian view, Jaynes (1976) drew on the distinction between the *I* and the *Me* in describing the self as a *mind-space*. The *I* constructs an analog space and metaphorically sees the *Me* moving in this space. When we plan to visit somebody, we imagine the place where we are going and see ourselves talking to that person. Narrating is not simply explicitly telling a story, but is an essential characteristic of all of our activities. Seated where I am, Jaynes explained, I am writing a book, and this activity is embedded in the story of my life, "time being spatialized into a journey of my days and years" (p. 63). In Jaynes' view, the conscious mind and the self, in particular, are a spatial analogue of the world, and mental acts are analogues of bodily acts. The self functions as a space where the *I* observes the *Me*, and orders the movements of the *Me* in a storylike fashion.

From a phenomenological point of view, Minkowski (1936) introduced the concept of *original space* in order to emphasize that we live our lives in an "experiential space" in which not only our bodies move but also our thoughts. It is the space in which we not only travel to another country but also move in our dreams. There are objects, roads, rocks, obstacles, and interacting characters both in our dreams and waking lives. The concept of original space may help us to better understand the concept of imaginal space that was used in defining the dialogical self as a "dynamic multiplicity of *I*-positions in an imaginal landscape." The term *imaginal space* is not to be understood as a "purely imaginary space" or "inner space" that is conceived of as existing somewhere outside "real space." Imaginal space, like original space, transcends a simple subject–object dichotomy so characteristic of Cartesian thinking. Imaginal space is not simply "internal," because the experiencing subject and the experienced object (out there) are both functioning in a spatial field of which they are constituting parts. This view implies that space, in the sense of imaginal or original space, is common to the mind and its environment.

DIALOGUE AND SELF-INNOVATION

The spatial nature of the dialogical self and the relative autonomy of characters positioned in this spatial structure are crucial for understanding the self's innovative potentials. It is precisely the independent status of the other that permits the author to disclose an extra spatial realm, for which Bakhtin used the notion of "surplus of vision" (Holquist, 1990). When two people meet each other at a particular place and at a particular moment in time, they see, to some extent, a common environment (e.g., the table between them). At the same time they are able to see things that the other does not see (e.g., A seeing the eyes of B, which B cannot see, and B seeing the eyes of A, which A cannot see). This aspect of the situation that the one person sees and the other not, represents what Bakhtin called our *surplus of vision*. He introduced this concept in order to underscore the independence of the characters as spatially and uniquely located partners in a dialogical relationship. In the dialogical relationship between person and other and between the person and him- or herself, language plays a crucial role. For Bakhtin, the use of language, in terms of the exchange of utterances from spatially located interlocutors, may lead to the innovation of meaning. Consequently, if the self is considered as a "multiplicity of voiced positions," new meanings are created on the border zone between different and opposed positions.

Mead (1934), another influential theorist of the self, was well in agreement with Bakhtin on the importance of self-innovation. He was aware of the problems that would have been raised if he had limited the social process to the internalization of the attitude of the other within the self (the generalized other). In that case the self would simply be a copy of external social roles and no more than a reflection of social institutions. Individuals would be considered as only conforming to social rules and function as "slaves of customs." Innovations that would bring social changes and renew institutions would then be impossible. Being aware of this problem, Mead (1934) introduced the distinction between *I* and *Me*:

> I have been undertaking to distinguish between the "I" and the "me" as different phases of the self, the "me" answering to the organized attitudes of the others which we definitely assume and which determine consequently

our own conduct so far as it is of a self-conscious character. Now the "me" may be regarded as giving the form of the "I." The novelty comes in the action of the "I," but the structure, the form of the self is one which is conventional. (p. 209)

On the basis of the *I–Me* distinction, Mead demonstrated that both the *I* and the *Me* function as sources of values, each in their own ways. The values of the Me are those that belong to the group: "The 'me' is essentially a member of a social group, and represents, therefore, the value of the group, that sort of experience which the group makes possible" (p. 214). The values of the I are found "in the immediate attitude of the artist, the inventor, the scientist in his discovery, in general in the action of the 'I' which cannot be calculated and which involves a reconstruction of the society, and so of the 'me' which belongs to that society" (p. 214). In Mead's view, the *I* prevents the *Me* (generalized other) from becoming purely conventional and makes it possible for individuals and groups to revitalize themselves. In agreement with Mead and Bakhtin, the dialogical self consists of a dynamic multiplicity of *I*-positions that allow innovative processes to develop.

Relational Schemas and the Problem of Innovation

A comparison between the dialogical self and the concept of "relational schema" may further elucidate the issue of self-innovation. After reviewing research in the area of social cognition, Baldwin (1992) proposed the term *relational schema* as a summary term of recent developments in this research domain. He defined a relational schema as a cognitive structure representing regularities in patterns of interpersonal relatedness. Rather than representations of self or others in isolation, relational schemas are generalized representations of self–other relationships.

Drawing on the work of early symbolic interactionists and recent impression management theorists, Baldwin started from the assumption that a sense of self is experienced in relation to some audience: people who are present or imagined, specific or generalized, actual or fantasized. Baldwin and Holmes (1987), for example, referred to the common observation that most people respond at different times to a range of different significant others, who often represent distinct ways of evaluating the self. Such an evaluating other functions as a "private audience" and can include such divergent figures as a spouse, best friend, religious leader, or business colleague. In one of Baldwin and Holmes's (1987) studies, some subjects vizualized the faces of two acquaintances from campus whereas other subjects vizualized the faces of two older members of their own family. Later all subjects were invited to read a sexually permissive piece of fiction.

When they were afterward asked to rate the enjoyableness of the story, they responded in ways that would be acceptable to their salient private audiences. Subjects who had thought of friends from campus reported more liking the story than those who thought of their older family members, who were supposed to be more moralistic.

A study by Andersen and Cole (1990) further underscored the influence of significant others in social perception. They examined the proposition that significant others are mentally represented as well-organized person categories that have the potential of influencing social perception even more than representations of nonsignificant others, stereotypes, or traits. Andersen and Cole found that significant other representations are richer (trigger more associations), more distinctive (have more unique features), and are more cognitively accessible (time required for retrieval of features) than the other categories (nonsignificant others, stereotypes, and traits). Baldwin's and Andersen's studies have in common that they suggest that significant others form rich, unique, and accessible internal representations that may function as a private audience that watches or listens to the person and responds to him or her with affect-laden evaluations. As this research indicates, self and other are composite parts of relational schemas.

A relational schema can become rather complex if the interaction is carried out to multiple iterations of if-then sequences. Baldwin (1992) gave the example of a teenage boy borrowing the keys to his mother's car. The goal of the boy is to borrow the car. At the same time, he expects that the goal of his mother is to make sure that he and the car are returned safely. If she is reluctant, he expects that the required behavior is to reassure his mother that he will act in a responsible way. In agreement with this expectation, he verbalizes phrases that have been successful in the past, such as, "I'll drive carefully" and "I'll be home before 1!" He expects that by his proceeding in this way, his mother will give him the keys. If not, he may try different routines, such as expressing his urgent need for transport, complaining about the unfairness of her behavior, and so on. In this way, multiple if–then sequences can be organized into a complete production system for guiding the behavior between interacting parties.

From a dialogical point of view, multiple if–then sequences are particularly significant. The boy's behavior can be described as a process of negotiation with the mother. If the first if–then sequence does not work (the mother refuses), the next sequence is started. In this succession of if–then sequences, the response from the mother at the end of the first sequence functions as a question for the boy to himself ("What shall I say now?"), which leads to an answer by his starting the next sequence. Considered in this way, the if–then sequences are not simply a temporally ordered succession of events; they are, rather, part of a process of question and answer between and within spatially and oppositionally organized positions.

An important theoretical advantage of the concept of relational schema is that it applies to a large variety of possible interactions. It ranges from conventional social role interactions, such as teacher–student or doctor–patient interaction patterns studied by script researchers, to highly idiosyncratic nuclear scenes (see Tomkins, 1978). There is, however, an important difference between relational schemas and the concept of the dialogical self. Relational schemas are based on "repeated experiences with similar interactions" (Baldwin, 1992, p. 468), and the two elements (self and other) are fixed as parts of a stable pattern. As such, a relational schema, like all similarly defined schemas, has a conservative nature. It lacks the explicit acknowledgment of innovation, an acknowledgment that has been emphasized, as we have seen, by such divergent theorists as Bakhtin and Mead.

The Process of Positioning and Repositioning

There are at least two factors that make the dialogical self sensitive to innovation. First, a central feature of dialogical relationships is that they are open to new information and knowledge as emergent from a process of interchange between existing positions in the system. As a result of this interchange, the position repertory as a whole may be reorganized. Second, dependent on the flux of interaction, a new position can be introduced into an existing repertory. Because of its relative autonomy, the new position can bring in new information and knowledge different from the information and knowledge associated with already existing positions in the self. In both cases the assumption is that as part of dialogical processes, agreement and disagreement, like question and answer, play a crucial role in pushing the self to a future that is to a significant degree unpredictable.

In contrast to the dialogical self, relational schemas function as stabilized repetitions that find, as internalized structures, their center in the past. As far as schemas are changed, they are changed by external factors, given their lack of internal potential for self-change and -renewal. The dialogical self, however, is continually challenged or plagued by questions, disagreements, conflicts, negotiations, and confrontations, because other people are represented in the self in the form of voiced positions functioning as centers of initiative. In more dynamical terms, the self has the capacity of multiple positioning with the possibility of emergence of new knowledge as a result of dialogical interchange. As such, the dialogical self can be described as parallel distributed processing (PDP) rather than in terms of a central processing unit (CPU) (see Foddy & Kashima, chap. 1, this volume).

The capacity of self-renewal and self-innovation allow the self to engage in an active process of positioning and repositioning. Given the self's capacity of renewal and innovation, it makes sense to make use of the more dynamic terms *position* and *positioning* rather than the more static term *role* as Harré and Van Langenhove (1991) argued. The use of the verb forms *positioning* and *repositioning* allows the dialogical self to take initiatives and to organize itself in new ways, as can be seen not only in the lives of artists and scientists, but also in the lives of all those people who renew themselves by breaking at times through the limits of custom and convention. (For extensive discussion of the issue of innovation in relation to James, Mead, and Bakhtin, see Hermans, 1999, and Hermans and Kempen, 1993.)

THEMES IN STORYTELLING

In accordance with the metaphor of the polyphonic novel, the dialogical self assumes that a person may tell different and even contrasting stories from different positions. Selves, like novels, movies, fairy tales, myths, program music, and other kinds of stories, may be organized around a broad variety of themes, such as jealousy, revenge, tragic heroism, injustice, unattainable love, the innocence of a child, inseparable friendship, discrimination, and so forth. This thematic variety, however, does not exclude the possibility that culture provides us with a limited amount of basic themes that function as organizing frames for the understanding and interpretation of life events. Such basic themes may help us to see the main structures in the self of one and the same person, and, moreover, may enable the researcher to compare the stories from different persons with each other. There are different ways of classifying themes as structuring devices of stories.

Frye (1957), for example, argued that themes in narratives are rooted in the experience of nature, and in the evolution of the seasons in particular. Spring has inspired *comedy*, expressing people's joy and social harmony after the threatening winter. Summer, bringing abundance and richness, gives rise to the *romance*, which depicts the triumph of good over evil, and of virtue over vice. Autumn, representing the decline of life and the coming death of the winter, instigates the *tragedy*. Finally, in the winter *satire* is born because this season makes people aware that one is ultimately a captive of the world, rather than its master. In the satire people find an outlet to criticize their own fate.

Although the movements of nature may lead to a cyclical classification of story themes, Gergen and Gergen (1988) proposed a classification of a more linear type. They considered narratives as changing over time toward a desirable end state. A *progressive narrative* is told if the story represents increments toward an end state. An individual telling such a narrative might say, "I am learning to overcome my shyness and be more open and friendly with people." A *regressive narrative* is focused on decrements in the orientation toward a desirable endpoint. An individual might say, "I can't control the events of my life anymore." Finally, in a *stable narrative* the individual remains essentially unchanged with respect to the valued end state. Somebody involved in such a narrative might say, "I am still as attractive as I used to be."

The psychological motives of the actors may also be taken as a starting point for the classification of narratives. Murray's (1938) system of needs and his use of the Thematic Apperception Test (TAT) may serve as a classic example (for review see Gieser & Stein, 1999). A TAT picture may invite subjects to tell stories with different themes (e.g., achievement, affiliation, dominance, sex, etc.). The guiding idea is that the themes, expressed in the stories, reflect the subjects' more or less unconscious needs. Inspired by Murray, later investigators used TAT procedures to assess people's motives or needs: achievement motive (McClelland, Atkinson, Clark, & Lowell, 1953), power (Winter, 1973), affiliation (Boyatzis, 1973), and the opposition of power and intimacy (McAdams, 1985). Such literatures reflect a close relationship between psychological motives and narratives.

In our own work (Hermans, 1988; Hermans & Van Gilst, 1991) we have assumed that there are two basic themes in collective stories, heroism (e.g., Alexander the Great, Achilles, Napoleon) and love (e.g., Orpheus and Eurydice, Romeo and Juliet, the love affair in the musical *Hair*). At the same time we have assumed that these themes are reflected in the psychological motives of individual people. In the tradition of Bakan (1966) two motives were distinguished, the striving for self-enhancement (i.e., self-maintenance and self-expansion), and the longing for contact and union with somebody or something else. In a study of affective reactions of subjects to Goya's serial painting *The Capture of the Bandit El Maragato* (Hermans, 1988), it was observed that this painting expressed the polarity of winning versus losing, representing the theme of self-enhancement. It was found that the same theme was present in the self-narratives of individual clients: The experience of winning was expressed in such statements as *My status position is acceptable but not enough; I want to go a few steps further,* or *My achievements were mine; they were valued (piano, sport, studying).* The experience of losing was expressed in statements like *I have the feeling that John can be strong by keeping me weak* or *Violence and aggression have knocked me down.*

A similar study was done on the affective meaning of the Narcissus myth (Hermans & Van Gilst, 1991). The central part of the myth, Narcissus looking into the water, was found to represent the experience of unfulfilled love, and can be considered as an expression of an existential longing for contact and union with other people and with oneself. On the basis of affective patterns derived from the central part of the myth, we explored whether similar patterns exist in the individual narratives of clients. It was found that the theme of unfulfilled longing was also present in specific statements present in the clients' self-narratives, like "I think it's too bad that I couldn't remove some of my mother's loneliness with my cheerfulness" or "First, I meant everything to him; now he means everything to me; the roles are now reversed." The Goya study and the Narcissus study suggest that basic themes, expressed in collective stories, are present in the self-narratives of individual people as well.

In summary, in contrast to the diversity and variety of *I*-positions, both within one and the same self and between different selves, a limited amount of basic themes or motives can be assumed that are common to the lives of many people in different periods of their lives. A narrative theme functions as an organizing principle in the structure of the story and serves as a criterion for highlighting certain events and positions as more relevant than other.

A MODEL FOR THE PROCESS OF POSITIONING

As we have argued, the *I* is not a central agency hovering above a great variety of positions, but the *I* itself is always positioned in time and space. The term *I-position* expresses this intrinsic boundedness of the mentally sounding concept of *I* and the materialized and spatialized concept of *position*. The *I* moves in an imaginal space from the one to the other position, creating dynamic fields in which self-negotiations, self-contradictions, and self-integrations result in a great variety of meanings.

In Fig. 4.1 the self is represented as a space composed of a multiplicity of positions (represented by dots within a circle). Internal positions are felt as parts of myself (e.g., "I as a mother," "I as an ambitious worker," "I as somebody who likes to engage in sports"), whereas external positions are felt as part of the environment ("my wife," "my colleagues," "my friend John"). External positions refer to people and objects in the environment that are, in the eyes of the individual, relevant from the perspective of one or more of the internal positions. In reverse, internal positions receive their relevance from their relation with one or more external positions. That is, internal and external positions receive their significance as emerging from their mutual transactions over time. Dependent on the dialogical process between existing positions, and the introduction of new ones, the self is involved in a process of innovation. From a theoretical perspective, all positions (internal and external) are *I*-positions because they are part of a self that is intrinsically extended to the environment and responds to self-relevant selections in the environment. At the vertical line

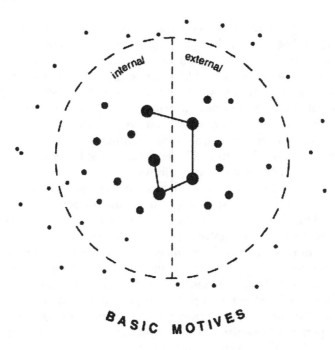

FIG. 4.1.   Model of positions in the self.

in Fig. 4.1, the internal and external parts of the system meet at their front sides. They are inseparably united as the two parts of a circle.

The lines between some of the positions in Fig. 4.1 refer to the dialogical relations that may develop between particular internal and external positions (e.g., "As a father I help my children if they need me"). They can, however, also exist between different internal positions ("I disagree with myself because as an ambitious worker I neglect my duties as a father") or between different external positions ("My son and daughter had a terrible argument"). The lines between the positions, representing dialogical relations, are placed near the dividing line in the circle indicating the front field of activity between positions. Other positions that show no dialogical relationships in a particular period or at a particular moment are in the background of the system. They are, as part of the repertoire, accessible for dialogical relationships at some other moment in time. The larger the dots, the more the positions move to the front of the system.

The positions that are placed within the circle are accessible as parts of the self (e.g., "When my friend invites me for a game, the sport fanatic is aroused in myself"). Many positions, however, are simply outside the subjective horizon of the self and simply fall beyond the person's awareness (dots outside the circle). As possible positions, however, they may enter the self space at some moment in time dependent on changes in the situation. For example, when the person finds a partner and establishes a family, a variety of new external positions (e.g., offspring) and internal positions (I as a mother or father) will be introduced as part of the self.

The model presented in Fig. 4.1 is based on the idea of moving positions, implying that the dots should be seen as moving. For example, external positions may move from the external to the internal space: A child may identify with a hero in a story to such a degree that the child becomes that hero (internalization). Or, an adolescent may create a new character in a story or a piece of art, in which his or her own self-preoccupations are expressed and materialized (externalization).

Basic motives as general story themes are also reflected in the model. These motives are supposed to influence the organization of the position repertory. They determine which positions move to the front of the system or to the background. For example, when a person hears that he will be dismissed from his job, his self-enhancement motive will be threatened. As a result the threatened (internal) position "I as an employee" will move immediately to the front of the system. At the same time, the contact motive will lead to the relevance of particular people who might be of help or support as relevant (external) positions. The opposite movement may take place if a person is brought into a position that is unbearable (e.g., a person who was forced to do an immoral job during the war). In that case the threatened position moves to the background of the system. The basic motives also determine if possible positions move from the outside into the system. If they are relevant for one or more basic motives, there is a greater chance that they move into the system than when they are not. In other words, the basic motives determine the relevance of internal and external positions and the nature of their dialogical relationships.

Changes in culture also can be reflected in changes of positions. In our present era, often labeled as *postmodern*, we are faced with an intensified flow and flux of positions moving in and out of the self-space within relatively short time periods. Such a cultural change evokes intriguing questions such as, does this flow lead to an "empty self" (Cushman, 1990) or a "saturated self" (Gergen, 1991) or does it lead to a reorganization of the self in such a way that an intensified flow of positions is counteracted by an increasing need for more stable positions that guarantee a basic consistency of the self-system? Such questions create the need for social psychological theories and methods that are suited for studying the relationship between culture and self.

The presented model is also sensitive to the emergence of biculturalism (LaFromboise, Coleman, & Gerton, 1993) or multiculturalism (Fowers & Richardson, 1996). When people are raised in one culture and then migrate to another, this leads to a self-organization in which two or more internal positions (e.g., I as an Indonesian and I as a Dutch person) transact with a multiplicity of external positions (e.g., the family of one's culture of origin and individuals and groups representing the second culture). Such cultural positions may be felt as conflicting or as coexisting in relatively independent ways. They may even fuse so that hybrid combinations in the form of multiple identities emerge (e.g., Algerian women playing soccer in an international competition) (Hermans & Kempen, 1998).

NANCY'S CASE: FROM A CHILD POSITION TO AN INDEPENDENT POSITION

As an illustration of the presented model a client involved in a psychotherapeutic process is described. This choice is made because a successful psychotherapy may be expected to include an innovation of the self during the time in which the client is involved in the psychotherapeutic process. This process implies the introduction of a new external position (the therapist) into the system with the intention to reorganize the system as a whole.

The client is Nancy, a 47-year-old woman, mother of two adolescent children and working as a secretary. She contacted a psychotherapist (Els Hermans-Jansen) in a period in which she suffered from several psychosomatic problems, such as frequent headaches and muscular tensions. She said that she felt permanently under pressure to defend her place in the world and felt overly dependent on the approval and evaluation by others, both in her work situation and at home. As a result of her strong need to be recognized and confirmed by others, she was always striving for perfection and experienced a large amount of guilt feelings when this perfection was not achieved.

After half a year of psychotherapy there was not much change in her condition and the described problems continued to impair her daily life. In order to give the process a new impulse, the psychotherapist, in cooperation with the author of the present chapter, invited Nancy to explicate her position repertory as a basis for taking new initiatives that may facilitate the psychotherapeutic process. With that aim in mind, Nancy was provided with a list of 40 internal positions and was instructed to mark those positions that she recognized in her own life. Some of the internal positions as chosen by Nancy are listed in Table 4.1. The two final positions were added by Nancy herself in her own language.

In the subsequent sessions, Nancy's internal positions were examined in close relation to her experiences in her daily life. She was requested to keep a diary in which she not only told about her daily experiences but also indicated which parts of her self (internal positions) and which people and groups (external positions) were involved. After some sessions it be-

TABLE 4.1
Nancy's Position Repertory: Some Examples

1. The fighter
2. The vulnerable figure
3. The self-surrendering figure
4. The recognition seeker
5. The moral figure
6. The jealous figure
7. The freedom seeker
8. The dreamer
9. The critic
10. The child
11. The aggressive figure
12. The relativizing figure

came evident that the internal position of the "child" played a central role in her daily life. In order to examine this position more deeply, it was decided to perform a self-investigation from the perspective of this particular position. That is, Nancy was invited to construct, from the position of the child in herself, some valuations referring to important meaning units in her past, present, and future (see the left side of Table 4.2). These valuations are expressed in sentences in which Nancy describes in her own words a variety of experiences or circumstances which are meaningful to her in a positive (pleasant) or negative (unpleasant) way. The valuations are aroused by open questions that refer to past, present, and future. An example of such a question is: "Has there been anything of major significance in your past that still continues to exert a strong influence on you?" Similar questions are posed about the present and the future. The psychotherapist helps the client with formulating an answer in such a way that the answer is in agreement with the client's intention. The psychotherapist helps the client to formulate a valuation in the client's own terms (for a detailed procedure, see Hermans & Hermans-Jansen, 1995).

It is supposed that each valuation has an affective connotation in which basic motives are expressed (Hermans & Hermans-Jansen, 1995). This affective connotation is measured by four indexes (see Table 4.2): index S referring to self-enhancement (e.g., pride and self-esteem), index O referring to contact and union with somebody or something else (e.g., love and tenderness), index P referring to positive affect (e.g., enjoyment and happiness), and index N referring to negative affect (e.g., anxiety and anger). After the construction of the valuations, the client rates all these valuations with a list of affect terms, which includes the four types of affect (S, O, P, and N). The rationale behind these indexes is that on their way to gratify their basic motives (S and O in this case), people meet obstacles that prevent this gratification. If they succeed in overcoming these obstacles, posi-

TABLE 4.2
Valuations From the Child and Independent Positions Constituting Part of Nancy's Position Repertoire

Valuations from the child position	S	O	P	N	Valuations from the independent position	S	O	P	N
1. I want attention and I want recognition	0	2	3	32	1. Yes, then you should do it in a good way; not by nagging but by staying realistic; I determine what happens, often in consultation	12	2	16	12
2. I'm dependent on others or their approval of me	2	1	5	34	2. You do not have to be; e.g., my new training: my brother-in-law has his suspicions, this touches the dependent child; I say: I can do it; I am who I am now and I can do it	16	3	21	14
3. My brothers and sisters are my rivals; they also demand attention from the one who I could also get attention from	2	1	5	38	3. [does not play a role in the current situation]				
4. My mother plays us against each other: I really feel pushed aside; I do my best to be even sweeter	1	0	0	41	4. Then I try to involve the independent one somewhat more and get some distance; this still plays a role; it is a pitfall; I have to be really alert, she [the mother] still does it	9	0	7	22
5. As a teenager, my father did not allow me to do much; he was strict and hot-tempered; I was never allowed to say what I thought; he didn't allow me to have any contact with him; I never noticed that he liked me	0	2	5	30	5. I can relativize this [no contact] from the position of independence; he's been dead for a long time; I see better now what happened; I think he was a coward 'cause he clearly chose for my mother; he thought he had to, that he had no choice	10	7	12	10

(Continued)

TABLE 4.2
(Continued)

Valuations from the child position	S	O	P	N		Valuations from the independent position	S	O	P	N
6. I feel quickly rejected (e.g., Jim went to his son and stayed away longer); I immediately think that he likes his son better than me; I pull myself down really quickly	2	5	5	31	6.	I use the independent to relativize this; the child now gets her fingers slapped: "don't put on such an act"; but this is still really hard	13	4	14	15
7. I have wrestled so long with the unrecognized child; I see no future whatsoever (I have also not succeeded with any other therapy)	1	1	0	34	7.	What I learned here is this therapy: that the child asked too much attention and still does; from the independent position, I now say: you just stay where I put you (this is where the independent really comes forward very strongly)	14	6	21	14
8. The child feels best when I am doing creative (painting) and, during vacations, the satisfied part of the child comes out	6	8	30	10	8.	Yes, doing creative work, that's allowed by the independent one, that playfulness is there too, that is really good, that helps the independent one to relativize. I have more control over that child, then the child can play more of a prominent role	14	11	28	2
9. How do I generally feel as a child	4	4	10	14	9.	How do I feel as an independent	13	0	21	16
10. How would I like to feel as a child?	16	16	40	4	10.	How do I like to feel as an independent?	20	14	47	2

Note. S = feelings of self-affirmation; O = feelings referring to contact and union with the other; P = positive; N = negative. The S and O indexes range from 0 to 20 and the P and N indexes range from 0 to 50.

tive affect predominates, and if these obstacles are insuperable, negative affect predominates.

As Table 4.2 shows, the valuations from the child position are typically associated with low levels of S and O affect in combination with high levels of N affect. This suggests that Nancy's child position is not able to gratify the self-enhancement motive nor the contact motive, and, as a result, much negative affect is aroused. The main reason seems to be that the unbridled and extreme nature of the child's wishes and pretensions (e.g., see Valuations 1 and 3) prevents them to be successfully realized in the adult world. A notable exception is Valuation 8, in which the creative aspects of the child position are associated with a predominance of positive affect. In other words, the child position is not negative or undesirable irrespective of circumstances. On the contrary, the child position may be positive or desirable in particular situations (e.g., during vacation). Although the child position has some positive experiences to offer, the general trend is quite negative. This is also indicated by the "general feeling" (number 9), which has low S and O affect and a slight predominance of N affect. The strong discrepancy, moreover, between the "general feeling" and the "ideal feeling" suggests that the child's valuation system typically reflects the theme of unfulfilled self-enhancement in combination with unfulfilled contact with the other.

THE EMERGENCE OF THE "INDEPENDENT" POSITION AS INNOVATION OF NANCY'S SELF

Not only for Nancy but also for the therapist a most striking phenomenon was that, as a result of the self-investigation, Nancy reacted with a very strong opposition toward the child's extreme egocentrism and unrealistic pretensions. The self-investigation and the discussion of the results had a strong impact on Nancy, in that she became aware, as never before, of the fact that she did not want to continue her life as largely determined by the child's dictatorial claims. In her own words, Nancy objected to the child's pretensions with a firm counterreaction:

> It is a hole, that endlessly wanting to be confirmed, that excessive request to continually be considered nice . . . The feeling is that it is never enough. The child has too much power at hand and paralyzes things. An end has to come to that nagging. The child wants too much, my future is also paralyzed.

This was a remarkable statement from Nancy, who was so long plagued by the dominance of her child position that determined her life more than she wanted. In the past she had received psychotherapeutic assistance several times. What these endeavors had in common was the aim to gratify the wishes of the child on the supposition that the neglected child should be gratified as a compensation for the early lack of confirmation. After the self-investigation from the child's position, Nancy became more and more convinced that it was necessary to counterbalance the absolute demands of the child. It was this counterbalance that gave a strong innovative impulse to the further development of her self.

After a period during which Nancy experimented with her behavior from the perspective of several positions (e.g., the fighter), she felt a growing conviction that there was one position in particular that was of growing relevance to her daily life, the "independent" figure, that she introduced as a new position into her position repertory a few months after the investigation:

> The independent one is a new world for me, but I still have to learn it. In my work I am busy practicing this. Also, in converation with John [her partner], I sometimes have a different opinion. This is getting stronger. Before, if someone had another opinion, I started to doubt my own. Now, the independent is starting to really surface.

Six months after the investigation from the position of Nancy's child, it was decided to perform a second investigation, but now from her independent position. In order to stimulate the dialogical relationship between the two positions, Nancy was invited to give an answer, from her independent position, to the valuations that she had earlier formulated from the position of the child. These valuations are listed at the right sight of Table 4.2. From an affective point of view, the main difference between the two positions is in the presence of the self-enhancement motive. In all valuations of the independent position, affect referring to self-enhancement is stronger than affect referring to contact and union and in most cases; moreover, positive affect predominates negative affect. The most prominent type of valuation in this position can be labeled as *positive self-enhancement* (high S, low O, high P, and low N). This particular type of valuation was found to differentiate between a group of clients in psychotherapy and a group of nonclients (Van Geel, 2000). The nonclient group had more valuations with a positive self-enhancement pattern of affect than the client group. This finding implies that this type of valuations is lacking in many psychotherapy clients. The fact that Nancy developed precisely this type of valuation as part of her independent position suggests that she is more capable than previously to give an adequate answer to her problems that were associated with the dominance of her child position. Another finding in Van Geel's study was that valuations with the pattern low S, low O, low P, and high N were more typical of the client group than the nonclient group. The fact that this type of valuation is lacking in Nancy's independent position but overly represented in her child position again indicates that the independent position contributes more to the fulfillment of her self-enhancement motive than the child position could do.

Valuation 8 of the independent position is particularly interesting from a theoretical point of view. Here we see that the independent position does not always have a conflicting relationship with the child position. It shows that the two positions can cooperate well with one another, particularly in situations in which Nancy's creativity and playfulness is involved. The fact that Valuation 8 is positive both from the perspective of the independent and from that of the child reflects a welcome coalition between two positions that are otherwise strongly clashing and conflicting. This observation emphasizes a basic feature of the dialogical self: the coexistence of conflict and cooperation between opposed positions in the self. It also emphasizes that positions in a multivoiced self are rarely to be characterized as "undesirable" in any generalized way. Positions that may impair the person's development in a variety of situations may be helpful in other situations. This means that one should know the situation before one may draw conclusions about the undesirability of particular positions. "Bad" in one situation may be "good" in another.

From a spatial perspective, Valuation 7 is particularly relevant because it phrases, in Nancy's own terms, how the imaginal space of herself is organized. The expression "stay on your spot" suggests that the child position is limited by the increasing expansion of the independent position. The child position is allowed some space but not the total space. This observation may be compared with Straus's (1958) analyses of the self space of clients who are disturbed by auditory hallucinations. In these cases the *total* space of the client is occupied by the intruding voice so that the distinction between a "safety zone" and a "danger zone," typical of a normally functioning person, has been wiped out. For the hallucinating person there is no place left to hide, whereas for the normal person there is, in the case of a threat, the opportunity to move from the danger zone to the safety zone. In Nancy's case we see a similar spatial organization. Initially she lives in a space that is almost entirely occupied by the dictatorial expansion of the child position. As soon as she becomes able to establish an opposite independent position, she reorganizes her space into a differentiated, more articulated space that enables her to move more flexibly into different directions dependent on the needs and requirements of the situation at hand.

In summary, Nancy's case illustrates several concepts that are central to the preceding theoretical discussion of the dialogical self: space, position, voice, dialogue, and innovation. In the spatial construction of the self, the concept of position reflects the organization of the self in terms of *position* and *opposition*. Between different positions a field is created that enables the *I* to flexibly move into different directions. In principle, each position is endowed with a voice that is able to tell a story from the specific perspective of that particular position. Different stories can be told from different positions, which enables the individual to tell stories with a multithematic variety. Voices are able not only to tell stories and create units of meaning; they are also able to entertain dialogical relationships with one another. In Nancy's case, we have focused on the dialogue between two significant internal positions (the child and the independent), which could be organized in innovative ways as a result of the intervening influence of a new external position (the therapist). Two positions (the child and the independent) that are usually conceived of as successive developmental periods in the life of an individual are brought together as if in space rather than in time, and, as a result of this juxtaposition, dialogical relationships have an opportunity to develop. The dialogical self allows for the innovation of the self by the introduction of new voices in a multivoiced self, and by the emergence of new meanings as a result from dialogical processes between existing voices.

DECENTRALIZATION AND INNOVATION

Psychological literature shows an increasing interest in the self from the perspective of multivoicedness and dialogue (e.g., Barresi & Juckes, 1997; Cooper, 1999; Fogel, 1993; Gergen, 1991; Gregg, 1991; Hermans, 1996a; Josephs, 1996; Raggatt, 2000; Rappoport, Baumgardner, & Boone, 1999; Shotter, 1999; Valsiner, 1997). Although such authors may greatly differ in their conception of dialogue as constitutive of the self, they have in common a rejection of the self as a central processing unit (the CPU model). This theoretical shift has some significant implications for future conceptions of the self.

The inclusion of the notion of dialogue into future theorizing enables theorists to deal with psychological phenomena in ways that clearly deviate from the CPU model. The dialogical self contrasts, for example, with Higgins's (1987) theory, which implies that discrepancies between several domains of the self are (automatically) associated with emotional vulnerabilities. One of the merits of Higgins's theory is that it does not treat the self as an undifferentiated whole and as unified in itself but as differentiated and multifaceted. At the same time, however, the theory assumes a central organizing process that automatically reduces the tensions between the different parts of the self. Implicitly based on a tension reduction model, Higgins's theory suggests that depression results from discrepancies between particular components of the self and that well-being results from a reduction of these discrepancies. Moreover, like every tension reduction model, Higgins's theory implies that discrepancies are "solved" by bringing back the system into a state of reduced tension. That is, the system is, in essence, in the same state after the tension as it was before, and, in this sense, the self has no opportunity to renew and innovate itself. In the dialogical self, on the other hand, self-discrepancies, or indeed contrasts, conflicts, disagreements, and contradictions between components of the self, are seen as intrinsic to a well-functioning self in general and to its innovation in particular. Although conflicts and disagreements, between internal and external positions, within internal positions, and within external positions, may be associated with negative feelings, they have the inherent capacity to create new and integrative constructions, as we have seen in Nancy's case.

In the dialogical self the voiced positions are not only intersubjectively related, but they also differ in their relative dominance. When positions are followed over time, a drastic change in their relative dominance can be observed (Hermans, 1996b). In Nancy's case it could be noticed that in the course of therapy her independent position became more dominant in her life than her child position, resulting in a "dominance reversal." Such a reversal functions as an important facilitator of the innovation of the self. A voice that was hitherto silent, neglected, or suppressed becomes, in a certain period, dominant in the self and may influence the dialogical relations to a significant degree. As argued earlier (Hermans & Kempen, 1993), the notion of dialogue has two intrinsic features: intersubjective interchange, and dominance. When a voice that was located in the background of the self-system (see Fig. 4.1) comes to the foreground, it becomes more dominant in the polyphony of the voices and may present in the self-system a message or story that is new in its dialogical repercussions.

Individual, Societal, and Evolutionary History: A Perspective for Future Theorizing

The notion of voice is central to the concept of the dialogical self, as we have extensively argued. Voices can tell stories and, as part of a community, they emerge from history. As proposed earlier (Hermans & Kempen, 1995), we envision the future of social psychology as the study of the individual person from a theoretical framework that incorporates three kinds of history, as originally distinguished by the Russian social scientist Leont'ev (1959/1973): individual, societal, and evolutionary.

Going through an individual history, each individual develops a personal story or self-narrative (Bruner, 1990; Gergen & Gergen, 1988; Hermans & Kempen, 1993; McAdams, 1993; Sarbin, 1986). As we argued in this chapter, the self is "distributed" among several positions located in space, with the possibility of moving to and fro among them. In this highly dynamic conception of the self, the *I* has the capacity to move from a particular position to another position *and back*, even if there is a distance in time (Marková, 1987). This capacity implies that a particular position can be revisited, as we have seen with Nancy, who revisited her child position in order to give the independent position the chance to respond. This process of positioning and repositioning may result in the generation of a multiplicity of personal stories.

As part of a society, the embodied person is spatially located together with other human beings and participates in a collective history. This implies that the self is prestructured by preceding generations who have produced traditions and institutions that leave their imprint on the individual. In the line of Bakhtin (1929/1973), it is supposed that the self is speaking not only as an individual voice but also as a collective voice, reflecting the collective values implied in the stories people tell one another as members of the groups and cultures to which they belong. Nancy, for example, was educated as a woman in a traditional Dutch family, and, coming from this background, she was faced with many obstacles in her attempts to develop her independent position. Given the simultaneity of individual and collective voices, the values implied by the collective voices influence and constrain the personal valuations as expressed by the individual voices.

From an evolutionary point of view, the human body is well equipped to participate in dialogical processes. The hands, in particular, are refined instruments that, in combination with the eyes, provide the biological tools not only for gathering knowledge about the environment but also for interacting with the world. As Fogel's 1993 study of giving and taking in mother–infant interactions demonstrated, the use of the hands in human interactions can be considered as prelinguistic forms of dialogue. Such prelinguistic dialogues have, in their turn, a clear precursor in the evolution of higher animals and humans who came to a point where they were able to take an upright position and "distantiate" themselves from their immediate environment. The upright position freed the hands to grasp and isolate an object from its context, enabling the individual to make new combinations between different objects located in space (e.g., a chimp taking a banana, which is out of reach, with the help of a stick). In other words, in order to understand the genesis of dialogical processes, it is necessary to study the functioning body as emerging from our evolutionary history.

A promising way of incorporating evolutionary processes into future theorizing is to include motivational factors in dialogical models. People do not dialogue with each other in an entirely free space in which they can take any direction. Rather, they communicate with each other to achieve particular goals and to gratify their needs. They are "motivated storytell-ers" who are able to tell passionate stories (Hermans & Hermans-Jansen, 1995). Two basic motives have been discussed in this chapter, self-en-hancement, and contact and union, which are supposed to influence and organize the process of positioning and repositioning. There is ample evi-dence that similar motives are also found in animals. The self-enhance-ment motive may find its evolutionary precursor in competitive and aggressive behavior, whereas the contact and union motive finds its fore-runner in forms of cooperative behavior (Walters & Seyfarth, 1987) and in the existence of "reciprocal altruism" (Silk, 1987).

Studying dialogical processes from the perspective of the three forms of history has the prospect of enriching future social psychological theories. The self as a decentralized dialogical movement can be understood as emerging from the particular activity of an individual person, as resulting from a collective societal history, and as prestructured by our common evolutionary origin. Dialogue as an embodied practice not only preceded *Homo sapiens* but also made them.

ACKNOWLEDGMENT

I thank Els Hermans-Jansen for giving me the opportunity to function as a cotherapist for the client of the case study.

REFERENCES

Andersen, S. M., & Cole, S. W. (1990). "Do I know you?": The role of significant others in general social perception. *Journal of Personality and Social Psychology, 59*, 384–399.

Bakan, D. (1966). *The duality of human existence.* Chicago: Rand-McNally.

Bakhtin, M. (1973). *Problems of Dostoevsky's poetics* (2nd ed., Transl. R. W. Rotsel). Ann Arbor, MI: Ardis. (Original work published 1929 under the title *Problemy tvorchestva Dostoevskogo* [Problems of Dostoevsky's Art])

Baldwin, M. W. (1992). Relational schemas and the processing of social information. *Psycho-logical Bullletin, 112*, 461–484.

Baldwin, M. W., & Holmes, J. G. (1987). Salient private audiences and awareness of the self. *Journal of Personality and Social Psychology, 53*, 1087–1098.

Barresi, J., & Juckes, T. J. (1997). Personology and the narrative interpretation of lives. *Jour-nal of Personality, 65*, 693–719.

Boyatzis, R. E. (1973). Affiliation motivation. In D. C. McClelland & R. S. Steele (Eds.), *Hu-man motivation* (pp. 252–276). Morristown, NJ: General Learning Press.

Bruner, J. S. (1986). *Actual minds, possible worlds.* Cambridge, MA: Harvard University Press.

Bruner, J. S. (1990). *Acts of meaning.* Cambridge, MA: Harvard University Press.

Caughey, J. L. (1984). *Imaginary social worlds: A cultural approach.* Lincoln: University of Nebraska Press.

Cooper, M. (1999). If you can't be Jekyll be Hyde: An existential-phenomenological exploration of lived-plurality. In J. Rowan & M. Cooper (Eds.), *The plural self: Multiplicity in everyday life* (pp. 51–70). London: Sage.

Cushman, Ph. (1990). Why the self is empty: Toward a historically situated psychology. *American Psychologist, 45,* 599–611.

Damon, W., & Hart, D. (1982). The development of self-understanding from infancy through adolescence. *Child Development, 4,* 841–864.

Fogel, A. (1993). *Developing through relationships: Origins of communication, self, and culture.* Hertfordshire: Harvester Wheatsheaf.

Fowers, B. J., & Richardson, F. C. (1996). Why is multiculturalism good? *American Psychologist, 51,* 609–621.

Frye, N. (1957). *Anatomy of criticism.* Princeton, NJ: Princeton University Press.

Gergen, K. J. (1991). *The saturated self: Dilemmas of identity in contemporary life.* London: Sage.

Gergen, K. J., & Gergen, M. M. (1988). Narrative and the self as relationship. *Advances in Experimental Social Psychology, 21,* 17–56.

Gieser, L., & Stein, M. I. (1999). *Evocative images: The Thematic Apperception Test and the art of projection.* Washington, DC: American Pychological Association.

Gregg, G. S. (1991). *Self-representation: Life narrative studies in identity and ideology.* New York: Greenwood Press.

Harré, R., & Van Langenhove, L. (1991). Varieties of positioning. *Journal for the Theory of Social Behaviour, 21,* 393–407.

Hermans, H. J. M. (1988). On the integration of idiographic and nomothetic research methods in the study of personal meaning. *Journal of Personality, 56,* 785–812.

Hermans, H. J. M. (1996a). Voicing the self: From information processing to dialogical interchange. *Psychological Bulletin, 119,* 31–50.

Hermans, H. J. M. (1996b). Opposites in a dialogical self: Constructs as characters. *Journal of Constructivist Psychology, 9,* 1–26.

Hermans, H. J. M. (1999). Dialogical thinking and self-innovation. *Culture & Psychology, 5,* 67–87.

Hermans, H. J. M., & Hermans-Jansen, E. (1995). *Self-narratives: The construction of meaning in psychotherapy.* New York: Guilford Press.

Hermans, H. J. M., & Kempen, H. J. G. (1993). *The dialogical self: Meaning as movement.* San Diego: Academic Press.

Hermans, H. J. M., & Kempen, H. J. G. (1995). Body, mind, and culture: The dialogical nature of mediated action. *Culture & Psychology, 1,* 103–114. [Commentary on James Wertsch's paper]

Hermans, H. J. M., & Kempen, H. J. G. (1998). Moving cultures: The perilous problems of cultural dichotomies in a globalizing society. *American Psychologist, 53,* 1111–1120.

Hermans, H. J. M., Kempen, H. J. G., & Van Loon, R. J. P. (1992). The dialogical self: Beyond individualism and rationalism. *American Psychologist, 47,* 23–33.

Hermans, H. J. M., & Van Gilst, W. (1991). Self-narrative and collective myth: An analysis of the Narcissus story. *Canadian Journal of Behavioural Science, 23,* 423–440.

Higgins, E. T. (1987). Self-discrepancy: A theory relating self and affect. *Psychological Review, 94,* 319–340.

Holquist, M. (1990). *Dialogism: Bakhtin and his world.* London: Routledge.

James, W. (1890). *The principles of psychology* (Vol. 1). London: Macmillan.

Jaynes, J. (1976). *The origin of consciousness in the breakdown of the bicameral mind.* Boston: Houghton Mifflin.

Josephs, I. E. (1996). Mind as dialogue: A developmental perspective. *Polish Quarterly of Developmental Psychology, 2,* 215–222.

LaFromboise, T., Coleman, H. L. K., & Gerton, J. (1993). Psychological impact of biculturalism: Evidence and theory. *Psychological Bulletin, 114,* 395–412.

Leont'ev, A. N. (1973). *Probleme der Entwicklung des Psychischen* [Problems in the development of mind]. Frankfurt, Germany: Athenaeum Fischer. (Original work published 1959)

Marková, I. (1987). On the interaction of opposites in psychological processes. *Journal for the Theory of Social Behavior, 17,* 279–299.

McAdams, D. P. (1985). *Power, intimacy, and the life story: Personological inquiries into identity.* Chicago: Dorsey Press.

McAdams, D. P. (1993). *The stories we live by: Personal myths and the making of the self.* New York: William Morrow.

McClelland, D. C., Atkinson, J. W., Clark, R. A., & Lowell, E. L. (1953). *The achievement motive.* New York: Appleton-Century-Crofts.

Mead, G. H. (1934). *Mind, self, and society.* Chicago: University of Chicago Press.

Minkowski, E. (1936). *Vers une cosmologie: Fragments philosophiques* [Toward a cosmology: Philosophical fragments]. Paris: Fernand Aubier.

Murray, H. A. (1938). *Explorations in personality.* New York: Oxford University Press.

Raggatt, P. T. F. (2000). Mapping the dialogical self: Towards a rationale and method of assessment. *European Journal of Personality, 14,* 65–90.

Rappoport, L., Baumgardner, S., & Boone, G. (1999). Postmodern culture and the plural self. In J. Rowan & M. Cooper (Eds.), *The plural self: Multiplicity in everyday life* (pp. 93–106). London: Sage.

Sarbin, T. R. (1986). The narrative as a root methaphor for psychology. In T. R. Sarbin (Ed.), *Narrative psychology: The storied nature of human conduct* (pp. 3–21). New York: Praeger.

Shotter, J. (1999). Life inside dialogically structured mentalities: Bakhtin's and Voloshinov's account of our mental activities as out in the world between us. In J. Rowan & M. Cooper (Eds.), *The plural self: Multiplicity in everyday life* (pp. 71–92). London: Sage.

Silk, J. B. (1987). Social behavior in evolutionary perspective. In B. B. Smuts, D. L. Cheney, R. M. Seyfarth, R. W. Wrangham, & T. T. Struhsaker (Eds.), *Primate societies* (pp. 318–329). Chicago: University of Chicago Press.

Straus, E. W. (1958). Aesthesiology and hallucinations. In R. May, E. Angel, & H. F. Ellenberger (Eds.), *Existence. A new dimension in psychiatry and psychology* (pp. 139–169). New York: Basic Books.

Tomkins, S. S. (1978). Script theory: Differential magnification of affects. In R. A. Dienstbier (Ed.), *Nebraska symposium on motivation* (pp. 201–236). Lincoln: University of Nebraska Press.

Valsiner, J. (1997). Dialogical models of psychological processes: Capturing dynamics of development. *Polish Quarterly of Developmental Psychology, 3,* 155–160.

Van Geel, A. L. M. (2000). *Agency and communion: A psychometric study of the self-confrontation method.* Dissertation, University of Nijmegen, Nijmegen, the Netherlands.

Vasil'eva, I. I. (1988). The importance of M. M. Bakhtin's idea of dialogue and dialogic relations for the psychology of communication. *Soviet Psychology, 26,* 17–31.

Walters, J. R., & Seyfarth, R. M. (1987). Conflict and cooperation. In B. B. Smuts, D. L. Cheney, R. M. Seyfarth, R. W. Wrangham, & T. T. Struhsaker (Eds.), *Primate societies* (pp. 306–317). Chicago: University of Chicago Press.

Wekker, G. (1994). Eindelijk kom ik tot mezelf. Subjectiviteit in een Westers en een Afro-Surinaams universum. In J. Hoogsteder (Ed.), *Etnocentrisme & communicatie in de Hulpverlening* (pp. 45–60). Utrecht: Landelijke Federatie van Welzijnsorganisaties voor Surinamers.

Winter, D. G. (1973). *The power motive.* New York: Free Press.

SOCIAL PROCESSES

Social perspectives are represented in Part III. Although social psychology has long taken a perspective of methodological individualism, which assumes that all social processes should be reduced to individual activities, recent developments in social approaches to self have acknowledged that both individuals and groups can act as significant social agents. Here, therefore, the social process involving the self is divided into interpersonal, role-theoretic, and intergroup aspects.

Sedikides, Campbell, Reeder, Elliot, and Gregg's chapter 5 provides an intriguing introduction to the interpersonal nature of self-evaluation processes. They describe the paradox of narcissism as the codependence of extreme individualism on the presence of others. Despite narcissists' extreme self-absorption, and a subsequent lack of interest in others, their self-love is parasitic on interpersonal relationships to be exploited. Although challenging some of the features of the social cognitive model of the mind (e.g., invariance; accuracy motive), these authors take the view that the individualist self can be interpersonally socialized in an unproblematic way.

Chapter 6, written by Smith-Lovin, introduces a symbolic interactionist perspective, which takes seriously the socialized and institutionalized side of interpersonal behavior. Although this view may be relatively unfamiliar to psychologists, it is becoming more apparent that the set of concepts developed by sociologists to deal with self and identity provides an important intellectual resource that can be drawn on to develop a more social conception of the person. In particular, the concept of social role provides a key link between individual self-conceptions and social institutions, the latter largely ignored by psychologists. Smith-Lovin outlines one detailed program of research, affect control theory, to illustrate how affective processes control behaviors associated with role identities. In addition, she sketches its affiliation with parallel distributed processing (PDP) models of mind, opening up a range of future research possibilities.

In chapter 7, Onorato and Turner highlight the group aspect of the social, and outline a much more variable conceptualization of the self than do most other authors in the book. This variability is seen to arise from the primacy of the social in the formation of the self. They show that intergroup processes in particular, being highly variable and changing across contexts, alter the salience of different selves, with the result that the idea of a single, unified self or identity is strongly challenged. From this perspective, the central processing unit (CPU) metaphor appears severely limited. On this view, the related view of the self requires a revision that incorporates a highly context-dependent, variable self. Onorato and Turner present evidence from experimental paradigms initially designed to test theories of the individual self, in support of their claims for context variability of selves. Although they do not directly address the issue of which model of mind would be most consistent with their position, we would venture that the CPU model is less promising than the PDP approach, because of the latter's capacity to deal with "multiple selves."

Chapter 5

Do Others Bring Out the Worst in Narcissists?: The "Others Exist for Me" Illusion

Constantine Sedikides
University of Southampton

W. Keith Campbell
University of Georgia

Glenn D. Reeder
Illinois State University

Andrew J. Elliot
University of Rochester

Aiden P. Gregg
University of Southampton

> *"I hate every human being on earth. I feel that everyone is beneath me, and I feel they should all worship me."*
> —Roseanne Barr in an interview at *Gear* magazine, October 2000

The cognitive revolution gave social and personality psychology a heuristically useful metaphor, the central processing unit (CPU) (Foddy & Kashima, chap. 1, this volume). The CPU was considered a robust, powerful, and efficient controller of mental processes—so efficient, in fact, that it was assumed to process information about the self in a virtually identical manner as information about other persons, non-human animals, and inanimate objects (Ostrom, 1984). It was this one-controller-fits-all notion that permeated theorizing on the self in the late 1970s, 1980s, and even early 1990s. The assumption asserted the relative invariance both of the self as a cognitive structure (Greenwald & Banaji, 1989; Kihlstrom et al., 1988; Rogers, Kuiper, & Kirker, 1977) and of the sources of incoming information (social vs. nonsocial; Hamilton, 1988; Ostrom, 1984; Srull & Wyer, 1989).

The invariance assumption was based, in part, on a rather implicit thesis, namely, that the guiding force (i.e., motive) behind information processing is a concern for accuracy. Humans are truth seekers. They single-mindedly pursue knowledge that is accurate and impartial, regardless of whether such knowledge pertains to the self, other persons, or environmental objects. After all, the pursuit of accuracy is both rational and functional. It is rational because it follows logical rules. It is functional because it provides the individual with valuable insight not only into others but also into the individual's relative position in family systems, occupational hierarchies, and societal structures.

The invariance assumption was also based on research agenda priorities. Perhaps because it was considered a reasonable starting point, the top item on the agenda was intrapsychic processing. Research foci aimed at explicating processes such as how individuals reflect on themselves, ruminate, resolve internal conflict, set goals consistent with their self-concept, evaluate the success of their goals as a function of internal standards, and experience emotions on the basis of subjective evaluations of goal attainment.

However, by the mid 1990s, the shortcomings of the invariance assumption had come to light. The accuracy assumption was shown to be only half correct. Humans indeed have accuracy concerns, but mostly when they process information about unfamiliar persons or objects (Sedikides & Green, in press; Smith, 1998; Wyer & Carlston, 1994). When it comes to processing information about the self, accuracy concerns give way to positivity concerns. Humans strive to protect, retain, repair, or increase the positivity of the self-concept—in short, they are driven by the motive to self-enhance (Brown & Dutton, 1995; Sedikides & Strube, 1997; Wheeler & Miyake, 1992).

The accuracy assumption was also challenged by waves of research on the role of the self in relational (Murray, 1999), intra- or intergroup (Onorato & Turner, chap. 7, this volume), and cultural (Heine, Lehman, Markus, & Kitayama, 1999) contexts. Such research highlighted the complex interplay between intra-psychic processes on the one hand, and interpersonal, group, and cultural processes on the other. It became clear that context can change the individual self in remarkable ways (Foddy & Kashima, chap. 1, this volume; Sedikides & Brewer, 2001).

We believe that the research described in this chapter captures the zeitgeist of the late 1990s and the beginning of the new millennium. To begin with, we fully endorse the well-founded notion that thinking about the self is colored by the self-enhancement motive. In an effort to map out the boundaries of how this motive affects self-perception, we zero in on a rather extreme manifestation of the motive: narcissistic self-enhancement. At the same time, we give serious consideration to contextual influences, as we examine the extent to which narcissistic self-enhancement is constrained by the interpersonal milieu. What sort of influence does an interpersonal bond have on the narcissistic self, if any? We postulate the existence of a narcissistic illusion, which we term the "Others Exist for Me" illusion. Bearing out this illusion are research findings that point to narcissists becoming competitive in interpersonal contexts and using other persons for own psychological advantage. Stated otherwise, we use an extreme example of egocentricity and self-enhancement to argue that what is believed to be a personality trait (i.e., narcissism) is actually, at least in part, a critical interpersonal phenomenon, an interpersonal extension of the individual self. We review relevant research findings, draw implications, and discuss issues that warrant further research attention.

NARCISSISM

Conceptual Definition

The *Diagnostic and Statistical Manual of Mental Disorders* (*DSM–IV*; American Psychiatric Association, 1994) classified narcissism as a personality disorder that distorts several areas of psychological functioning. Narcissists are highly self-focused and egocentric, think of themselves in extraordinarily positive ways, have persistent needs for attention and admiration, have a strong sense of uniqueness, specialness, and entitlement, and have recurrent fantasies of power, success, and fame. In the classic personality and social psychological tradition (e.g., Emmons, 1987; Raskin, Novacek, & Hogan, 1991a; Rhodewalt & Morf, 1995), we conceptualize narcissism as a personality variable on which the population lies on a continuum.

Operational Definition

Narcissism has most commonly been operationalized via the Narcissistic Personality Inventory (NPI; Raskin & Hall, 1979). The NPI is a forced-choice scale that has adequate reliability and validity (Raskin & Terry, 1988; Rhodewalt & Morf, 1995). The scale consists of seven components: authority, entitlement, exhibitionism, exploitativeness, self-sufficiency, superiority, and vanity. Most of the research that we review in this chapter has used the NPI to sort out narcissists from their humbler brethren. For the purposes of this chapter, we consider "narcissists" those individuals who score above the median (or are relatively high) on the NPI, and "normals" those who score below the median (or are relatively low) on the NPI.

THE "OTHERS EXIST FOR ME" ILLUSION

We propose that narcissistic thinking about the self in relation to others is characterized by the "Others Exist for Me" illusion. At the core of this illusion are self-centeredness and self-admiration, perceptions of others as vastly inferior, and the belief that others care or should care as much about the narcissist's psychological welfare as the narcissist does. Other persons are expected to bow to narcissistic superiority, are exploited for personal gain (i.e., the affirmation of narcissistic perceptions of superiority), and are met with hostility when they display behaviors that the narcissist finds uncongenial.

We begin by providing a rationale for the "Others Exist for Me" illusion. We proceed with reviewing four classes of evidence that support the illusion. These are (a) narcissistic perceptions of one's own superiority, (b) narcissistic manifestations of one's own superiority in independent tasks, (c) narcissistic perceptions of others' inferiority, and (d) narcissistic use of others for self-enhancement in interdependent tasks.

Rationale

Underlying our proposal for the "Others Exist for Me" illusion is our conviction that the crucial distinction between narcissists and normals is not simply that narcissists engage in more blatant self-enhancement. Instead, the crucial distinction rests in the interpersonal price that narcissists are willing to pay in order to self-enhance. The price is damage to an interpersonal bond. In some sense, other persons bring out the worst in narcissists. Narcissists appear to be energized by others, to perceive the interpersonal situation competitively, to expect others to cater on them. They then take advantage of others, and become hostile when the script does not go as planned.

It is informative to consider normals as a reference point. Normals are prone to keeping their self-enhancement tendencies in check when an interpersonal bond has been formed, no matter how superficial this bond is. In other words, normals show contextual sensitivity. For example, they automatically describe themselves more humbly to persons who know them well (i.e., friends) than to strangers (Tice, Butler, Muraven, & Stillwell, 1995). On the contrary, the narcissistic self agenda remains uncompromisingly rigid and transparent: Narcissists ruthlessly pursue the aggrandizement of the individual self, even at the price of diminishing others and at the risk of sacrificing the interpersonal bond. The narcissistic self relates to the social world in fundamentally different ways than the normal self.

Why do narcissists fail to show contextual sensitivity? Why are they so rigid in their self-enhancement patterns? How have they formed the "Others Exist for Me" illusion in the first place? According to psychodynamic theorizing, one theme that runs through the life of the narcissists is the antagonism between the need for self-enhancement and the ability to maintain healthy interpersonal relationships—be it romantic relationships or friendships. This theme first appeared in Greek mythology when Narcissus forsook the advances of Echo and a host of prospective partners, and eventually fell in love with his own reflection in a pool of water. This theme was also central to Freud's (1914/1957) analysis of narcissism. Freud emphasized that love is a limited psychological resource. As a result of narcissists' libidinal cathexis with the self, libido becomes unavailable for cathexis with other objects. In plain English, narcissists spend all of their love on themselves, and, as a result, have none left over for close others.

Following Freud's lead, several psychodynamically oriented theorists, notably Kernberg (1975), Kohut (1977), and Millon (1981), focused on disfunctional parent–child relationships as the source of narcissism. Kernberg reckoned that the child's construction of an inflated self-concept was a defense against the emotional abandonment by parents and also the child's rage resulting from such abandonment. Narcissists use relationships to feel good about themselves, and thus avoid experiencing intense feelings of loss and anger. Kohut proposed that the child's construction and maintenance of an inflated self-concept were the outcome of unmet psychological needs (e.g., attention, comfort, love). Narcissists use relationships to feel good about themselves, and thereby compensate for the absence of loving attention that they received in childhood and the intense negative affect that accompanied it. Millon (1981), on the other hand, presented a dramatically contrasting view of narcissism. Narcissism is the result of parental over-attention, overly positive feedback, and excessive levels of admiration. The child is getting used to this royal treatment and generalizes the expectancies of deservingness and entitlement to adult relationships. When these expectancies are violated, the child feels betrayed and responds with rage, hostility, and aggression.

Narcissistic Perceptions of Own Superiority

Narcissists self-aggrandize to an extraordinary degree, as correlational evidence suggests. Narcissism is positively correlated with self-esteem (Jackson, Ervin, & Hodge, 1992; Raskin & Terry, 1988), body image (Jackson et al., 1992), belief of possessing extraordinary talents (Tobacyk & Mitchell, 1987), lack of a discrepancy between the actual and ideal self (Rhodewalt & Morf, 1995), self-focus (Emmons, 1987; Raskin & Shaw, 1988), agency (Bradlee & Emmons, 1992), need for uniqueness (Emmons, 1984), need for status and power (Bradlee & Emmons, 1992; Carroll, 1987), and machiavellianism (McHoskey, 1995).

Narcissistic Manifestations of Own Superiority in Independent Tasks. Independent tasks involve settings in which participants work alone (Sedikides, Campbell, Reeder, & Elliot, 1998). Self-enhancement in such tasks does not implicate others directly. That is, judgments about the self or attributions about one's performance do not necessitate a direct comparison with another person. Self-enhancement in independent tasks does not require the explicit derogation or diminishment of another person.

Independent tasks afford the researcher the opportunity of contrasting narcissistic with normal self-enhancement. As we have emphasized, the crucial distinction between narcissists and normals lies in the interpersonal price that narcissists are willing to pay in order to enhance the individual self. However, based on the already reviewed evidence for narcissistic self-perceived superiority, we maintain that narcissistic self-enhancement will surpass normal self-enhancement even in tasks that do not involve other persons: Narcissists will be more self-enhancing than normals on independent tasks. That is, although others are sufficient to energize narcissists and activate their superiority beliefs and competitive tendencies, they are not necessary.

A good portion of the literature is supportive of the proposition that narcissists self-enhance even on independent tasks. Gabriel, Critelli, and Ee (1994) asked participants to rate their own intelligence and physical attractiveness in relation to the average college student. The researchers compared these ratings both to the results of an intelligence test that participants took following the self-ratings and to judges' ratings of the participants' attractiveness. Relative to normals, narcissists overestimated the degree to which they were intelligent and attractive. Likewise, compared to normals, narcissists were overoptimistic about their current and final course grade, and about the success of their performance at an upcoming laboratory task (Farwell & Wohlwend-Lloyd, 1998).

Narcissists self-enhance in additional ways. Participants in a study by Kernis and Sun (1994) received randomly determined positive or negative interpersonal feedback and subsequently rated the diagnosticity of such feedback. Compared to normals, narcissists regarded the feedback as more diagnostic when it was positive and as less diagnostic when it was negative. John and Robins (1994) examined the perceptions of master's of business administration (MBA) students participating in a group discussion task. At the end of the discussion, participants evaluated their own overall positive contribution to the group in comparison to their fellow discussants' positive contributions. In disagreement with observers or peers, narcissists, relative to normals, rated their own performance as more impactful. These findings were conceptually replicated by Gosling, John, Craik, and Robins (1998), and by Raskin and Shaw (1988).

Nevertheless, other lines of research seem to blur the clear picture that these findings present. This research examines attributions for one's own performance, and specifically the empirically robust self-serving bias. This valid signature of the self-enhancement motive refers to individuals taking responsibility for successful task outcomes, but denying responsibility (by displacing it to other persons or circumstances), for unsuccessful task outcomes (Arkin, Cooper, & Kolditz, 1980; Campbell & Sedikides, 1999; Mullen & Riordan, 1988).

In a study by Rhodewalt and Morf (1995, Study 1), participants filled out the Attributional Style Questionnaire (Rhodewalt, Strube, Hill, & Sansone, 1988), in which they made attributions for hypothetical negative or positive events. Participants attributed the cause of each event to factors that were internal versus external, stable versus unstable, and global versus specific. Participants also indicated the extent to which they were responsible for each event. True to form, narcissists manifested a self-serving attributional pattern with regard to positive outcomes: They attributed such events to internal, stable, and global causes. Surprisingly, however, narcissists did *not* differ from normals in their attributions for negative outcomes. That is, narcissists did not surpass normals in attributing these events to external, unstable, and specific causes.

We supplemented this correlational study with several experimental investigations of narcissistic self-enhancement in independent tasks. (Note that in this, as in all of our experiments, we statistically removed from narcissism the contribution of self-esteem.) Participants in one of our published studies (Campbell, Reeder, Sedikides, & Elliot, 2000, Experiment 2) took the "Lange-Elliot Creativity Test," an ostensibly well-validated measure of "individual creativity" (Bartis, Szymanski, & Harkins, 1988). Each participant listed as many uses as possible for two objects: a brick and a candle. The number of unique object uses that each participant generated would be her or his score on the test. Upon test completion and scoring, each participant received false success or failure feedback. Next, participants were told that creativity is a function of many factors, and it is near impossible to tell what percentage of their score is due to test-taker characteristics or to chance circumstances. Thus, participants were asked to estimate the degree to which they thought that they were individually responsible for their score on the test. They also indicated whether the test outcome was due to internal factors (ability and effort) or to external factors (difficulty and luck). We derived an overall measure of internal attributions by subtracting the scores on the external factors from the scores on the internal factors (e.g., Stephan, Rosenfield, & Stephan, 1976).

Finally, participants indicated the degree to which they regarded creativity as an important trait to have. This constitutes an indirect measure of self-enhancement (Wyer & Frey, 1983). A self-enhancing pattern would be one in which participants valued the trait more following success than following failure.

In general, participants manifested the self-serving bias: Those who succeeded assumed more responsibility for the outcome of the test than those who failed. In addition, success feedback participants made more internal attributions, and valued creativity more, than failure feedback participants. However, none of these effects was qualified by narcissism to a statistically significant degree. Apparently, narcissists were as likely as normals to display the self-serving bias, to make an internal attribution for the successful completion of the test, and to value creativity mostly in the face of success. We conceptually replicated these findings both in a published study (Campbell, Reeder, Sedikides, & Elliot, 2000, Experiment 1) and in an unpublished experiment (Campbell, Reeder, Sedikides, & Elliot, 2001).

Taken together, evidence for the proposition that narcissists self-enhance on independent tasks is somewhat mixed. Narcissists are not invariably and robustly more self-enhancing than normals. Instead, narcissists manifest a mildly higher self-enhancement pattern than normals on independent tasks.

Narcissistic Perceptions of Others' Inferiority

Correlational studies provide suggestive evidence for the proposal that narcissists do not consider others as equals. Narcissism is inversely related to perspective taking or empathy (Watson, Grisham, Trotter, & Biderman, 1984), need for intimacy (Carroll, 1987), agreeableness (Hendin & Cheek, 1997; Rhodewalt & Morf, 1995), affiliation (Bradlee & Emmons, 1992), and gratitude (Farwell & Wohlwend-Lloyd, 1998). In fact, narcissists seem to have antagonistic relational patterns with others. Narcissism is positively related to competitiveness (Raskin & Terry, 1988), exploitativeness (Bennett, 1988; Biscardi & Schill, 1985), anger (McCann & Biaggio, 1989), hostility (Rhodewalt & Morf, 1995; Raskin, Novacek, & Hogan, 1991b), and aggression (Baumeister, Bushman, & Campbell, 2000). Furthermore, narcissists enjoy competitive tasks more than normals do (Morf, Weir, & Davidov, 2000).

Narcissistic Use of Others for Self-Enhancement in Interdependent Tasks

Interdependent tasks involve collaboration between or among participants (Sedikides et al., 1998). Success or failure of the dyad (or the team) depends on the joint rather than unique contribution of its members.

When performance is evaluated, the feedback refers to the quality of the dyadic, rather than the individual, performance. As such, interaction, co-ordination of effort, and an amiable working relationship between dyad members are prerequisites for an optimal task outcome. Importantly, self-enhancement in interdependent tasks implicates the real or imagined presence of other persons. That is, judgments about the self or attributions about one's performance require a direct comparison with another person. Thus, self-enhancement in interdependent tasks necessitates the derogation or belittlement of another person.

At the core of the "Others Exist for Me" illusion is the tenet that narcissistic self-enhancement will be substantially and robustly discrepant from normal self-enhancement in interdependent tasks. Narcissists will devalue the interpersonal bond, and will opt to boost their self-concept even at the expense of the working relationship. Bluntly put, they will have no qualms about using the relationship for individual psychological gain (i.e., self-enhancement). Thus, the narcissistic self thrives in interpersonal settings. Narcissists frame the interpersonal situation in a way that it will allow them to gain a competitive advantage.

Direct evidence is strongly supportive of the already mentioned tenet. In one of our published studies (Campbell, Reeder, Sedikides, & Elliot, 2000, Experiment 1), participants completed the "Lange–Elliot Creativity Test" in dyads. They were told that each unique object use that they had generated would count toward scores on a dyadic creativity test. The experimenter had no way of knowing individual input to the test. The feedback would pertain to the success and failure of the dyad as a unit, not of individual members. Following completion of the test, participants received false success or failure feedback at the dyadic level (e.g., "your dyad did well," or "your dyad did poorly.") Next, participants made a comparative judgment: They indicated who (i.e., the participant vs. the other dyad member) was more responsible for the combined performance and outcome of the test. This relativistic attribution measure allowed us to determine whether participants were willing to denigrate their partner's performance for own gain. Finally, participants expressed the importance that they assigned to the creativity test. This measure was considered to reflect an individual (i.e., noncomparative) judgment. Participants did not need to belittle the other dyad member in order to assert their perceived superiority.

The results were revealing. In the comparative measure, narcissists manifested the self-serving bias. They regarded themselves more responsible than normals for the dyadic success, but less responsible than normals for the dyadic failure. Narcissists were fired up by the competitive situation and strove to take the psychological lead over their partner. However, in the noncomparative measure, narcissists did not differ significantly from normals, as the two categories of participants assigned equivalent importance to creativity following success and equivalent importance to it following failure. This finding conceptually replicates previously reviewed experiments utilizing independent tasks: Narcissists do not necessarily self-enhance more than normals, unless an opportunity of gaining a competitive advantage over another person is provided.

In an unpublished experiment (Campbell et al., 2001), we replicated and extended these findings. The procedure and dependent measures were identical to those of the already mentioned study (i.e., Campbell, Reeder, Sedikides, & Elliot, 2000, Experiment 1). However, we included two additional measures. First, we asked participants whether the outcome of the test was due to internal factors (ability and effort) or external factors (difficulty and luck). We derived an internal attribution index by subtracting the external factors score from the internal factors score. Second, we asked participants to provide free responses both immediately following feedback (i.e., "list all thoughts that cross your mind") and on completion of the dependent measures (i.e., "justify your responses on the prior scale").

We begin by reporting our findings on the outcome responsibility measure (Table 5.1). When the dyad succeeded, narcissists tended to take greater responsibility for the outcome of the creativity test than when the dyad failed. Normals, in contrast, allocated responsibility in a more even-handed manner. Clearly, narcissists were willing to denigrate the partner's performance for individual gain.

However, the results on the internal attribution index told another story. Note that this measure is a noncomparative measure of self-enhancement. It is not necessary to diminish the partner in order to elevate the self. In replication of previous findings, narcissists did not differ significantly from normals: They were equally likely to attribute the successful task outcome to internal qualities, and to attribute the unsuccessful task outcome to forces beyond their control. This pattern was also obtained with the importance measure, another indicator of noncomparative judgment. Narcissists and normals were equally likely to brand creativity an important trait when they succeeded, and to brand it a relatively unimportant trait when they failed.

TABLE 5.1
Responsibility for Task Outcome as a Function of Narcissism
and Feedback in Campbell, Reeder, Sedikides, and Elliot (2001)

	Success Feedback	Failure Feedback
Narcissists	6.22	5.10
Normals	5.80	5.76

Note. Higher scores indicate perceptions of greater personal responsibility.

Of particular interest were the free-response measures, as they are likely to provide additional insight into the reasons that may make narcissists behave the way they do. All free responses were coded by two research assistants. The two free-response tasks were coded on several dimensions, two of which yielded statistically significant results and are particularly relevant to the present discussion. With regard to the free-response task following feedback, the relevant dimension was presence of thoughts regarding the partner (100% coder agreement). With regard to the free response task following the dependent measure, the relevant dimension was presence of positive thoughts regarding the self (91% agreement, with the few disagreements resolved through discussion).

We analyzed these two indexes using hierarchical regression analyses. Independent variables were feedback (success, failure) and narcissism. On the free-response task following feedback, narcissism was negatively related to the presence of thoughts regarding the partner. Thus, to the extent that participants were narcissistic, they were less likely to think about their partner after getting either success or failure feedback. When we entered presence of thoughts regarding the partner into a regression equation with self-esteem, narcissism, and feedback, thoughts regarding the partner did not predict outcome responsibility. Moreover, we obtained no evidence of mediation when we entered the interaction of feedback and thoughts regarding the partner into the full model. Clearly, thoughts about the partner did not mediate the relation between narcissism and the self-serving bias.

On the free-response task following the completion of the dependent measures, narcissism was related positively to the presence of favorable thoughts regarding the self. Thus, narcissists justified their self-serving attributions by making positive statements about the self. We were unable to conduct conclusive mediational analyses because participants made their justifications after the measurement of the self-serving bias. Nevertheless, we went ahead and examined the role of positive statements as a mediator. When we entered the interaction of positive self-statements and feedback into the full model (along with the positive self-statements main effect), evidence of mediation emerged. Specifically, the interaction between positive self-statements and feedback was significant, whereas the significance of the interaction between narcissism and feedback dropped to marginality. In an effort to better understand this effect, we examined the success and failure conditions separately. In the success condition, positive self-statements were related positively to taking responsibility for the task outcome. In the failure condition, positive self-statements were related negatively to taking responsibility for the task outcome.

In summary, the free-response measures yielded some clues as to why narcissists display the self-serving bias. Narcissism was related negatively to thinking about one's partner, and narcissism was related positively to justifying responses on the dependent measure by referring favorably to oneself. Further analyses revealed that thinking about the partner did not mediate the relation between narcissism and the self-serving bias. On the other hand, positive thoughts about oneself did mediate the relation between narcissism and the self-serving bias. Because this justification measure was taken after the dependent measure, however, its role as a mediator can not be confirmed conclusively. We believe that the gist of these findings is that the rigidity of narcissistic self-enhancement in interdependent tasks is partly due to narcissists' undue focus on the self (and thus overvaluation of their own contribution) at the expense of their partner.

Corroborating Evidence

Although we were unable to locate any other studies that examined narcissistic self-enhancement in interdependent tasks, we wish to report on a handful of investigations that focused on the ways narcissists respond socially to unfavorable feedback. In some of these experimental settings, narcissists were given the opportunity to express their views of the evaluator. The study by Kernis and Sun (1994) is a case in point. Narcissists who received negative feedback at a performance task rated the evaluator (in comparison to normals) as incompetent and unlikeable. Smalley and Stake (1996) replicated these findings.

In another experimental setting, narcissists were offered the opportunity to express their views of a participant who outperformed them. Morf and Rhodewalt (1993) examined the role of narcissism in self-evaluation maintenance (SEM; Tesser, 1988). The SEM model predicts that individuals will attempt to retain a positive self-evaluation by derogating close others who perform well on a task that is highly self-relevant. Participants engaged in a self-relevant task (i.e., a test of "social sensitivity"), after which they were informed that they had performed worse than a close other. Of course, the feedback was bogus. Narcissists were more likely than normals to derogate the successful close other.

Not only do narcissists express negativity toward unfavorable evaluators, they also behave aggressively toward them. In a study by Bushman and Baumeister (1998), narcissists and normals wrote an essay and were informed that their essay would be evaluated by another participant. In actuality, it was the experimenter who provided a written essay evaluation. The feedback consisted either of negative or positive ratings on organization, originality, argument persuasiveness, writing style, clarity of expression, and overall quality. A negative ("This is one of the worst essays I have read") or positive ("No suggestions, great essay!") written comment accompanied the corresponding type of feedback. Next, participants engaged in a competitive reaction time task (Taylor, 1967), which was actually a measure of aggression. Participants learned that the faster respondent on each trial would be in a position to punish the slower respondent by controlling the intensity and duration of a blast of noise. The combination of these two measures constituted the aggression index. On the first and most telling trial, narcissists were more aggressive toward the fictitious competitor than normals, but only when the feedback was unfavorable (Experiment 1). Furthermore, this aggression was not displaced; instead, it was targeted to the specific assumed source of unfavorable feedback (Experiment 2).

THE "OTHERS EXIST FOR ME" ILLUSION: IMPLICATIONS

Next, we evaluate the empirical status of the "Others Exist for Me" illusion and discuss its implications for narcissistic patterns of relatedness.

Summary

The fundamental aspect of narcissistic self-enhancement is the nature of responsiveness (or non-responsiveness!) to interpersonal context. Narcissists build an inner shrine to themselves. They consider themselves to be at the epicenter of their social world, a world that is, or should be, their fan club. They expect all inhabitants of this world to be devoted to promoting their emotional welfare. When their naive expectancies are not met, they react with rage and hostility—as the opening Roseanne Barr quote illustrates.

We believe that the "Others Exist for Me" illusion captures the essence of narcissistic self-enhancement. Narcissists self-enhance when they engage in independent tasks or make noncomparative judgments, but their enhancement patterns are only equivocally more pronounced than those of normals. Narcissists, however, self-enhance rigidly when they perform in interdependent tasks or make comparative judgments. The distinctive feature of narcissists is that they pursue self-enhancement even when doing so means detracting from the accomplishments of a coworker. Narcissists selfishly exploit the interpersonal context in pursuit of this self-enhancement. They sacrifice interpersonal bonds in general, and diminish close others in particular, to feel better about themselves.

Perhaps Millon (1981) captured the gist of narcissistic self-enhancement. He emphasized that narcissists feel entitled in their interpersonal relationships. Indeed, narcissistic entitlement, interpersonal exploitativeness, and forcefully negative responding to disapproval are all indicators (albeit indirect) of overgeneralized relatedness patterns. An important reason why narcissists expect the royal treatment from adult partners may be that they were socialized in such a treatment.

Narcissists and Relationships Do Not Mix

How is narcissistic self-enhancement received by others? Are others forgiving or unforgiving of narcissistic behavior? When first encountered in social settings, narcissists give off a positive impression. They appear energetic, confident, and intense. However, as interpersonal encounters accumulate (indeed, by the seventh weekly social interaction: Pauhlus, 1998), narcissists are perceived as show-offs (conceited and self-centered), who are more interpersonal liabilities than interpersonal assets (Buss & Chiodo, 1991; Leary, Bednarski, Hammon, & Duncan, 1997; Schlenker & Leary, 1982). Narcissists manage to alienate others by violating rules of politeness and norms of social conduct.

The bitter aftertaste that narcissistic exploitativeness leaves in others will naturally have repercussions for narcissists' interpersonal relationships (e.g., coworkers, friendships, romantic partnerships). The most obvious repercussion is that narcissists are likely to drive away many relational partners, assuming that few persons are interested in a relationship with an individual who is nongracious when it comes to sharing collective credit and achievement. The second, and perhaps more subtle, repercussion is that narcissists' relationships will lack the mutuality of status, caring, and respect that characterizes functional adult relationships. Narcissists will have trouble being genuinely concerned for their partner (i.e., lack of communal or prosocial orientation: Clark & Mills, 1979; Van Lange, Agnew, Harinck, & Steemers, 1997), incorporating the partner into their self-concept (Aron & Aron, 1997), trusting the partner (Holmes & Rempel, 1989), committing to the partner (Campbell & Foster, 2000), accommodating to the partner's need (Rusbult, Verette, Whitney, Slovik, & Lipkus, 1991), and sacrificing for the partner (Van Lange et al., 1997). Narcissists believe that they are intrinsically superior to their relationship partners, and this belief will likely cut short their chances of having a close relationship.

Yet narcissists cannot help but have spells of closeness and intimacy, assuming that the "need to belong" (Baumeister & Leary, 1995) is a universal motive among humans. If so, how do narcissists fulfill their closeness and intimacy needs? It is likely that, in the initial stages of romantic courtship, narcissists look for a partner who appears to have the potential for facilitating their pursuit of self-enhancement. A narcissist may seek out a partner who not only accepts narcissistic claims of the lion's share of credit for the various successful projects on which the couple engages, but also displays open admiration for him or her (similar to Kohut's [1977] concept of "mirroring"). Alternatively, a narcissist may also be attracted to highly successful or attractive others so that he can bask in their reflected glory (Cialdini et al., 1976) or gain self-esteem via reflection processes (Tesser, 1988; see also Kohut's [1977] concept of "idealization"). Moreover, a narcissist may be repelled by prospective partners who offer intimacy, because this intimacy does not fit with the narcissists' view of relationships as an arena for competition and self-inflation. All these narcissistic patterns of relatedness were supported empirically by Campbell (1999).

Narcissism may influence the course of romantic relationships as well. One possibility is that the narcissistic self-orientation leads to relatively short-lived romantic involvements. The relationship may be quick to end once the romantic partner finds out that, under the initially appealing exterior, the narcissist thinks only of himself. Another area of inquiry is the development of the narcissistic self in the context of romantic involvement. Theory and research point to the role of romantic relationships in the maintenance of the self-concept (Drigotas, Rusbult, Wieselquist, & Whitton, 1999; Murray, 1999; Swann, de la Ronde, & Hixon, 1994), but the role of narcissism in this process has not been examined. Perhaps narcissists will remain in relationships with persons who are willing to constantly show them attention and admiration. The one type of person who would be most unwilling to play the role of admirer, however, is another narcissist. This suggests the possibility of a pattern of assortative mating, with narcissists selecting those partners who are particularly low on narcissism.

How Narcissists Navigate the Interpersonal Realm

We have discussed so far the apparent troubles that narcissists have in their relationships. A set of important issues needs to be addressed: Are narcissists aware of others' (frequently tacit) rejection of them? Do narcissists even care about the possibility of being rejected? Are they affected by rejection?

Existing evidence, although neither plentiful nor definitive, points to narcissists being aware of the interpersonal costs of unabashed self-enhancement: Narcissists are as accurate as normals in perceiving unfavorable feedback as such (Kernis & Sun, 1994; Smalley & Stake, 1996). Narcissists likely know, at some level, that they overstay their welcome. Still, why do narcissists seem not to learn from feedback? Why are they so unresponsive to interpersonal context? Why do they self-enhance so rigidly at the expense of the interpersonal bond? Why do they seem not to care about social rejection?

Explanations for the rigidity of narcissistic self-enhancement in interpersonal settings (i.e., for the "Others Exist for Me" illusion) converge in proposing that narcissists engage in implicit or explicit cost-benefit analysis. Narcissists calculate the benefits of maintaining psychological stability and the cost of alienating others, and the self-favoring side wins out. According to one explanation, narcissists, due to their unduly positive but fragile self-concept and self-esteem, are invested in intensely seeking self-affirmation from other persons, with interpersonal bonds being often times the unfortunate victim (Morf & Rhodewalt, 2001). According to another explanation, narcissists regulate their self-esteem by manifesting interpersonal patterns of dominance, grandiosity, and hostility (Raskin et al., 1991b).

Sedikides and Gregg (2001) proposed another explanation, which is complementary to the already mentioned ones. Sedikides and Gregg used the analogy of "high functioning autistics" to characterize narcissists, as these individuals appear to be unable to appreciate fully the long-term repercussions of social rejection, to benefit from constructive feedback, and to improve. Furthermore, Sedikides and Gregg called for investigations that explored neuroanatomical correlates of narcissistic responding to social rejections.

Are narcissists affected, in the long run, by interpersonal rejection? Apparently, they are not affected as much as one would expect. In fact, narcissists may even emerge unscathed from social rejection, a feat that would explain their persistent self-enhancement patterns in social settings. How is it possible for narcissists to remain unaffected? To begin with, "there is somebody for everybody," a catchphrase that may be applicable to narcissists. As discussed earlier, narcissists likely date those persons who pay attention to them and express admiration for them, especially if these persons are successful (Campbell, 1999). Narcissists may also manage to establish a small network of admiring (and certainly nonnarcissistic!) friends. In fact, not only do narcissists report equivalent levels of social support with normals, but they surpass normals in reporting self-esteem support. That is, narcissists believe that there is a good number of persons who think highly of them (Rhodewalt & Morf, 1995, Study 3). This belief may partially explain why narcissists seem to manifest levels of psychological adjustment (i.e., subjective well-being, loneliness, sadness, anxiety) that parallel those of normals (Rudich & Sedikides, 2001).

CONCLUDING COMMENTS

In line with the central theme of this volume, our chapter highlights motivational systems and the interpersonal context. Furthermore, our chapter conceptualizes motivation and interpersonal context as a two-way street. The context can affect how (at least some) individuals think of themselves, and self-views can also shape some parameters of the social context.

We attempted to accomplish our objectives by focusing on narcissism. This practice allowed us to challenge the plausibility of the CPU metaphor, to test both relatively flexible and rigid forms of self-enhancement, and to explore the nature of boundary (i.e., contextual) constraints on self-enhancement. The CPU metaphor is outdated, as it does not take sufficiently into account motivational concerns, such as the concern to self-enhance. The self-enhancement motive can be manifested both flexibly and rigidly. For example, normals self-enhance in independent tasks, but tend to refrain from self-enhancement in interdependent or interpersonal tasks. On the other hand, narcissists self-enhance rigidly regardless of contextual subtleties.

We believe that the present review has several implications for our understanding of self-enhancement. Traditionally, research has focused on either documenting self-enhancement (Brown & Dutton, 1995) or testing its prevalence over other self-evaluation strivings, such as the striving for self-concept accuracy (self-assessment motive) or the striving for self-concept consistency (self-verification motive) (Sedikides, 1993). Although this approach has yielded interesting insights, empirical attention has recently been redirected at other questions (Sedikides & Strube, 1997). Central to these questions is the search for moderators of the self-enhancement motive.

Classes of relevant moderators are person moderators (i.e., who is most likely to self-enhance?) and situational moderators (i.e., in what situations is self-enhancement most likely to occur?). An example of research addressing person moderators is that of Roney and Sorrentino (1995), who showed that participants who score high on the need to resolve uncertainty are less likely to self-enhance. An example of research addressing situational moderators is that of Dunning (1993) demonstrating that participants are more likely to self-enhance on ambiguous than unambiguous tasks. The research reviewed in support of the "Others Exist for Me" illusion adds to this growing body of literature by presenting a model of self-enhancement that includes both a person moderator (i.e., narcissism) and a situational moderator (i.e., independent versus interdependent tasks). Person and situational factors have a synergistic relation—a relation that needs to be fully explored for a more complete understanding of self-enhancement phenomena.

REFERENCES

American Psychiatric Association (1994). *Diagnostic and statistical manual of mental disorders* (4th ed.). Washington, DC: Author.
Arkin, R., Cooper, H., & Kolditz, T. (1980). A statistical review of the literature concerning the self-serving attribution bias in interpersonal influence situations. *Journal of Personality*, *48*, 435–448.

120

SEDIKIDES ET AL.

Aron, A., & Aron, E. N. (1997). Self-expansion motivation and including other in the self. In S. Duck (Ed.), *Handbook of personal relationships: Theory, research and intervention* (2nd ed., pp. 251–270). Chichester: John Wiley & Sons.

Bartis, S., Szymanski, K., & Harkins, S. G. (1988). Evaluation and performance: A two-edged knife. *Personality and Social Psychology Bulletin, 14*, 242–251.

Baumeister, R. F., Bushman, B. J., & Campbell, W. K. (2000). Self-esteem, narcissism, and aggression: Does violence result from low self-esteem or from threatened egotism? *Current Directions in Psychological Science, 9*, 26–29.

Baumeister, R. F., & Leary, M. R. (1995). The need to belong: Desire for interpersonal attachments as a fundamental human motivation. *Psychological Bulletin, 117*, 497–529.

Bennett, J. B. (1988). Power and influence as distinct personality traits: Development and validation of a psychometric measure. *Journal of Research in Personality, 22*, 361–394.

Biscardi, D., & Schill, T. (1985). Correlations of narcissistic traits with defensive style, Machiavellianism, and empathy. *Psychological Reports, 57*, 354.

Bradlee, P. M., & Emmons, R. A. (1992). Locating narcissism within the interpersonal circumplex and the five-factor model. *Personality and Individual Differences, 13*, 821–830.

Brown, J. D., & Dutton, K. A. (1995). Truth and consequences: The costs and benefits of accurate self-knowledge. *Personality and Social Psychology Bulletin, 21*, 1288–1296.

Bushman, B. J., & Baumeister, R. F. (1998). Threatened egotism, narcissism, self-esteem, and direct and displaced aggression: Does self-love or self-hate lead to violence? *Journal of Personality and Social Psychology, 75*, 219–229.

Buss, D. M., & Chiodo, L. M. (1991). Narcissistic acts in everyday life. *Journal of Personality, 59*, 179–215.

Campbell, K. W. (1999). Narcissism and romantic attraction. *Journal of Personality and Social Psychology, 77*, 1254–1270.

Campbell, K. W., & Foster, C. A. (2001). *Narcissism and commitment in romantic relationships: An investment model analysis.* Manuscript under review, University of Georgia, Athens, Georgia.

Campbell, K. W., Reeder, G., Sedikides, C., & Elliot, A. J. (2000). Narcissism and comparative self-enhancement strategies. *Journal of Research in Personality, 34*, 329–347.

Campbell, K. W., Reeder, G., Sedikides, C., & Elliot, A. T. (2001). *Further evidence for the absence of the self-serving bias in independent tasks.* Unpublished manuscript, University of Georgia, Athens, GA.

Campbell, K. W., & Sedikides, C. (1999). Self-threat magnifies the self-serving bias: A meta-analytic integration. *Review of General Psychology, 3*, 23–43.

Carroll, L. (1987). A study of narcissism, affiliation, intimacy, and power motives among students in business administration. *Psychological Reports, 61*, 355–358.

Cialdini, R. B., Borden, R. J., Thorne, A., Walker, M. R., Freeman, S., & Sloan, L. R. (1976). Basking in reflected glory: Three (football) field studies. *Journal of Personality and Social Psychology, 34*, 366–375.

Clark, M. S., & Mills, J. (1979). Interpersonal attraction in exchange and communal relationships. *Journal of Personality and Social Psychology, 37*, 12–22.

Drigotas, S. M., Rusbult, C. E., Wieselquist, J., & Whitton, S. W. (1999). Close partner as sculptor of the ideal self: Behavioral affirmation and the Michelangelo phenomenon. *Journal of Personality and Social Psychology, 77*, 293–323.

Dunning, D. (1993). Words to live by: The self and definitions of social concepts and categories. In J. Suls (Ed.), *Psychological perspectives on the self* (Vol. 4, pp. 99–126). Hillsdale, NJ: Lawrence Erlbaum Associates.

Emmons, R. A. (1987). Narcissism: Theory and measurement. *Journal of Personality and Social Psychology, 52*, 11–17.

Farwell, L., & Wohlwend-Lloyd, R. (1998). Narcissistic processes: Optimistic expectations, favorable self-evaluations, and self-enhancing attributions. *Journal of Personality, 66*, 65–83.

Freud, S. (1957). On narcissism: An introduction. In S. Strachey (Ed. and Trans.), *The standard edition of the complete psychological works of Sigmund Freud* (Vol. 14, pp. 67–104). London: Hogarth Press. (Original work published 1914)

Gabriel, M. T., Critelli, J. W., & Ee, J. S. (1994). Narcissistic illusions in self-evaluations of intelligence and attractiveness. *Journal of Personality, 62*, 143–155.

Gosling, S. D., John, O. P., Craik, K. H., & Robins, R. W. (1998). Do people know how they behave? Self-reported act frequencies compared with on-line codings by observers. *Journal of Personality and Social Psychology, 74*, 1337–1349.

Greenwald, A. G., & Banaji, M. R. (1989). The self as a memory system: Powerful but ordinary. *Journal of Personality and Social Psychology, 57*, 41–54.

Hamilton, D. L. (1988). Casual attribution viewed from an information processing perspective. In D. Bar-Tal & A. W. Kruglanski (Eds.), *The social psychology of knowledge* (pp. 359–385). Cambridge, England: Cambridge University Press.

Hendin, H. M., & Cheek, J. M. (1997). Assessing hypersensitive narcissism: A reexamination of Murray's Narcissism Scale. *Journal of Research in Personality, 31*, 588–599.

Heine, S. J., Lehman, D. R., Markus, H. R., & Kitayama, S. (1999). Is there a universal need for positive self-regard? *Psychological Review, 106*, 766–794.

Holmes, J. G., & Rempel, J. K. (1989). Trust in close relationships. In C. Hendrick (Ed.), *Review of personality and social psychology* (Vol. 10, pp. 187–220). London: Sage.

Jackson, L. A., Ervin, K. S., & Hodge, C. N. (1992). Narcissism and body image. *Journal of Research in Personality, 26*, 357–370.

John, O. P., & Robins, R. W. (1994). Accuracy and bias in self-perception: Individual differences in self-enhancement and the role of narcissism. *Journal of Personality and Social Psychology, 66*, 206–219.

Kernberg, O. (1975). *Borderline conditions and pathological narcissism*. New York: Jason Aronson.

Kernis, M. H., & Sun, C. (1994). Narcissism and reactions to interpersonal feedback. *Journal of Research in Personality, 28*, 4–13.

Kihlstrom, J. F., Cantor, N., Albright, J. S., Chew, B. R., Klein, S. B., & Niedenthal, P. M. (1988). Information processing and the study of the self. In L. Berkowitz (Ed.), *Advances in experimental social psychology* (Vol. 21, pp. 145–177). New York: Academic Press.

Kohut, H. (1977). *The restoration of the self*. New York: International Universities Press.

Leary, M. R., Bednarski, R., Hammon, D., & Duncan, T. (1997). Blowhards, snobs, and narcissists: Interpersonal reactions to excessive egotism. In R. M. Kowalski (Ed.), *Aversive interpersonal behaviors* (pp. 111–113). New York: Plenum Press.

McCann, J. T., & Biaggio, M. K. (1989). Narcissistic personality features and self-reported anger. *Psychological Reports, 64*, 55–58.

McHoskey, J. (1995). Narcissism and machiavellianism. *Psychological Reports, 77*, 755–759.

Millon, T. (1981). *Disorders of personality*. New York: Wiley.

Morf, C. C., & Rhodewalt, F. (1993). Narcissism and self-evaluation maintenance: Explorations in object relations. *Personality and Social Psychology Bulletin, 19*, 668–676.

Morf, C. C., & Rhodewalt, F. (2001). Unraveling the paradoxes of narcissism: A dynamic self-regulatory processing model. *Psychological Inquiry, 12*, 177–196.

Morf, C. C., Weir, C., & Davidov, M. (2000). Narcissism and intrinsic motivation. *Journal of Experimental Social Psychology, 36*, 424–438.

Mullen, B., & Riordan, C. A. (1988). Self-serving attributions for performance in naturalistic settings: A meta-analytic review. *Journal of Applied Social Psychology, 18*, 3–22.

Murray, S. L. (1999). The quest for conviction: Motivated cognition in romantic relationships. *Psychological Inquiry, 10*, 23–34.

Ostrom, T. M. (1984). The sovereignty of social cognition. In R. S. Wyer, Jr., & T. K. Srull (Eds.), *Handbook of social cognition* (Vol. 1, pp. 1–38). Hillsdale, NJ: Lawrence Erlbaum Associates.

Paulhus, D. L. (1998). Interpersonal and intrapsychic adaptiveness of trait self-enhancement: A mixed blessing? *Journal of Personality and Social Psychology, 74*, 1197–1208.

Raskin, R., & Hall, C. S. (1979). A narcissistic personality inventory. *Psychological Reports, 45*, 590.

Raskin, R., Novacek, J., & Hogan, R. (1991a). Narcissism, self-esteem, and defensive self-enhancement. *Journal of Personality, 59*, 19–38.

Raskin, R., Novacek, J., & Hogan, R. (1991b). Narcissistic self-esteem management. *Journal of Personality and Social Psychology, 60*, 911–918.

Raskin, R. N., & Shaw, R. (1988). Narcissism and the use of personal pronouns. *Journal of Personality, 56*, 393–404.

Raskin, R. N., & Terry, H. (1988). A principle components analysis of the Narcissistic Personality Inventory and further evidence of its construct validity. *Journal of Personality and Social Psychology, 54*, 890–902.

Rhodewalt, F. T., & Morf, C. (1995). Self and interpersonal correlates of the narcissistic personality inventory. *Journal of Research in Personality, 29*, 1–23.

Rhodewalt, F. T., Strube, M., Hill, C., & Sansone, C. (1988). Strategic self-attribution and Type A behavior. *Journal of Research in Personality, 22*, 60–74.

Rogers, T. B., Kuiper, N. A., & Kirker, W. S. (1977). Self-reference and the encoding of personal information. *Journal of Personality and Social Psychology, 35*, 677–688.

Roney, C. J. R., & Sorrentino, R. M. (1995). Self-evaluation motives and uncertainty orientation: Asking the "who" question. *Personality and Social Psychology Bulletin, 12*, 1319–1329.

Rudich, E. A., & Sedikides, C. (2001). *It's a matter of self-esteem: Narcissism as predictor of emotional nondistress*. Unpublished manuscript. University of South Hampton.

Rusbult, C. E., Verette, J., Whitney, G. A., Slovik, L. F., & Lipkus, I. (1991). Accommodation processes in close relationships: Theory and preliminary evidence. *Journal of Personality and Social Psychology, 60*, 53–78.

Schlenker, B. R., & Leary, M. R. (1982). Audiences' reactions to self-enhancing, self-denigrating, and accurate self-presentations. *Journal of Experimental Social Psychology, 18*, 89–104.

Sedikides, C. (1993). Assessment, enhancement, and verification determinants of the self-evaluation process. *Journal of Personality and Social Psychology, 65*, 317–338.

Sedikides, C., & Brewer, M. B. (2001). *Individual self, relational self, collective self*. Philadelphia: Psychology Press.

Sedikides, C., Campbell, W. K., Reeder, G., & Elliot, A. J. (1998). The self-serving bias in relational context. *Journal of Personality and Social Psychology, 74*, 378–386.

Sedikides, C., & Green, J. D. (2000). On the self-protective nature of inconsistency/negativity management: Using the person memory paradigm to examine self-referent memory. *Journal of Personality and Social Psychology, 79*, 906–922.

Sedikides, C., & Gregg, A. P. (2001). Narcissists and interpersonal feedback: Motivational surfeits and a motivational deficits. *Psychological Inquiry, 12*, 237–239.

Sedikides, C., & Strube, M. J. (1997). Self-evaluation: To thine own self be good, to thine own self be sure, to thine own self be true, and to thine own self be better. In M. P. Zanna (Ed.), *Advances in experimental social psychology* (Vol. 29, pp. 209–269). New York: Academic Press.

Smalley, R. L., & Stake, J. E. (1996). Evaluating sources of ego-threatening feedback: Self-esteem and narcissism effects. *Journal of Research in Personality, 30*, 483–495.

Smith, E. R. (1998). Mental representation and memory. In D. T. Gilbert, S. T. Fiske, & G. Lindzey (Eds.), *The handbook of social psychology* (Vol. I, pp. 391–445). New York: Oxford University Press.

Srull, T. K., & Wyer, R. S., Jr. (1989). Person memory and judgment. *Psychological Review, 96*, 58–83.

Stephan, W. G., Rosenfield, D., & Stephan, C. (1976). Egotism in males and females. *Journal of Personality and Social Psychology, 34,* 1161–1167.

Swann, W. B., de la Ronde, & Hixon, J. G. (1994). Authenticity and positivity strivings in marriage and courtship. *Journal of Personality and Social Psychology, 66,* 857–869.

Taylor, S. P. (1967). Aggressive behavior and physiological arousal as a function of provocation and the tendency to inhibit aggression. *Journal of Personality, 35,* 297–310.

Tesser, A. (1988). Toward a self-evaluation maintenance model of social behavior. In L. Berkowitz (Ed.), *Advances in experimental social psychology* (Vol. 21, pp. 181–227). New York: Academic Press.

Tice, D. M., Butler, J. L., Muraven, M. B., & Stillwell, A. M. (1995). When modesty prevails: Differential favorability of self-presentation to friends and strangers. *Journal of Personality and Social Psychology, 69,* 1120–1138.

Tobacyk, J. J., & Mitchell, T. E. (1987). Out-of-body experience status as a moderator of effects of narcissism on paranormal beliefs. *Psychological Reports, 60,* 440–442.

Van Lange, P. A., Agnew, C. R., Harinck, F., & Steemers, G. E. M. (1997). From game theory to real life: How social value orientation affects willingness to sacrifice in ongoing close relationships. *Journal of Personality and Social Psychology, 73,* 1330–1344.

Van Lange, P. A. M., Rusbult, C. E., Drigotas, S. M., Arriaga, X. B., Witcher, B. S., & Cox, C. L. (1997). Willingness to sacrifice in close relationships. *Journal of Personality and Social Psychology, 72,* 1373–1395.

Watson, P. J., Grisham, S. O., Trotter, M. V., & Biderman, M. D. (1984). Narcissism and empathy: Validity evidence for the narcissistic personality inventory. *Journal of Personality Assessment, 45,* 159–162.

Wheeler, L., & Miyake, K. (1992). Social comparison in everyday life. *Journal of Personality and Social Psychology, 62,* 760–773.

Wyer, R. S., Jr., & Carlston, D. E. (1994). The cognitive representation of persons and events. In R. S. Wyer, Jr., & T. K. Srull (Eds.), *Handbook of social cognition: Basic Processes* (Vol. 1, pp. 41–98). Hillsdale, NJ: Lawrence Erlbaum Associates.

Wyer, R. S., & Frey, D. (1983). The effects of feedback about self and others on the recall and judgments of feedback-relevant information. *Journal of Experimental Social Psychology, 19,* 540–559.

Chapter 6

Roles, Identities, and Emotions: Parallel Processing and the Production of Mixed Emotions

Lynn Smith-Lovin
University of Arizona

The sociological study of self and identity has struggled with two central questions throughout its history. First, how can people be so different in different social settings (in effect, be different "people" in those different settings) yet have a coherent, self-reflexive sense of a unitary self? Second, how can people play social roles in a predictable manner so as to allow smooth coordination of the social system, while responding with considerable creativity in interactions that require it? Because of the tension between a structurally shaped, role-driven actor and an agentic, creative self-reflexive actor, sociologists in the 1950s and 1960s tended to concentrate their attention either (a) on the study of social statuses and their rights and obligations vis a vis other statuses (role theory) or (b) on the process of creative social action in relatively unstructured settings (processual symbolic interactionism) (see an excellent review in Stryker, 1981). Only in the last three decades have sociologists developed a set of interrelated theories that are capable of incorporating both the highly predictable, structured nature of most social life and the incredible creativity of social action when individuals make or alter roles in unusual circumstances.

These developments within sociology have paralleled a number of the important insights from the cognitive revolution in psychology. Sociologists have integrated a view of multiple selves, each dependent on the social relationships in which ego is embedded, with a view of a unitary, internally organized self that prioritizes certain types of relations. And sociologists, like psychologists, have embraced a cybernetic control model of the self. Identity meanings, evoked by social situations, act as reference levels for interpreting the ongoing social interactions (and remembered past interactions). Actors plan, carry out, and perceive actions that serve to maintain these meanings. Emotions act as signals about how well events maintain identities. Where sociologists differ from psychologists is (a) in their greater attention to the social structural elements that go into forming the self, (b) in their image of how affect and cognition are linked in the production of social actions, and (c) in their model of how the self system produces emotions.

In this chapter, I briefly review three interrelated theories that represent this new consensus about the social self among sociological social psychologists. Stryker's identity theory links the self to the social network in which an individual is embedded, and the social structure that strongly shapes that network. Heise's and Smith-Lovin's affect control theory shows how affect and cognition link role identities to actions and emotions. Burke's identity control theory suggests another, more cognitive model of how identities and actions are linked, with somewhat different predictions about emotion. In the final section, I suggest that the recent sociological work is more consistent with a connectionist view of human cognitive processing (see chap. 2, this volume) than with the serial processing/central processing unit model that is dominant in psychology (see chap. 1). Adopting the connectionist view leads to two important insights consistent with sociological thought about self and identity. First, it allows us to deal effectively with selves as mutliple identities within a situation. In particular, it allows us to understand the frequent experience of mixed emotions in response to social events, which become interpretable as the simultaneous processing of a single occurrence from the standpoint of multiple identities, while integrating these experiences in terms of their emotional implications for a central self. Second, it allows us to see identity meanings as cultural elements, incorporated into the self through repeated interactions and through the observation of others' emotional reactions.

SOCIOLOGISTS LOOK AT THE SELF: SYMBOLIC INTERACTIONISM

Almost all sociologists who focus their attention on self and identity share some central assumptions. These assumptions derive primarily from the work of George Herbert Mead (1934; see Miller, 1973, for an annotated bibliography) and his fellow pragmatists John Dewey, William James, and

Charles Pierce. Herbert Blumer (1969) coined the term *symbolic interactionism* for this set of ideas.[1] The three guiding principles are:

1. People act toward things, including each other, in terms of the meanings that those things have for the actor.
2. The meanings of things derive primarily from social interaction.
3. People manage and transform meanings in their social worlds through an interpretive process. In other words, people make sense of the interactions in which they participate (behaviorally, cognitively or emotionally) based on learned meanings.

A focus on the active interpretation of meanings made symbolic interactionists distinctive within sociology during the era when structural–functional theories stressed the orderly acquisition and performance of social roles. Role theory (Heiss, 1981) presented a picture of relatively static behavioral expectations vis-à-vis particular role alters. Symbolic interactionists brought the individual actor as an active processor back into the social fabric. However, the interactionists' concentration on the creative, negotiated character of social life led to criticisms that they were ignoring the impact of social structure—forces like institutional role constraints, power differences, and other regularities in social structure that could not be negotiated away by individual action (see Reynolds, 1993; chap. 9, for a review of these criticisms). Theory and research on the structured, orderly aspect of social institutions and on the active, creative aspect of negotiated action tended to proceed in parallel, but with little dialogue. Only in the last three decades has a view of self, identity, and role emerged that can simultaneously capture the orderly and the creative. There are really two interrelated theories necessary to bridge the gap: Stryker's (1980) view of the self as an organized, hierarchical set of role identities, and a cybernetic control model of how identities are related to social actions and emotions (Heise, 1979; Smith-Lovin & Heise, 1988; Burke 1991).

---

[1]Many who share the basic theoretical assumptions articulated by Blumer (and outlined here) would reject Blumer's methodological prescriptions, which largely eschewed the scientific method and argued for the inductive development of "sensitizing concepts" instead of hypothetical deductive theory. Blumer did not believe that social psychology (at least in its current stage of development) was capable of generating broad, abstract theoretical statements about social processes that would hold across situations and times. The more structural symbolic interactionists whose work I describe here begin with the same fundamental view of the social actor, but proceed to generate abstract theoretical principles, which they then examine with evidence from a variety of methods (qualitative, survey, and experimental).

FROM ROLES TO IDENTITIES:
STRYKER'S IDENTITY THEORY

Sheldon Stryker (1968, 1980) developed a highly successful attempt to bring social structure and roles back into a systematic treatment of identity. Stryker's identity theory adopted the basic symbolic interactionist assumption that the self reflects society, and argued that this fact implied a multifaceted self that reflected the variety of network contacts in which an individual participated. A person who had connections to five alters—a wife, a son, an employer and two coworkers—would have four identities corresponding to those role relationships (husband, father, employee, and coworker). People have as many identities as they have network ties in which they occupy a social position and play an associated role.[2]

This central conception of the self as a configuration of identities corresponding to role relationships is linked to two levels, one more macro-structural and the other more microindividual. At the macro level, the theory recognizes that people live their lives in circumscribed networks of social relationships that are largely determined and bounded by the structure of the larger social system (Stryker & Burke, 2000). Roles generally determine the types of networks and the relationships to others within them. These roles are, essentially, expectations (vis-à-vis others) attached to positions occupied in networks of relationships.

Although recognizing that the internalized role expectations of these role identities would lead to different actions in settings that evoked them, Stryker also recognized that the self had a more unitary character. Individuals make active role choices by choosing a course of action when two or more positions are simultaneously available (the microindividual-level process). The key element of Stryker's theory is the hierarchical organization of role identities into a salience structure. He defined identity salience in behavioral terms—the probability that a given identity will be evoked across a variety of situations.[3] Following much work in cognitive psychology (Markus, 1977), Stryker viewed identities as cognitive schemas with a variety of stored meanings and information. They served as frameworks for defining situations and interpreting experience. The higher the salience of an identity in the self structure, the more likely that a situation would be defined using that role's institutional framework, and the higher the probability that behavioral expectations associated with that role

---

[2]Later researchers like Stets (1995) argued that personal identities (basically individually held self-conceptions about characteristics that one possesses) have a theoretical status similar to role identities, in that they also have meanings that are maintained in interaction.

[3]Alternatively, one can think of salience as the probability across persons that an identity will be evoked, given a specific situational configuration.

would be enacted (relative to other, less salient role-identity options within the setting).[4]

True to his symbolic interactionist assumptions, Stryker looked to the social environment for determinants of the self structure. He used a network conception of social structure, and argued that several features of a network relationship influenced the salience of the identity evoked by that role relationship. He defined commitment as the dependence of a person's relationships on a particular role identity. It was measured by the degree of loss entailed by abandoning a role identity (in terms of number and centrality of relationships to alters). The more frequent and rewarding a tie, the more salient was the identity that it activated. In simple terms, Stryker's theory translates the Meadian dictum that society shapes the self, into this: Network commitments shape identity salience shapes role choice behavior (Stryker & Burke, 2000).

Because the concept of value is contained implicitly in both commitment and salience,[5] careful measurement is necessary to keep from confounding the two. Fundamentally, these two aspects of identity—the structural and the intrapersonal—are easiest to separate with data over time that follow individuals through changes in social environments. One of the most impressive studies of this sort followed freshmen university students for 6 months as they moved from their home environments into university life (Serpe, 1987; Serpe & Stryker, 1987). As the theory predicts, there was stability of the self structure over time, and the new students made attempts to seek new relationships in which to play out their most salient identities. In the face of significant change in their social environments, however, individuals shifted their self structures over time. The salience of identities that were not supported by network ties in the new environment faded, whereas identities that were supported increased in importance.

Although students have been the focus of much identity theory research (largely because their identities and social environments are in flux), other research on more general populations also supported the theory's basic proposition. The salience of religious identities (Stryker & Serpe, 1982), the blood donor identity (Callero, 1985), the mother identity (Nuttbrock & Freudiger, 1991), and the feminist identity (Kroska, 1997) all predict, to

---

[4]Stryker's concept of identity salience is related to, but not equivalent to, the concept of psychological centrality. See Stryker and Serpe (1994) for a study that distinguishes both the measurement and predictive power of the two concepts.

[5]The idea of loss from the absence of an identity in commitment implicitly contains the notion of how valuable the relationships based on that identity are for ego. The hierarchical aspect of salience also implies a valuelike ranking of the importance of identities within the self structure. Stryker, however, defines both commitment and salience in behavioral terms.

varying degrees, the amount of time spent in activities that enact those identities. The roles that are more institutionally constrained (like wife and mother) show somewhat lower levels of prediction than those that allow more choice (like religion and blood donation).

Stryker's main contribution was to link the stable social structure and its role requirements with the self structure and its active choice behavior. He brought the symbolic interactionist principles back to their roots in society, answering the criticisms of the perspective as one that ignored the larger social framework and its powerful force in shaping social interaction. In recent years, however, attention within structural symbolic interaction has shifted from Stryker's emphasis on the structured sources of the self and the self's active role in selecting and defining situations to the cybernetic control system through which identity meanings shape actions within interaction.

THE MEANING OF ROLE IDENTITIES

As interest shifted from the selection of identities and how that selection is shaped by social structural forces to the process through which identities shape action, the problem of how to measure identities became central. Based on the symbolic interactionist tenet that people respond to things (including other people and themselves) in terms of their meanings, researchers looked for a systematic, general, reliable way to measure the meanings of role-identities. Both Heise (1965, 1969, 1970, 1977) and Burke (1980; Burke & Tully, 1977) adopted the general framework for representing meaning developed by Osgood and his colleagues (Osgood, Suci, & Tannebaum, 1957; Osgood, May, & Miron, 1975). The semantic differential technique developed by Osgood viewed meaning as a general, affective response to a stimulus (in this case, an identity) that could reliably be measured by ratings on bipolar scales anchored by sets of opposing adjectives.

Heise and Burke took somewhat different approaches to using Osgood's semantic differential technique, however. Heise embraced Osgood's finding that general affective meanings had a common dimensional structure across concept domains and across cultures. Heise (1965, 1969, 1970) used these common dimensions—evaluation (good vs. bad), potency (powerful vs. powerless), and activity (lively vs. quiet)—to represent both role identities and interpersonal behaviors so that both could be represented within the same common meaning space. Later extensions of the theory represented emotions, traits, and behavior settings, within the same dimensional system (Smith-Lovin, 1990; Smith-Lovin & Heise, 1988). This use of a common dimensional structure allowed Heise to develop a powerful, general model that described how identities and actions were connected in a cybernetic control system (see next section).

Burke measured self meanings within specific institutional domains like gender (Burke, 1977), university student life (Burke & Reitzes, 1981), and old age (Mutran & Burke, 1979). He argued that different dimensions were relevant for different institutional domains and their role sets. For example, in the university student domain Burke and Reitzes (1981) found four dimensions: academic responsibility, intellectualism, sociability, and personal assertiveness. Using different dimensions in each role domain means that Burke's own version of a cybernetic control theory can only be applied *after* assessing the role identity dimensions and meanings that are relevant for that particular domain.

After structural symbolic interactionists developed a reliable format for measuring identity meanings, the next step was to relate meaning to action. Simple causal frameworks had produced unsatisfactory results, and researchers concluded that more situated, contextualized, processual approaches were needed (see reviews of related literature in Alexander & Wiley, 1981, and Hill, 1981). Few of these approaches were general and powerful, however. A marked exception is Heise's affect control theory.

INTERPERSONAL BEHAVIOR AS THE CONTROL OF IDENTITY

David Heise (1977, 1979) proposed that identity meanings, evoked by an interpersonal situation, acted as reference levels in a cybernetic control system. As a symbolic interactionist, Heise posited that the identity meanings—viewed on the three dimensions of evaluation, potency and activity—develop from past interactions. They are largely determined by one's culture, and were learned through watching others perform roles, direct experience with role occupants, observation of others' emotional reactions to events, and physical cultural materials like books, films, and television. Once a situation evokes an identity—for example, a woman enters a classroom and becomes a professor interacting with a student—the meanings of the professor and student identities on the three dimensions are called up from memory to act as reference levels for guiding and interpreting events within the situation.

Because identities, behaviors, and other event elements are all measured on the same three dimensions, Heise and his colleagues could explicitly model the effect of potential actions on the meanings within the situation (Heise, 1969, 1970; Smith-Lovin & Heise, 1988). They used meanings from identities and behaviors rated in isolation ("a professor," "a student," and "to compliment someone") to predict the ratings of meanings when they are presented in the context of events described by simple sentence ("a professor compliments the student"). An event like "the professor challenges the student" might produce very little movement from the original meanings, whereas an event like "the professor hits the student" would produce massive changes. Heise called the square of the differences between the culturally acquired meanings called from memory and the situational meanings produced by an event, when summed across all three dimensions and all of the event elements (actor, behavior and object-person), a *deflection*. The key prediction of his affect control theory is that actors will act (and perceive events) in ways that maintain the reference meanings. Therefore, people will act to minimize deflections. This minimization is represented in the theory by a mathematical model that solves for the three-number evaluation, potency, and activity profile of a behavior that will minimize the deflection, given the current state of the system (its reference levels and current situated meanings).

Affect control theory suggests that people maintain their identities through actions when that is institutionally possible. Of course, sometimes it is not possible to act to restore meanings—either we are physically unable to act, or perhaps powerful others constrain our freedom to act. When actions are constrained by such structural factors, redefinition of the situation (cognitive labeling) is likely to occur. The theory can easily incorporate this type of processing, by solving the mathematical model for the type of person (the three-number evaluation, potency, and activity profile associated with an identity) who would do (or receive) such an action. Later versions of the theory (Smith-Lovin, 1990, Smith-Lovin & Heise, 1988) incorporated emotional responses, traits, and status characteristics into the model. Minor deflections may result in attributions of moods or personality traits. In effect, the mathematical model looks for a qualifier that, when combined with an identity, produces a composite evaluation, potency, and activity profile that "makes sense" of the events that have occurred. For example, a professor might not be expected to criticize a student without prior events, but an irritated professor might do such a thing after he or she had been deflected downward on the evaluation and potency dimensions. The qualifier *irritated* changes the meaning of the identity *professor* in systematic ways (Heise & Thomas, 1989).

The amalgamation of qualifying adjectives and identities allows the theory to predict emotional states as indicators of discrepancies between reference meanings of identity and the situated meanings. Basically, people are predicted to experience emotions that indicate the direction and extent of deflection. In this way, emotions indicate how well current events are maintaining one's identity (Smith-Lovin, 1990). When events are maintaining identity meanings, emotions are determined almost completely by the culturally given reference meanings of the identity that is occupied. In a courtroom setting, for example, a judge might feel secure (moderate evaluation, high potency, and low activity) whereas the criminal who is convicted might feel angry, self-conscious, or aggravated (low evaluation, moderate potency, high activity). When events disturb meanings, however, emotions show the effects of the disturbance. So a criminal who has attacked a judge should feel afraid, insecure, and cowardly—the result of having done something nasty to someone who is basically good, potent, and quiet.

Predictions like these come from a computer simulation INTERACT developed by David R. Heise to implement the affect control cybernetic model (see Heise, 1990, for a brief description of the technical aspects of the model).[6] The program translates between verbal presentations and quantitative formulations by using corpuses of the average evaluation, potency, and activity ratings of a large number of identities, social behaviors, emotions, and other events elements. Corpuses are available for the United States, Canada, Germany, Japan, and China. Average ratings of identities, behaviors, and emotions are used in the simulation because in affect control theory individuals are often used as replicates of one another within a subculture to get estimates of reference levels—even though these are theoretically intraindividual entities. That is, because only situated meanings can be assessed at any given period of time, role identity (and other) meanings from many individuals within the same subculture are assessed, then averaged, under the assumption that any disturbance that has occurred for any of them will likely be counteracted by an opposing disturbance experienced by another subculture member. Thus, distributions on these meanings can represent the degree of cultural consensus, the existence of subcultural meanings within the group, and so on. This view is consistent with the doubly distributed processing mechanisms presented by Kashima, Kashima, and Aldridge (2001): Meanings not only are represented in the memory system of each individual, but also are distributed across individuals in society. Institutional forms, like the layout of a building or the grading practices of a university, are cultural artifacts that support and regenerate the meanings of role-identities for new members of the culture.

The cybernetic control ideas in affect control theory grew out of work on perception and behavior by William T. Powers (1973). It is similar to psychological theories that involve the assessment of discrepancies created by social life and the motivation to reduce those discrepancies, such as Higgins's (1989) self-discrepancy theory. Affect control theory is considerably more sociological, however, in that it deals with reference levels set by role identities that are evoked by specific institutional contexts. Higgins

---

[6]A version of the simulation is available on the web at http://www.indiana.edu/~socpsy/ACT/.

suggested that people compare cognitive representations of the actual self with representations of the ideal or ought self. Although the "ought" self contains a serious social, normative element, the representations of self are more global than situational in Higgins's theory. In contrast, affect control theory does not privilege a unitary self. People are seen as acting in different identities in different settings. In this sense, it is much closer to the Jamesian view of the individual actor as multiple social selves. Only when linked with Stryker's idea of a hierarchical self-structure of identities does affect control theory's emphasis on situated identities create a coherent cross-situational influence of the individual actor.

The impact of the self in affect control theory must operate either through the definition of the situation or through idiosyncratic meanings. In the first case, individual differences in identity salience may motivate a definition of situation (as salience of identities determines the probability that any given identity will be enacted). For example, if I am inclined to take on a professorial role identity even in social settings, the salience of *professor* in my self hierarchy will influence my behavior as I attempt to maintain that identity across situations. Alternatively, individuals may hold different meanings for role identities or behaviors—idiosyncratic reference meanings that may have been built up as a result of personal interaction history. Children who have grown up in abusive families, for example, often have meanings for family role identities that differ from those of mainstream culture. We would expect them to behave differently in family settings, as they try to maintain these idiosyncratic reference meanings.

The view of affect in affect control theory is also somewhat different from that in psychological theories. Most psychological literature has concentrated on how cognitions affect emotional response (Fiske, 1982; Frijda, 1986) or how mood influences the retrieval of information from memory (Isen, 1987; Isen, Nygren, & Ashby, 1988). In affect control theory, affect and cognition are inseparable (MacKinnon, 1994). An event cannot be cognitively processed without calling up affective meanings (on the three semantic differential dimensions). Conversely, the affective processing that occurs as events are perceived, remembered, or planned influences in very concrete ways the types of cognitions that are possible to envision. Thus, cognition and affect are not separate systems but two sides of the same coin, inherently inseparable in their effects on thought, behavior, and perception.

There is also a difference in how emotions are viewed in affect control theory and current psychological perspectives. In Higgins's self-discrepancy theory, discrepancies between ideal and actual performance are presumed to create anxiety and dejection. In most psychological cybernetic models, the discrepancy between the reference levels and current experience is presumed to cause some degree of tension or negative emotion. In affect control theory, emotions are characterized on the same three dimensions as identities and behaviors. Some deflections can result in quite positive (high evaluation) emotions. For example, a professor who has been admired by a student will experience positive deflection on all three dimensions, and will feel charmed, satisfied, and cheered as a result of the unexpected positive appreciation. The criminal who is rehabilitated by a judge is likely to feel awestruck, rather than his or her usual usual angry emotions. However, actors in affect control theory are not predicted to maximize positive feelings. Although positive emotion results from disconfirming interactions that deflect one upward on evaluation and potency, such deflections still motivate action to restore identities meanings for self and others. In this sense, the affect control approach is very similar to Swann's work on self-consistency (Swann, Griffin, Predmore, & Gaines, 1987; Swann, Pelham, & Krull, 1989). In Swann's formulation, too, people experience positive emotion but seek self-confirmation when they occupy negatively evaluated identities.

Affect control theory's predictions about behavior have been tested using experimental methods. Wiggins and Heise (1987) showed that undergraduate subjects used positive and negative behaviors toward interaction partners to restore their self-esteem after being criticized. A secretary (actually a confederate) berated an undergraduate subject for using incorrect procedures in filling out a questionnaire. The student then had the opportunity to interact with another confederate who was labeled either as another student or as a juvenile delinquent. Affect control theory correctly predicted that positive actions would be directed at esteemed interaction partners (the other student), whereas deviant interaction partners (the juvenile delinquent) would be treated negatively to restore self-esteem. Robinson and Smith-Lovin (1992), using an experimental design very similar to Swann's self-consistency paradigm, showed that positive deflection could lead to both positive emotion and the selection of an interaction partner who offered confirming, negative evaluations. Robinson, Smith-Lovin, and Tsoudis (1994) showed that people used emotion displays to make inferences about an actor's identity after a negative event. When a criminal showed remorse during his confession, he was judged to be less likely to commit another crime and was given a lighter sentence. Tsoudis and Smith-Lovin (1999) showed that the same affective dynamics shaped the impressions formed of the victim's identity in a court case. Victims who showed negative emotion (indicating downward deflection from the negative event) were seen as more fundamentally positive people than victims who took the crime in stride with little emotion. Robinson and Smith-Lovin (1999) demonstrated these identity attribution effects in more general terms, examining how emotions led to identity inferences when perceivers used them as indications of deflection.

Two decades of theoretical development and empirical research on affect control theory demonstrate clearly the value of a cybernetic approach to identity, action and emotion. Its value lies in its ability to explain the variability of social action across settings, while acknowledging the central meanings that consistently guide that action. The theory accounts for a great deal of what we know about how people play social roles, how they perceive and label others, how they attribute moods and personality characteristics to others, and how they experience emotions. Indeed, the fundamental cybernetic structure of affect control theory was appealing enough to generate alternative models that used some of the same basic structure.

One of these alternative sociological cybernetic models, developing out of the structural symbolic interactionist tradition and building even more directly on Stryker's identity theory, is perhaps closer to dominant psychological views. Burke's identity control theory shares many features with affect control theory, but its differences place it closer to the classical psychological perspective.

ANOTHER VIEW OF IDENTITY CONTROL

Burke (1991) also based his identity control theory on Powers's (1973) model of perception. As in affect control theory's earlier formulation, identity meanings associated with named positions in social structure act as reference levels in Burke's theory. Here, meanings can have any number of dimensions, depending on the relevant criteria for assessing the institutional domain (e.g., academic responsibility might be relevant for the student identity, but not for the assessment of the elderly's age-based identity). Actors compare role identity meanings to the perceptions of self-relevant meanings produced in the situation. The differences between the identity standard and the perceived self-meanings from the situation lead to a process of self-verification, as the person acts in ways to bring the situational meanings into line with the standard. One important difference from affect control theory, however, is the more limited scope of the reference level that motivates action to decrease discrepancy. In affect control theory, the cultural meanings associated with one's own identity, with others' identities in the situation, and with the meanings of social actions all act as reference levels to be maintained. In identity control theory, only one's own identity standard operates as a reference signal to guide action. The identities of others, and their actions, are relevant only insofar as they constitute a self-relevant environmental signal that is consistent with or discrepant from self-identities.

As in affect control theory, discrepancies from the identity standard lead to emotions in identity control theory (Burke, 1991). However, the predictions in identity control theory are closer to those made by Higgins's self-discrepancy theory. Identity disconfirmation leads to negative emotion and stress, regardless of what type of disconfirmation occurs. Presumably, being treated much better than one would expect, given one's identity, would lead to as much discomfort and stress as the equivalent amount of disconfirmation in a negative direction.[7]

Identity control theory has been tested most often using survey data. A study of newly married couples in Washington state that followed husbands and wives for 3 years was particularly useful. Burke and Stets (1999) found that problems in verifying the spousal identity within the context of marriage led to depression and anxiety, and lowered commitment to the marriage. The longitudinal marriage study has been particularly effective at showing how higher level control systems serve to reset identity standards. For example, Burke and Cast (1997) found that the gender identities of newly married couples changed in response to changes in basic family structure with the birth of a first child. Tsushima and Burke (1999) found that mothers with more resources developed high-level (more abstract, value-directed) identity standards, and that these higher level standards were more effective in directing effective child care. Most interesting in linking the identity control theory back to Stryker's original formulation were studies that looked at how verification and interruption shaped future network relationships. Cast and Burke (1999), for example, found that the feelings of self-worth that result from the mutual self-verification of married couples are able to act as a buffer against future self-verification problems.

Burke's identity control theory is decidedly more cognitive than affect control theory. It uses a much more denotative conceptualization of meaning, and a much more situation-specific determination of what types of signals from the environment will be self-discrepant. Although its predictive power in empirical research has been impressive, it is much less generative in its application to new situations than affect control theory. In addition, processes like attribution, labeling and maintaining the meanings of others' role identities, are only implicitly treated within the theory.

Both cybernetic theories risk losing the social structural power of Stryker's approach by concentrating so much on the proximate cognitions and affective processing of individuals. Future theoretical developments need to link the internal processing back to the social networks that give rise to the role identities. In particular, the theories need to be elaborated to ac-

---

[7]In practice, it is difficult to resolve the conflicting predictions of affect control theory and identity control theory about emotions. Just as in the debate between self-verification and self-enhancement, the fact that most people occupy very positive identities means that most maintenance activity also will serve to enhance self-esteem.

count for how people manage multiple identities simultaneously, both within and across situations.

NEW DIRECTIONS: THE RELATIONSHIP TO COGNITIVE PSYCHOLOGY

Affect control theory and identity control theory share a basic cybernetic imagery that is consistent with the dominant psychological conception of the individual as an information processor. I now consider which of the two information-processing models—the central processing unit or the connectionist parallel processor—fits best with the sociological model.

At first glance, it might seem that the role identity theories developed by the sociologists are consistent with the central processing view that currently dominates psychology. Both Heise's (1977, 1979) and Burke's (1991) formulations grew directly out of Powers's perceptual control model, which has a heavily hierarchical, centralized character. However, there are several indications in recent theoretical discussions that a connectionist model might be more consistent with the new challenges that the theories face in the future. Theorists in both traditions have identified the problem of multiple identities as one of the primary issues for future theory development (Smith-Lovin & Heise, 1988; Stryker & Burke, 2000). Affect control theory and identity control theory currently treat the self in a given situation as occupying a single identity, with actors operating to maintain the meanings associated with that identity by reducing discrepancies that arise in interaction. But Stryker's conception of the self as a hierarchical set of many identities raises the question of whether or not more than one identity might be activated at any given time within a situation. If the self consists of multiple identities, why would only one of these be active in guiding behavior at one time? The fact that gender, race, and other transituational identities can influence interactions over a wide variety of settings and in a wide variety of role identities (Ridgeway & Smith-Lovin, 1999) lends credence to the idea that several identities may operate simultaneously (e.g., "when the doctor is a 'lady' "—the title of a now-classic conversational analytic article on gender and interruptions [West, 1984]). Affect control theory has dealt with multiple identities in a simple manner by averaging the meanings of those identities to form a new, composite identity (e.g., averaging the meanings of *lady* and *doctor*) or by using one identity as a qualifier for the other (a *female doctor*). But these technical solutions have little theoretical structure behind them. They are an attempt to force a multiplex self into a single reference level. Identity control theory researchers have dealt with multiple identities as multiple independent variables in a multiple regression format (Stets, 1995, 1997), but have not developed a theoretical model of how multiple identities guide action within an interpersonal interaction.

The connectionist processing model offers the possibility of a more sound representation of multiple identities. The distributed representations that are possible within the connectionist model (see Humphreys and Kashima, chap. 2, this volume) are well suited to characterizing Stryker's multiple-identity self. And the parallel processing offers a potential answer to the problem of how multiple identities operate within a given situation. Multiple aspects of the self—multiple role identities that are potentially relevant to the situation, or a mix of more general self-conceptions and specific role identity meanings—can be activated by a situation. Events can be perceived and processed simultaneously from the point of view of multiple identities.

One phenomenon that this multiple-identity processing could explain is the common experience of mixed emotions (Hochschild, 1989). If the sociological cybernetic identity models are correct, emotions are experienced primarily as the result of the confirmation or disconfirmation of role identities that are activated within a setting. If an actor is occupying more than one identity simultaneously, and experiencing events from those multiple perspectives, it is natural that a mixture of emotions (some of which might be quite different in character) would be felt as a result of events. For example, a directive action that would support the identity of "judge" might produce negative deflection on the evaluation and positive deflection on the potency dimension for "woman." This might produce a mixture of feelings of being tense (the judge) and being bitchy (the woman).

The connectionist representation is also quite consistent with affect control theory's view of the relationship between individuals and the culture from which they derive identity meanings. Consider the view that each individual represents a variety of self-conceptions (role identities) within a parallel distributed processing system, and that the meanings associated with these self-conceptions is shared with other individuals and represented symbolically by cultural artifacts like books, films and language use (Kashima et al., 2001; chap. 2, this volume). This distributed cognition model captures several features that are central to affect control theory and closely related sociological theories that grew out of Meadian symbolic interactionism. First, it accurately represents the relationship between the individual and the collective. Individual meanings are developed out of contact with society (in both its personal and artifactual forms). Furthermore, individuals act as both learners, carriers, and (within limits) innovators of cultural meanings.

CONCLUSION

In this chapter, we have shown how sociological perspectives on identity, action, and emotion draw on and complement developments in psychology's cognitive revolution. It seems reasonable to end by summarizing the value added by a sociological approach, over and above closely related psychological perspectives like Higgins's self-discrepancy and Swann's self-consistency theories. The chief difference between the psychological and sociological models is, appropriately, the degree of attention that they pay to the social structural roots of the self. Psychologists often conceptualize the self as having just a few (admittedly complex) components (e.g., Higgins's "ideal" and "ought" selves), whereas sociologists emphasize the multiple selves that are elicited by different network ties and different institutional settings. Even psychologists who recognize multiple identities based on the social environment (e.g., Tajfel & Turner, 1979) usually base those identities on category membership rather than role identities. Sociologists (and anthropologists), with their greater attention to the functioning of the overall social system, have been more likely to focus on roles, relationship to role alters, and the rights and obligations that are central to roles' meanings.

The rise of cybernetic processing models has brought the two approaches closer together by focusing on how role identities are represented and maintained within individuals. Additional work analyzing how other types of social categories (e.g., group memberships) and personal identities are maintained along with role identities will strengthen the connection. Similarly, a newly developing focus on how multiple identities combine within the self will strengthen the connection of the new cybernetic models back to their social structural origins in social networks (Stryker & Burke, 2000, pp. 292–293; Smith-Lovin, 2001).

REFERENCES

Alexander, C. N., & Wiley, M. G. (1981). Situated activity and identity formation. In M. Rosenberg & R. H. Turner (Eds.), *Social psychology: Sociological perspectives* (pp. 269–289). New York: Basic Books.

Blumer, H. (1969). *Symbolic interactionism: Perspective and method.* Englewood Cliffs, NJ: Prentice-Hall.

Burke, P. J. (1980). The self: Measurement implications from a symbolic interactionist perspective. *Social Psychology Quarterly, 43*, 18–29.

Burke, P. J. (1991). Identity processes and social stress. *American Sociological Review, 56*, 836–849.

Burke, P. J., & Cast, A. D. (1997). Stability and change in the gender identities of newly married couples. *Social Psychology Quarterly, 60*, 277–290.

Burke, P. J., & Reitzes, D. C. (1981). The link between identity and role performance. *Social Psychology Quarterly, 44,* 83–92.

Burke, P. J., & Stets, J. E. (1999). Trust and commitment in an identity verification context. *Social Psychology Quarterly 62,* 347–360.

Burke, P. J., & Tully, J. (1977). The measurement of role/identity. *Social Forces, 55,* 881–897.

Callero, P. L. (1985). Role-identity salience. *Social Psychology Quarterly, 48,* 203–214.

Cast, A. D., & Burke, P. J. (1999). *Integrating self-esteem into identity theory.* Portland, OR: Pacific Sociological Association.

Fiske, S. T. (1982). Schema-triggered affect: Applications to social perception. In M. S. Clark & S. T. Fiske (Eds.), *Affect and cognition: The 17th annual Carnegie symposium on cognition* (pp. 55–78). Hillsdale, NJ: Lawrence Erlbaum Associates.

Frijda, N. H. (1986). *The emotions.* London: Cambridge.

Heise, D. R. (1965). Semantic differential profiles for the 1000 most frequent English words. *Psychological Monographs, 70*(8) (whole no. 601).

Heise, D. R. (1969). Affective dynamics in simple sentences. *Journal of Personality and Social Psychology, 11,* 204–213.

Heise, D. R. (1970). Potency dynamics in simple sentences. *Journal of Personality and Social Psychology, 16,* 48–54.

Heise, D. R. (1977). Social action as the control of affect. *Behavioral Science, 22,* 163–177.

Heise, D. R. (1979). *Understanding events.* New York: Cambridge University Press.

Heise, D. R. (1990). Affect control theory: Technical appendix. In T. D. Kemper (Ed.), *Research agendas in the sociology of emotions* (pp. 271–80). Albany, NY: State University of New York Press.

Heise, D. R., & Thomas, L. (1989). Predicting impressions created by combinations of emotion and social identity. *Social Psychology Quarterly, 52,* 141–148.

Heiss, J. (1981). Role theory. In M. Rosenberg & R. H. Turner (Eds.), *Social psychology: Sociological perspectives* (pp. 94–132). New York: Basic Books.

Higgins, E. T. (1989). Self-discrepancy theory: What patterns do self-beliefs cause people to suffer? In L. Berkowitz (Ed.), *Advances in experimental social psychology* (pp. 93–136). New York: Adademic Press.

Hill, R. J. (1981). Attitudes and behavior. In M. Rosenberg & R. H. Turner (Eds.), *Social psychology: Sociological perspectives* (pp. 347–377). New York: Basic Books.

Hochschild, A. (1989). *The second shift: Working parents and the revolution at home.* New York: Viking.

Isen, A. M. (1987). Affect, cognition and social behavior. *Advances in Experimental Social Psychology, 20,* 203–253.

Isen, A. M., Nygren, T. E., & Ashby, F. G. (1988). Influence of positive affect on the subjective utility of gains and losses: It is just not worth the risk. *Journal of Personality and Social Psychology, 55*(5), 710–717.

Kashima, Y., Kashima, E., & Aldridge, J. (2001). Towards cultural dynamics of self-conceptions. In C. Sedikides & M. B. Brewer (Eds.), *Individual self, relational self and collective self: Partners, opponents or strangers* (pp. 123–143). Philadelphia, PA: Psychology Press.

Kroska, A. (1997). The division of labor in the home: A review and reconceptualization. *Social Psychology Quarterly, 60,* 304–322.

MacKinnon, N. J. (1994). *Symbolic interactionism as affect control.* New York: SUNY Press.

Markus, H. (1977). Self-schemata and processing of information about the self. *Journal of Personality and Social Psychology, 35,* 63–78.

Mead, G. H. (1934). *Mind, self and society.* Chicago: University of Chicago Press.

Miller, D. L. (1973). *George Herbert Mead: Self, language and the world.* Austin, TX: University of Texas Press.

Mutran, E., & Burke, P. J. (1979). Personalism as a component of old age identity. *Research on Aging, 1,* 37–64.

Nuttbrock, L., & Freudiger, P. (1991). Identity salience and motherhood: A test of Stryker's theory. *Social Psychology Quarterly, 54,* 146–157.

Osgood, C. E., May, W. H., & Miron, M. S. (1975). *Cross-cultural universals of affective meaning.* Urbana: University of Illinois Press.

Osgood, C. E., Suci, G. J., & Tannebaum, P. H. (1957). *The measurement of meaning.* Urbana: University of Illinois Press.

Powers, W. T. (1973). *Behavior: The control of perception.* Chicago: Aldine.

Reynolds, L. T. (1993) *Interactionism: Exposition and critique* (3rd ed.). Dix Hills, NY: General Hall.

Ridgeway, C., & Smith-Lovin, L. (1999). Interaction in the gender system: Theory and research. *Annual Review, 25,* 191–216.

Robinson, D. R., & Smith-Lovin, L. (1992). Selective interaction as a stategy for identity maintenance: An affect control model. *Social Psychology Quarterly, 55,* 12–28.

Robinson, D. R., & Smith-Lovin, L. (1999). Empathy, liking, and emotional display during self-disclosure. *Motivation and Emotion, 23,* 73–104.

Robinson, D. T., Smith-Lovin, L., & Tsoudis, O. (1994). Heinous crime or unfortunate accident: Emotion displays and reactions to vignettes of criminal confessions. *Social Forces, 73,* 175–190.

Serpe, R. T. (1987). Stability and change in self: A structural symbolic interactionist explanation. *Social Psychology, Quarterly, 50,* 44–55.

Serpe, R. T., & Stryker, S. (1987). The construction of the self and reconstruction of personal relationships. In E. Lawler & B. Markovsky (Eds.), *Advances in group processes* (pp. 41–66). Greenwich, CT: JAI Press.

Smith-Lovin, L. (1990). Emotion as confirmation and disconfirmation of identity: An affect control model. In T. D. Kemper (Ed.), *Research agendas in the sociology of emotions* (pp. 238–270). Albany, NY: SUNY Press.

Smith-Lovin, L. (2001, April). *The self, multiple identities, and the production of mixed emotions.* Paper presented at Conference on Self and Identity in Honor of Sheldon Stryker, Bloomington, IN.

Smith-Lovin, L., & Heise, D. R. (Eds.). (1988). *Analyzing social interaction: Research advances in affect control theory.* New York: Gordon and Breach.

Stets, J. E. (1995). Role identities and person identities: Gender identity, mastery identity and controlling one's partner. *Social Psychology Quarterly, 60,* 185–217.

Stets, J. E. (1997). Status and identity in marital interaction. *Social Psychology Quarterly, 60,* 185–217.

Stryker, S. (1968). Identity salience and role performance. *Journal of Marriage and the Family, 4,* 558–564.

Stryker, S. (1980). *Symbolic interactionism: A social structural view.* Menlo Park, CA: Benjamin Cummings.

Stryker, S. (1981). Symbolic interactionism: Themes and variations. In M. Rosenberg & R. H. Turner (Eds.), *Social psychology: Sociological perspectives* (pp. 3–29) New York: Basic Books.

Stryker, S., & Burke, P. J. (2000). Identity theory: Past, present and future. *Social Psychology Quarterly, 65,* 284–297.

Stryker, S., & Serpe, R. T. (1982). Commitment, identity salience and role behavior: A theory and research example. In W. Ickes & E. S. Knowles (Eds.), *Personality, roles and social behavior* (pp. 199–218). New York: Springer-Verlag.

Swann, W. B., Jr., Griffin, J. J., Jr., Predmore, S. C., & Gaines, B. 1987. The cognitive-affective crossfire: When self-consistency confronts self-enhancement. *Journal of Personality and Social Psychology, 52*(5), 881–889.

Swann, W. B., Jr., Pelham B. W., & Krull, D. S. 1989. Agreeable fancy or disagreeable truth: Reconciling self-enhancement and self-verification." *Journal of Personality and Social Psychology, 57*(5), 782–791.

Smith-Lovin, L., & Heise, D. R. (1998). *Affect control theory: Research advances*. New York: Gordon and Breach.

Stryker, S., & Serpe, R. T. (1994). Identity salience and psychological centrality: Equivalent, overlapping or complementary concepts? *Social Psychology Quarterly, 57,* 16–35.

Tajfel, H., & Turner, J. C. 1979. An integrative theory of intergroup conflict. In W. G. Austin & S. Worchel (Eds.), The Social Psychology of Intergroup Relations (pp. 33–47). Monterey, CA: Brooks-Cole.

Tsoudis, O., & Smith-Lovin, L. (1999). How bad was it? Identity and emotion display in mock jury deliberations. *Social Forces, 77,* 695–722.

Tsushima, T., & Burke, P. J. (1999). Levels, agency, and control in the parent identity. *Social Psychology Quarterly, 62,* 173–189.

West, C. (1984). When the doctor is a 'lady': Power, status and gender in physician-patient exchanges. *Symbolic Interaction, 7,* 87–106.

Wiggins, B., & Heise, D. R. 1987. Expectations, intentions and behavior: Some tests of affect control theory. *Journal of Mathematical Sociology, 13,* 153–169.

Chapter 7

Challenging the Primacy of the Personal Self: The Case for Depersonalized Self-Conception

Rina S. Onorato
John C. Turner
*Flinders University of South Australia
and Australian National University*

During the last two decades, the idea that the self can be treated as a central processing unit (CPU) rather like a centralized "schema" or "prototype" has come to be widely accepted within social psychology. In particular, social cognition has focused on the intrapsychic structures and processes that constitute the self. Intrapersonal aspects of the self—particularly the cognitive structures that constitute the *Me* self—have tended to be viewed as somewhat more fundamental than social aspects, such as interpersonal components. More recently, however, researchers have argued for the need to go beyond the intrapsychic level of analysis, to consider the influence of the interpersonal context on self-conception, including the effect of interpersonal relationships, social comparison, and real or imagined audiences (Baldwin & Holmes, 1987; Baumeister, 1998; Hardin & Higgins, 1996; Tice, 1992; see also Sedikides, Campbell, Reeder, Elliot, & Gregg, chap. 5, this volume). Self-categorization theorists have taken this argument a step further, maintaining that intergroup processes are also important, in addition to interpersonal processes. Indeed, this perspective "asserts the interdependence of individuality and shared, collective identity . . . [and argues] that individual and group must be reintegrated psychologically before there can be an adequate analysis of either" (Turner & Oakes, 1989, p. 270; see also Simon & Kampmeier, 2001; Spears, 2001).

In keeping with the rest of this volume, the broad aim of this chapter is to explore the limitations of the schema model that remains prevalent in social cognition. Our own critique is informed by self-categorization theory principles. The schema model implies the primacy of personal identity over other self-aspects, and this is, in our view, one of its main limitations. There are several indicators of the presumed primacy of personal identity in social cognition. For instance, it is commonly assumed that personal identity is the (only) appropriate level of analysis when it comes to the study of the self, and further, that personal identity regulates all major cognitive, affective, motivational, and behavioral processes (e.g., see Brown, 1998; Markus & Wurf, 1987; Sedikides & Skowronski, 1997; Smith, 1984).

In contrast, we believe that multiple levels of self-categorization are possible, that self-perception is always varying between these levels, and that the personal level of identification is no more critical or central to self-definition than are other levels. Importantly, we argue that to the extent that one's attention is directed away from one's own individuality, and toward an identity that is socially shared with others (e.g., gender identity or national identity), self-conception will be *depersonalized*; that is, the self will be experienced as relatively interchangeable with other ingroup members, rather than as unique and individuated. Much of the evidence for depersonalized self-conception has accumulated within the intergroup relations literature rather than within standard self-concept paradigms. Nevertheless, it is possible to examine the implications of this evidence for understanding the nature and functioning of the self-concept. This is our strategy in this chapter.

SELF AS A PERSONALIZED, CENTRAL SCHEMA

Social cognition research has focused on developing a cognitive analysis of the structure and functioning of the self-concept (for reviews, see Baumeister, 1998; Fiske & Taylor, 1991; Greenwald & Pratkanis, 1984; Higgins & Bargh, 1987; Kihlstrom & Cantor, 1984; Kihlstrom, Cantor, Albright, Chew, Klein, & Niedenthal, 1988; Linville & Carlston, 1994; Markus & Wurf, 1987; Sherman, Judd, & Park, 1989). Research conducted within this broad framework has converged on a view of the self as "a collection of at least semi-related and highly domain-specific knowledge structures" (Fiske & Taylor, 1991, p. 182). This view is perhaps most readily illustrated by Markus's self-schema approach (Markus, 1977) and Rogers, Kuiper, and Kirker's (1977) self-prototype model. Self-schema theory asserts that the core self comprises one's *self-schemata*. Self-schemata are defined as "knowledge structures developed by individuals to understand and explain their own social experiences" (Markus & Sentis, 1982, p. 45). Importantly, these core self-structures are described as stable and chronically accessible (Markus & Wurf, 1987). It is assumed that they are "derived from the repeated categorizations and evaluations of behavior by oneself and others" (Markus & Sentis, 1982, p. 45). Individuals are said only to develop self-schemata about aspects of their behavior that are important to them in some way, for instance, their distinctive personality traits or behavioral tendencies (e.g., one's independence, extroversion, or masculinity). Once formed, self-schemata integrate all the information known about the self in a given behavioral domain (Markus & Sentis, 1982). It is further proposed that self-schemata facilitate the processing of information that is congruent with the schema, and resist information that is incongruent with the schema; self-schemata are therefore implicated in self-concept maintenance and in cross-situational consistency in behavior (Markus, 1977).

Along similar lines, Rogers and his colleagues conceptualized the self as "a superordinate schema that contains an abstracted record of a person's past experience with personal data" (Rogers et al., 1977, p. 685). As a prototype or schema, the self was believed to contain general terms (e.g., personality traits) and situation-specific aspects of self-perception (e.g., memories of specific behaviors and events) (Rogers, 1981). Moreover, the self-structure was presumed to be stored somewhere in the memory system; hence in judging whether a specific trait term applies to the self, one simply compares the stimulus trait with the stored prototype to determine if it "fits" into the structure (see Rogers, 1981, p. 196). Rogers argued that another way of thinking about the self-prototype is to say that it functions "as an anchor point or immobile point of reference for deciphering and interpreting personal information. This follows directly from our definition of the self as a cognitive structure" (Rogers, 1981, p. 199).

The perspectives of Markus and Rogers et al. have a great deal in common. The major difference is that Markus studied domain-specific self-schemata (e.g., self-schemata for independence) and accordingly drew conclusions about the information-processing consequences of particularistic self-schemata, while Rogers and his colleagues preferred to study the self-concept as an abstract mental representation containing various trait descriptors, and accordingly drew conclusions about the effects of self-referencing in general. Whether a specific schema or a general schema, both perspectives focus on delineating the structure of the self-schema and its role in information processing. Markus's (1977) empirical strategy was to examine the speed with which self-referential judgments are made in specific behavioral domains, and the degree to which these judgments are consistent with past self-appraisals. Rogers et al.'s (1977) strategy was to examine whether self-referencing at the time of encoding trait adjectives facilitates the recall of these trait terms (see also Rogers, 1981). These paradigms produced much evidence that is consistent with the view that a personal, highly central schema may mediate self-referential judgements

(Markus & Sentis, 1982; Rogers, 1981), although this conclusion has not gone unchallenged (Greenwald & Banaji, 1989; Higgins & Bargh, 1987; Klein & Kihlstrom, 1986; Rudolph, 1993).

Markus (1977) and Rogers et al. (1977) demonstrated how individual differences in the cognitive content of the self-concept could be empirically investigated. The fact that the notion of "self-concept" has practically been replaced with that of "self-schema" in the contemporary literature (Greenwald & Pratkanis, 1984) is testimony to their influence. Recent advances within social cognition have developed, consolidated, and refined the self-schema notion, particularly ideas about its content, structure, and functions, but the basic notion of a cognitive structure, with its associated information-processing properties, has not undergone a major metamorphosis since its inception and early exploration in the late 1970s. The notion of a self-schema thus remains the dominant model of the personal self within contemporary social psychology:

> Social psychologists currently think of the self-concept as a cognitive structure that organises experiences and guides action. It is a dynamic structure, constantly acquiring new cognitions that are related to existing cognitions about the self and are therefore more likely to add stability to that structure. Indeed, the acquisition of knowledge that stabilises the self-concept is fostered, whereas knowledge inconsistent with a person's self-concept is likely to be rejected. This basis is common to almost all current treatments of the self-concept. (Hormuth, 1990, p. 67)

Self-categorization theory, in contrast, places less emphasis on stipulating the *structural* properties of the self than on understanding the dynamic psychological *processes* involved in self-referential judgments. In fact, this perspective rejects the view that the self takes the form of a central cognitive structure located somewhere in the individual's memory system, which functions like a fixed vantage point from which all personal and social judgments emanate.

CHALLENGING THE PRIMACY OF PERSONAL IDENTITY: THE SELF-CATEGORIZATION ANALYSIS

There are many aspects to the self-categorization analysis as it applies to the self (for recent treatments see Onorato & Turner, 2001; Turner, 1999; Turner, Oakes, Haslam, & McGarty, 1994; Turner & Onorato, 1999). One central aspect of the analysis is the concept of the *psychological group*. Specifically, the theory is based on the understanding that groups do not just exist in the physical or social sense; groups are also "real" in the psychological sense. A psychological group is a group that is psychologically significant for its members, that individuals privately accept membership in, and from which they derive their norms and values (Turner, Hogg, Oakes, Reicher, & Wetherell, 1987). This concept is critical to an understanding of where self-categorization theory departs from the dominant schema metaphor. In short, the self-concept (including its individual and group aspects) is assumed inter alia to be derivative of psychological group memberships. The psychological group may be some large-scale collective entity such as the society or culture we see ourselves as belonging to, or it may be more definite and specific, such as membership in the social category "we Australians" rather than "the Germans, French, or Swiss." In any case, it is assumed that the psychological group is implicated in the experience of all self-concepts. Hence in this perspective, there is no sense of self that does not at some level imply a psychological relationship between self and other, between the perceiver[1] and his or her group (Onorato & Turner, 2001); it is in this sense a truly *social* theory.

Self-categorization theory provides a cognitive as well as a social account of the self. At the level of cognition, the self is said to take the form of *self-categorizations*, that is, cognitive groupings of oneself and some class of stimuli as identical, in contrast to some other class of stimuli (Turner et al., 1987). Indeed, from the perspective of self-categorization theory, the term *self-concept* is used to refer to one's current self-categorization(s). Self-categorizations are the variable and context-dependent products of "a dynamic [reflexive] process of social judgement" (Turner et al., 1994, p. 458). Traditionally, the term *self-concept* has implied a long-term knowledge structure, which represents "me" and differentiates "me" from "not me." This long-standing emphasis within social psychology has implied that the self is "set" or functioning at one level—the personal level—and further, that the content of this personal self is stable and embodied in long-term memory. In contrast, self-categorization theory rejects the view that there is an enduring, one-to-one correspondence between a particular preformed cognitive structure (or set of structures) and the self-concept.

It assumes that self-categories are constructed on the spot as a function of a creative interaction between the perceiver's motives, expectations, background knowledge and theories, and the particular social relationships between self and others being represented. Self-categories are, as we

---

[1]In using the term *perceiver* we do not intend to indicate singularity of the self (cf. Twenge & Baumeister, chap. 3, this volume). The perceiver in our analysis is not a self-referential term as such; it refers simply to the individual person or physical being that is actively perceiving and interpreting their social world. There is no single self in our view; indeed, multiplicity is assumed at each level of identification. Clearly though, there are single individuals in which self processes occur. In short, "perceiver" should not be read as interchangeable with "self" within the self-categorization analysis.

show later, comparative, social contextual representations of the perceiver
and hence vary as a function of the social context within which the
perceiver is defined. This social variability of the self provides human beings with great behavioral and cognitive flexibility. One of the fundamental ways in which self-categories vary is in terms of the level of inclusiveness
of the self, and it is assumed that this kind of variation (from "I" and "me"
to "we" and "us" and back again) is normal and ever present. It is this constant variability of self-categorizing in the service of a reflexive, social,
reality-oriented self-representation which functions to provide adaptive
self-regulation that leads self-categorization theory to reject the idea of
self-experience as the expression of the activation of a fixed cognitive
structure. The theory should not be misread as denying the existence of
long-term knowledge structures in memory. Undoubtedly this complex
knowledge base includes information about the self. However, a critical
point from this perspective is that this long-term knowledge (like other
cognitive resources, such as values, norms, ideologies) is recruited flexibly
when we come to categorize self and others (Turner et al., 1994). Sometimes one's current self-categorization will be consistent with aspects of
that long-term knowledge (e.g., my current self-category may confirm the
knowledge that I have behaved independently on numerous occasions in
the past), and sometimes it will be inconsistent with it. Sometimes it may
be inconsistent with memories of past selves but still embody indirectly the
generic knowledge and theories derived from such memories. The point
is that the traditional assumption of a preexisting cognitive structure
called the "self-concept" has been abandoned. A self-category is not assumed to be a self-category because of how and where it is stored in the
cognitive system, but because of its functional property of being reflexive,
of defining the person who is doing the defining.

This perspective further asserts that self-categorizations exist as part of
a hierarchical system of classification. That is, self-categories form at different levels of abstraction such that the more inclusive the self-category,
the higher the level of abstraction. Although levels higher and lower are
postulated, Turner et al. (1994) stated that "for purposes of theoretical exposition" at least three levels of self-categorization are important when
considering the functioning of the self-concept: the *superordinate level* (self-
definition as a human being in contrast to other forms of life), the *intergroup level* (self-definition as a member of some ingroup in contrast to
some outgroup), and the *interpersonal level* (self-definition as a unique individual in contrast to other ingroup members). Importantly, the self is not
fixed at any level within this analysis.

For present purposes, our interest lies in the distinction between personal and group self-aspects (or personal and social identity) as two components of the self. Personal identities are salient when interpersonal in-

teractions take place, whereas social identities are psychologically salient in intergroup settings. More formally, it can be said that

> Personal identity refers to self-categories that define the individual as a unique person in terms of his or her individual differences from other (ingroup) persons. Social identity refers to . . . self-categories that define the individual in terms of his or her shared similarities with members of certain social categories in contrast to other social categories. (Turner et al., 1994, p. 454)

Personal identity, as conceived within this theoretical framework, is not the same thing as a person-specific self-schema. Personality models of the self imply stable knowledge structures, or enduring individual *differences* (see Turner & Onorato, 1999). In contrast, in Turner's (1985) analysis, category formation (including the formation of personal self-categories) is not a matter of differences, but a matter of *relative similarities and differences*. Personal identity is made possible because of self-other differentiation in terms of some shared higher order identity that provides a context for social comparison. This implies quite clearly that similarity and difference go hand in hand in defining the personal self. Thus, even at the personal level, self-definition is inherently social, contextual, and relational. This emphasis represents an important point of departure from dominant social cognitive models of the personal self, which treat self-schemata as absolute, rather than relative, properties of the perceiver.

According to self-categorization theory, self-conception is the product of the categorization of self vis-à-vis others, which implies *social comparison.* Categorization and comparison are interdependent processes. Specifically, the division of stimuli into categories depends on perceived similarities and differences, but stimuli can only be compared insofar as they have already been categorized as similar at some higher level of abstraction, which in turn presupposes a prior process of comparison and so on (see Turner et al., 1987). This idea is central to the theory and suggests the important hypothesis that "self-categorizations at any level tend to form and become salient through comparisons of stimuli defined as members of the next more inclusive (higher level) self-category" (Turner et al., 1987, p. 46). Presumably the personal self may be experienced as quite stable if the perceiver habitually compares his or her personal attributes and qualities to the same ingroup category. Likewise it follows that the personal self may be experienced quite differently when the ingroup category that provides the context for social comparison changes (Onorato & Turner, 1997; Reynolds & Oakes, 1999).

Self-categorization theory further postulates that self-perception tends to vary from the perception of self as a unique individual to the perception of self as an ingroup member. Self-perception is likely to occur at the mid-point of this continuum much of the time (cf. Brewer, 1991), such that individuals will tend to define themselves as:

> moderately different from ingroup members, who in turn will be perceived as moderately different from outgroup members. . . . Personal self- and ingroup–outgroup categorizations, then, are not mutually exclusive. On the contrary, *they will tend to operate simultaneously most of the time, but their perceptual effects are inversely related.* (Turner et al., 1987, p. 50, emphasis added)

On this point, it is important to avoid confusion. Self-categorization theory argues that one level of self-categorization depends on another, implying a positive relationship between personal and social identity. For instance, it is likely that to a degree we infer the attributes of our ingroup from our own personal attributes, and our personal attributes from the attributes of our ingroup; hence personal and social identity are likely to be interdependent and correlated. At the same time, however, there is a negative relationship across situations between the tendency to categorize self at the personal versus the group level (Turner & Oakes, 1989). In some social situations I will tend to categorize myself more as a group member (e.g., at the Sydney Olympics, in following my national team compared to the teams of other nations), whereas in others I will tend to categorize myself more as an individual (e.g., when taking a tertiary entrance exam and thinking about how I will do compared to my fellow students).

In this connection, Turner (1982) pointed out that "the possibility arises that social identity may on occasion function nearly to the exclusion of personal identity, i.e. that at certain times our salient self-images may be based solely or primarily on our group memberships" (p. 19). This brings us to the next key point of the analysis: Specifically, factors that tend to enhance the salience of ingroup-outgroup categorizations tend to enhance the perception of self as similar to or interchangeable with other ingroup members, and so *depersonalize* individual self-perception. Depersonalization (or self-stereotyping) is not a loss of personal identity, as some developmental and clinical theories suggest (e.g., Mellor, 1988; Rosenberg, 1987), nor a submergence of the self in the group (see Turner et al., 1987, p. 51); rather, it represents "a cognitive redefinition of the self—from unique attributes and individual differences to shared social category memberships and associated stereotypes" (Turner, 1984, p. 528). This mechanism, then, is seen to make all group behavior possible, including ethnocentrism, stereotyping, collective action, and so on. In the past, it has been these applications that have piqued the interest of investigators. In contrast, our present interest in depersonalization stems from its conception as an important type of "*change in the nature and content of the self-concept* corresponding to the functioning of self-perception at a more inclusive level of abstraction" (Turner et al., 1987, p. 51, emphasis added).

Following Bruner (1957), it is argued that the salience of some ingroup–outgroup categorization (or other self-categorization) in a given situation is always a function of an interaction between the perceiver's readiness to use a categorization as the basis for perception or action, and the fit between the stimulus input and category specifications (Oakes, 1987; Turner, 1985). It is argued that individuals are predisposed to using certain categorizations of self; in particular, categorizations that have prior meaning or significance, or that are relevant to the perceiver's current goals, motives, values and needs, may be highly accessible (Haslam, 2001). The centrality of a given self-category to the perceiver is an important factor here (Simon, 1999).

Fit has two aspects, comparative and normative. *Comparative fit* is defined by the principle of *meta-contrast*, which states that a collection of stimuli is more likely to be categorized as an entity (or higher order unit) to the degree that the average differences perceived between them are less than the average differences perceived between them and the remaining stimuli that comprise the frame of reference. The process of categorizing self and others is thus understood to be a dynamic, inherently comparative and context-dependent process. The principle of comparative fit predicts that when intrapersonal (within-individual) differences are less than intragroup (within-group) differences, personal identity will tend to be salient (i.e., the self-representation that I refer to as "me," or some aspect of such a self-category, such as my traits and dispositions); in contrast, social identity will come to the fore when intergroup (between-group) differences are greater than interindividual differences within the ingroup (e.g., when I observe the behavior of women, including my own, to be distinctly different from that of a group of men).

Normative fit is assessed by asking whether the instances being represented match the category label in terms of substantive content. To categorize a group of people as Australians versus Italians, as men versus women, and so on, the first group must not only differ (in attitudes, behavior, etc.) from the second group more than from each other (this is comparative fit), but they must also do so in the right direction on specific content dimensions of comparison. For instance, "emotionality" is normatively fitting for the category Italians but not for Australians, who are, by comparison, emotionally subdued. Thus this pattern of covariation (i.e., emotional Italians, unemotional Australians) represents a situation of high normative fit, because differences are consistent with our normative beliefs about the substantive social meaning of the relevant categories. In contrast, low normative fit refers to the observation of similarities and differences that conflict with normative beliefs about the substantive content of the relevant categories (e.g., unemotional Italians, emotional Australians).

EVIDENCE OF DEPERSONALIZED SELF-CONCEPTION

One idea that is clearly central to the self-categorization analysis of the self is the notion that individual self-perception is depersonalized in settings that involve intergroup encounters (e.g., Blacks vs. Whites, men vs. women, "Aussies" vs. "Poms"). Depersonalization, or self-stereotyping, is the process "whereby people come to perceive themselves more as the interchangeable exemplars of a social category than as unique personalities defined by their individual differences from others" (Turner et al., 1987, p. 50). Depersonalization implies that under certain conditions, self-conception may derive entirely or predominantly from group membership. In other words, knowledge of one's personal position on some trait dimension (e.g., independence) need not have any bearing on self-descriptions obtained in an intergroup context, where the perceiver is rating him- or herself in terms of some higher order, shared group identity. Evidence that the personal level of identification can be "bypassed" in this manner would therefore appear inconsistent with the view that personal identity is somehow more fundamental, central, or important than other components of the self.

Evidence that a salient social identity depersonalizes the perception of self (and others) is now quite extensive (for overviews, see Ellemers, Spears, & Doosje, 1999; Haslam, 2001; Hogg, 1992; Oakes, Haslam, & Turner, 1994; Spears, Oakes, Ellemers, & Haslam, 1997; Turner et al., 1994). This research has demonstrated that social category salience:

1. Leads one to ascribe to the self the characteristics of the ingroup (e.g., Biernat, Vescio, & Green, 1996; Dion, Earn, & Yee, 1978; Hogg & Turner, 1987; James, 1993; Lorenzi-Cioldi, 1991; Onorato & Turner, 1996, 1997; Rosenkranz, Vogel, Bee, Broverman, & Broverman, 1968; Simon, 1993; Simon, Glassner-Bayerl, & Stratenwerth, 1991; Simon & Hamilton, 1994; Simon, Pantaleo, & Mummendey, 1995).

2. Leads one to ascribe attitudes or values characteristic of the ingroup to the self (e.g., Abrams, Sparkes, & Hogg, 1985; Charters & Newcomb, 1952; Haslam, Oakes, Reynolds, & Turner, 1999; Salancik & Conway, 1975).

3. Leads one to behave more like an interchangeable group member (e.g., Abrams et al., 1985; Branscombe & Wann, 1994; Levy, 1996; Turner, 1975, 1978; Turner, Hogg, Turner, & Smith, 1984).

4. Accentuates perceptions of a self–ingroup match, intragroup homogeneity, or intragroup similarity (e.g., Hardie & McMurray, 1992; Lau, 1989; Simon & Hamilton, 1994; Smith, Coats, & Walling, 1999; Smith & Henry, 1996), particularly when ingroup identification is high (e.g., Doosje & Ellemers, 1997; Doosje, Ellemers, & Spears, 1995; Ellemers, Spears, & Doosje, 1997; Kelly, 1989; Spears, Doosje, & Ellemers, 1997).

5. Produces self–ingroup assimilation and self–outgroup contrast (e.g., Brewer & Weber, 1994; David & Turner, 1992; Haslam & Turner, 1992, 1995; Wilder & Thompson, 1988).

6. Accentuates perceptions of within-group similarities and between-group differences (e.g., Brown & Turner, 1996; Haslam & Turner, 1992, 1995; Hensley & Duval, 1976; Hogg, 1992; Oakes et al., 1994; Turner, 1978; Wilder, 1984).

7. Heightens perceived ingroup and outgroup homogeneity (e.g., Ellemers & van Knippenberg, 1997; Haslam, Oakes, Turner, & McGarty, 1996; Simon, 1992; Simon & Brown, 1987; Wilder, 1984).

8. Produces consensual stereotypes of the ingroup and the outgroup (e.g., Haslam, Oakes, McGarty, Turner, Reynolds, & Eggins, 1996; Haslam, Turner, Oakes, McGarty, & Reynolds, 1998; Haslam, Turner, Oakes, Reynolds, Eggins, Nolan, & Tweedie, 1998).

Two broad classes of evidence of depersonalization can be extrapolated from this list. Firstly, there are those studies that look for an effect of depersonalization at the level of the ingroup only (i.e., depersonalized self-ratings, attitudes, values, or behavior; enhanced self–ingroup match, intragroup similarity, or intragroup homogeneity). Taken together, these studies illustrate one key aspect of the depersonalization process, namely, *intragroup homogenization*. That is, they show how depersonalization changes the perceived psychological distance between self and other ingroup members. Equally importantly though, depersonalization has implications for *perceptions of the ingroup vis-à-vis the outgroup*. Accordingly, the second broad class of studies are those that simultaneously look for effects of depersonalization at the level of the ingroup and outgroup (e.g., accentuation of within-group similarity and between-group contrast; accentuation of ingroup and outgroup homogeneity; the consensualization of ingroup and outgroup stereotypes).

Multiple, diverse operationalizations have clearly been utilized in the literature. In addition, some studies used artificially created groups to study depersonalization, whereas others studied this process in relation to preexisting group memberships. This research has taught us a great deal about group processes. For present purposes, however, our primary interest in depersonalization stems from the fact that it illustrates the form that self-perception takes at a more inclusive level of abstraction than personal identity, which has been the traditional focus in self-concept research. In the next section, a handful of studies drawn from this expansive literature will be described. Given our present aims, our selective coverage will focus mainly on studies that provide evidence of depersonalized self-conception in relation to meaningful, preexisting social categorizations that clearly constitute a part of the self-concept (such as religious affiliation, gender identity, student identities, national identity, and political affiliations). Although far from exhaustive, the following review does demonstrate that conditions that enhance the salience of "us" versus "them" categorizations in turn facilitate the emergence of depersonalized self-conception.

Depersonalized Self-Conception in Relation to Preexisting Social Categorizations

Early studies by Dion et al. (1978) demonstrated that depersonalized self-conception arises in group contexts. Focusing on ethnicity as a component of the self, these investigators found that Jewish participants who could attribute their failure at a task to discrimination on the part of opponents who they had categorized as Gentiles subsequently endorsed positive aspects of the ingroup stereotype more strongly in their self-descriptions than did Jewish participants who perceived their opponents as individuals. These results were replicated with other groups that possess (or arguably possess) minority-group status. For instance, female participants dealt with perceived prejudice from men by identifying with the positive pole of the ingroup stereotype. Dion et al.'s research illustrated that conditions which heighten awareness of group membership (i.e., perceived threat from the outgroup) can increase identification and depersonalization (see also Lorenzi-Cioldi, 1991; Simon et al., 1991; Simon & Hamilton, 1994); interestingly, this was the common response to perceived prejudice rather than attempts to refute the stereotype held by the dominant group.[2]

Hogg and Turner (1987) further investigated depersonalized self-perception in a context that rendered gender identity salient. There were two experimental conditions in Hogg and Turner's study. Individuals participated either in discussion dyads in which two people of the same sex disagreed with each other (the intragroup condition) or in four-person discussion groups in which two men disagreed with two women (the intergroup condition). In the intragroup condition, the within-category differences in attitudes are greater than the within-person differences; in con-

---

[2]It should be noted, however, that this was not found in a study where Chinese participants were the minority group. The authors concluded that "highly visible" minority groups (like the Chinese, who have distinctive physical characteristics) may not respond to prejudice in the same manner as "less visible" [sic] minorities (e.g., Jews).

trast, in the intergroup condition the between-category differences are greater than the within-category differences. That is, the meta-contrast makes individual differences salient in the first condition, and group membership salient in the second condition (Turner et al., 1994). Depersonalization was measured by examining individual's self-descriptions in terms of stereotypical male or female traits. As predicted, depersonalization (the ascription of ingroup-defining traits to one's own person) was more pronounced in the intergroup than the intragroup condition.

James (1993) likewise studied depersonalization in relation to gender identity. He proposed that depersonalization will be stronger (and individual differences weaker) when the situation focuses attention on group membership rather than one's individuality. Female participants who were either high or low in personal self-esteem had their attention focused (via an essay-writing task) either on their unique characteristics or their gender-group identity. Their perceptions of their own levels of characteristics that correlate with group membership were then assessed. Masculinity and femininity scores on the Bem (1974) Sex-Role Inventory served as the dependent measures. It was expected that individual differences in self-esteem would interact with situationally induced salience of gender identity to influence self-description on masculine and feminine traits. Specifically, it was predicted that individual differences would emerge in the individuality focus condition; in contrast, these differences were expected to be lessened or even eliminated in the gender-group focus condition. As expected, in the individuality focus condition high self-esteem women had higher masculinity and lower femininity scores than low self-esteem women, but these differences disappeared in the gender-group focus condition. The group that was most affected by the gender-group salience manipulation was of course the high self-esteem women; these individuals initially diverged from the ingroup stereotype, but under conditions of a salient group identity, they self-stereotyped on gender-relevant traits.

Smith and Henry (1996; see also Smith et al., 1999) recently used pre-existing university student groups (liberal arts vs. engineering majors; fraternity/sorority members vs. nonmembers) to test whether ingroup attributes can become a part of the self, as suggested by the depersonalization hypothesis. More specifically, the question was whether self-ratings would be facilitated for characteristics where there is a self–ingroup match, and inhibited for responses where there is a self–ingroup mismatch. This pattern of reaction-time facilitation and inhibition, the researchers reasoned, would suggest that the ingroup is cognitively linked to the self. In contrast, if the self and the ingroup are represented in separate cognitive structures, no differences in reaction times would be expected between self–ingroup matching and mismatching attributes.

Timed self-descriptiveness judgements were collected for various trait dimensions. In addition, participants rated the applicability of the same trait terms to the ingroup and to the relevant outgroup (the order of ratings was randomly determined across participants). The response-time analysis revealed that responses for traits on which individuals perceived a self–ingroup match were faster than responses for mismatching traits. However, responses that indicated a self–outgroup mismatch, or a self–ingroup match coupled with an self–outgroup mismatch, were not significantly facilitated. Thus in the context of this experiment, it appeared that intergroup differences were not particularly salient (this was probably a function of task requirements); rather, traits that defined Purdue students in general (i.e., the higher order categorization in terms of which the ingroup and outgroup could be compared) were emphasized. The observed pattern of reaction times (facilitation of responses for traits on which self and ingroup match, and inhibition of responses for traits on which self and ingroup mismatch) was interpreted as evidence that the ingroup can be psychologically represented as part of the self—a mechanism that is clearly implicated in depersonalization of the self-concept.

Along similar lines, Biernat et al. (1996) asked sorority and fraternity members to rate their own sorority/fraternity, sororities/fraternities in general, themselves as individuals, and finally, students in general, on attributes that were stereotypic of sororities/fraternities. The instructions focused participants' attention on sorority or fraternity memberships; therefore it was assumed that this ingroup identity was the most salient at the time that dependent measures were collected. Under these conditions, participants displayed "selective self-stereotyping"; that is, they endorsed positive stereotypes of their own sorority/fraternity as highly descriptive (e.g., fun-loving, sociable), but rejected negative stereotypes (e.g., conforming, snobbish), for *themselves* and for *their own sorority/fraternity*. Although they did not deny that there was some truth to the negative stereotypes, they displayed creativity (see Tajfel & Turner, 1979) by ascribing these negative attributes to a higher order categorization—sororities or fraternities in general—thereby presumably diminishing the immediate relevance of these negative ascriptions to the self and their closest ingroup. The investigators thus concluded that "nested category membership may allow individuals to protect themselves against social identity threats by selectively self-stereotyping" (Biernat et al., 1996, p. 1207).

Levy (1996) examined the potential implications of depersonalization for the self-concepts of the elderly. Specifically, she examined the implicit homogenization of attitudes and behaviors on the part of elderly participants (mean = 73 years) in a context that made their group membership salient. Given the prevalence of ageism in society at large, Levy proposed that these (predominantly negative) stereotypes may be internalized into the self-image of the elderly without their awareness (i.e., implicitly), irrespective of their explicit beliefs about old age. She demonstrated that the implicit activation of negative self-stereotypes among the elderly (using subliminally presented primes such as senile, incompetent, decrepit) can have a negative impact on memory performance, memory self-efficacy, and attitudes toward aging, whereas the activation of positive self-stereotypes (wise, learned, alert, etc.) can enhance these things. In an extension of this work, Chiu, Hong, Lam, Fu, Tong, and Lee (1998) similarly established that incidental exposure to gender-related environmental cues increases gender-consistent self-descriptions, or depersonalization, among men and women.

Kelly (1989) studied depersonalization in relation to preexisting political identities. She found a positive relationship between the salience of political identity, as indexed by strength of political affiliation, and level of depersonalization, as indexed by ratings of perceived ingroup and outgroup homogeneity. More specifically, British Labour Party members perceived both their ingroup and the Conservative Party outgroup to be more homogeneous than did nonmembers. Furthermore, ingroup homogeneity was more pronounced on those items that served to best differentiate the ingroup from the psychologically relevant outgroup. Research along these lines has established that perceptions of the ingroup and the outgroup and, moreover, the perceived psychological distance between the ingroup and the outgroup are affected by social identity salience.

People's stereotypic views of their own national ingroup, and how these views change in response to significant historical events, have also recently been studied. For instance, Reicher, Hopkins, and Condor (1997) studied the historical correlates of self-stereotypes in the context of the 1992 General Election in Scotland. A topic of much debate at this time was the constitutional question of whether Scotland should move toward independence from England. Reicher and his colleagues closely analyzed political discourse gathered at numerous public meetings and interviews throughout the period of the election campaign and immediately afterward. They observed that there was very little consensus among Scots as a whole over the meaning of the identity "Scottish" at this time. The self-stereotype of "Scottishness" was highly contentious and highly variable. In support of self-categorization theory principles, people with different political allegiances and motives defined Scottishness in different ways at different times. Second, Reicher et al., found that this variability in self-stereotypes served political ends; shared social identities and the associated self-stereotypes make possible social influence on a large scale (Haslam, Turner, Oakes, McGarty, & Reynolds, 1998; Oakes et al., 1994; Turner, 1991). Third, Reicher et al.'s analysis of the complex social and political functions of self-stereotypes confirmed the limitations of purely (fixed) trait theories of stereotypes (see Brown & Turner, in press; Turner, 1982). Group stereotypes may be expressed as traits in particular conditions, but fundamentally they are variable products of an interplay between perceivers' motives, expectations, background theories and knowledge, and stimulus reality, and can take any social categorical form (Turner & Onorato, 1999).

Within the Australian context, Haslam and his colleagues (Haslam, Oakes, Reynolds, & Mein, 1999) similarly studied the historical correlates of change in Australian students' self-stereotypes. These investigators sampled a student population from 1992 to 1997. During this time, the political scene in Australia changed dramatically. The Labor government lost the federal election in 1996 for the first time in 13 years, and was succeeded by a more conservative Liberal–National coalition. Several significant policy changes followed, most notably a challenge to Aboriginal rights to native title. At the same time, a new right-wing political party called One Nation emerged in the political arena. Among other things, One Nation supporters strongly advocated an end to "special treatment" of indigenous Australians. The question was whether the new political climate had impacted on Australians' self-stereotypes. Student volunteers were asked to describe Australians (and only Australians) using the Katz–Braly (1933) checklist. As expected, domestic political conflict was associated with reduced *consensus* in stereotypes of the ingroup. The ingroup stereotype was also significantly less favorable in 1997, a time marked by internal social and political division. This study illustrated that stereotypes reflect perceived social reality (Oakes et al., 1994) and are sensitive to change in intergroup and intragroup relations (see also Simon et al., 1991).

Extending this work, Haslam, Oakes, Turner, and McGarty (1995) examined self-stereotyping among Australian participants, in either a restricted (intragroup) context or an extended (intergroup) context. Drawing on the meta-contrast principle, Haslam and his colleagues reasoned that as a general rule, perceived group homogeneity should tend to be accentuated on relevant dimensions when a group is rated in an intergroup context (the intergroup differences should tend to make salient the relevant social categorization, leading to perceived intracategory similarities), whereas rating a group in an intragroup context (i.e., on its own) should tend to make salient individual differences and enhance perceived group heterogeneity. They pointed out that outgroups usually tend to be rated in an intergroup context because they implicitly or explicitly will tend to be compared to the ingroup, but that ingroups can either be compared to an outgroup or to one's personal self. In sum, they suggested that an ingroup will tend to be perceived as less homogeneous than an outgroup where it is rated on its own (in isolation from the outgroup), but equally as homogeneous where it is rated explicitly in the context of the outgroup (just as the outgroup is rated in the context of the ingroup). In one study (see Haslam et al., 1995), participants assigned traits on a checklist either to a target ingroup (Australians) or to a target outgroup (Americans). They then estimated the percentage of people in the target group alone who had the assigned traits or, alternatively, the percentage of people in the target group and in the comparison group who had the traits that had just been assigned to the target group. As expected, when the target group (either Australians or Americans) was judged in isolation of a comparison group, a relative outgroup homogeneity effect was obtained. That is, stereotypic traits were believed to apply to more Americans than Australians (75% vs. 57%). In contrast, when ingroup and outgroup ratings were made at the same time, participants estimated that Australian-stereotypic traits (e.g., sportsmanlike) applied to 74% of Australians and, similarly, that American-stereotypic traits (e.g., nationalistic) applied to 74% of Americans. It follows from this analysis that relative ingroup homogeneity for minorities (e.g., homosexuals; the physically challenged) may be attributable to their tendency to make more intergroup comparisons. More generally, this research illustrates that the ingroup is perceived as less variable (or that ingroup members are perceived as more similar) in clear intergroup contexts.

Along similar lines, Haslam, Turner, Oakes, Reynolds, Eggins, Nolan, and Tweedie (1998) have demonstrated that increasing the salience of national identity among Australians produces consensual stereotypes of the ingroup (Australians) and the psychologically relevant outgroup (once again, Americans). To illustrate, in one study research participants selected traits from a checklist to describe both the ingroup (Australians) and the outgroup (Americans). Half of the sample described first the ingroup, then the outgroup; the other half described first the outgroup, then the ingroup. Drawing on the meta-contrast principle, Haslam and his colleagues reasoned that an intergroup context for the ingroup ratings (ingroup ratings *after* outgroup ratings) would effectively highlight intergroup differences and hence accentuate the salience of one's own national identity, relative to an intragroup context (ingroup ratings *before* outgroup ratings). It was predicted and found that the ingroup stereotype was more consensual (i.e., that there was more agreement across participants regarding trait ascriptions) in the intergroup context than in the intragroup context. Also as expected, the order manipulation had little effect on the sharedness of participants' stereotype of Americans; this made sense given that the outgroup was always by necessity rated in an intergroup context. Thus it appears that stereotypes of the (self-inclusive) ingroup ("us") and the outgroup ("them") become more consensual as the salience of social identity is increased.

In summary, research has established, on a range of dependent measures, that psychologically, individuals come to perceive themselves as

more similar to or interchangeable with other ingroup members as the salience of social identity is increased. Intragroup homogenization (in terms
of attitudes, beliefs, values, and behavior) is one indicator of depersonalization. Depersonalization also produces perceptions of outgroup homogeneity, and an accentuation of the perceived psychological distance between the ingroup and the outgroup. Together, these studies illustrate
that self-perception takes a special form in group contexts. The observation that intragroup similarities and intergroup differences serve as a basis
for self-definition in group contexts is of particular interest here.

    More specifically, depersonalized self-conception is, in our view, prob-
lematic for the dominant social cognitive model. The schema model
implies the primacy of personal identity; it implies that self-definition necessarily derives from or reflects interpersonal differences. The schema
model treats the self-concept as a fixed cognitive structure or immobile
reference point from which all social judgments—including all self-relevant judgments—emanate. However, evidence of depersonalization challenges the presumed primacy of personal identity. The depersonalization
studies illustrate that the self can come to be defined almost exclusively in
social identity terms in intergroup contexts. They demonstrate that the
position of the ingroup vis-à-vis the outgroup can sometimes serve as a
reference or anchor point for self-relevant judgments. In this case, the ref-
erent becomes "us" or "we," rather than "I" or "me," but it is nevertheless
a judgment of the self.

REVISITING THE PRIMACY ISSUE

The growing body of evidence pertaining to depersonalization, coupled
with the growing interest in social identity as a facet of the self (e.g.,
Brewer & Gardner, 1996; Deaux, 1996; Sedikides & Brewer, 2001; Tyler,
Kramer, & John, 1999), clearly raises the issue of the relative primacy or
status of personal and social identity in self-definition. This debate is taking place within cross-cultural perspectives (e.g., Chen, Brockner, & Katz,
1998; Markus & Kitayama, 1991; Trafimow, Triandis, & Goto, 1991;
Triandis, 1989) and in the more general literature on the self (e.g.,
Gaertner, Sedikides, & Graetz, 1999; Sedikides & Brewer, 2001; Simon,
1993; Simon et al., 1995; Taylor & Dube, 1986). Although self-categorization theory acknowledges our heavy reliance on self-ingroup comparisons as a basis for self-definition, the theory unequivocally states that
neither personal identity nor social identity takes precedence in defining
the self (e.g., see Turner et al., 1987, p. 46); the appropriate level of self-
categorization (of which personal and social identity are only two) depends on perceiver factors in interplay with social context. Other perspec-

tives argue for the prepotency of personal identity. For instance, Simon's (1993) "egocentric social categorization" model argues that the personal self, or "me versus not me" categorization, is the basic level of self-categorization, at least in individualistic Western cultures. In contrast to Simon, Brewer's (1991) optimal distinctiveness extension of self-categorization theory argues for "the relative prepotency of group identity over personal identity" (p. 478). According to Brewer, social identity is prepotent because it simultaneously satisfies one's need for assimilation with others and one's need for differentiation from others through intragroup and intergroup comparisons respectively. Both Brewer and Simon present evidence to support their positions.

Studies have been documented that were designed to "pit" the personal self against the collective self, in order to ascertain the degree to which one or the other is primary in self-perception. One illustration of this from the cross-cultural stream is the work of Trafimow et al. (1991). North American and Chinese student volunteers (all drawn from a North American University) completed a self-description task that required them to complete 20 sentences that began "I am." Before this task was completed, the investigators primed either the individual self or the collective self. Participants' responses were coded according to whether they referred to the individual self (e.g., personality attributes, interpersonal behavior) or the collective self (e.g., demographic categories, group memberships). The results were that Chinese students listed more collective selves than American students, and those individuals whose collective self rather than individual self had been primed listed more collective selves. In addition, participants generally tended to list more individual than collective self-descriptions. Trafimow et al. attributed this to the fact that all participants had spent considerable time in the individualistic culture of North America (p. 651), but other researchers have interpreted this finding as evidence of the primacy of the individual self (e.g., Gaertner et al., 1999).

A more recent illustration of research designed to "pit" the personal self against the collective self is provided by Gaertner et al. (1999). These investigators conceived the individual self as "a self-definition that is independent of group membership," whereas the collective self was conceived as "a self-definition derived from membership in a social group" (p. 5). To establish which self is motivationally primary, Gaertner et al. examined how experimental participants respond in the face of a threat (i.e., negative feedback) directed either at the personal or the collective self. Gaertner et al. reasoned that if the individual self is prepotent, "participants will regard a threat to the individual self as more severe than a threat to the collective self" (p. 8). The opposite pattern was expected if the collective self is prepotent. The results indicated that when the individual self was threatened, participants downplayed their uniqueness and identified more strongly with the ingroup, presumably in order to protect the individual self from the immediate threat. However, analogous effects were not observed when the collective self was threatened (i.e., participants did not highlight their uniqueness and identify less strongly with the ingroup), leading the researchers to conclude that the individual self was primary.

One interesting feature of this research is Gaertner et al.'s operationalization of the *collective self*. In order to tease apart collective and individual self-aspects, they controlled the information directed at the collective self such that it did not contain feedback about the individual participant (Investigations 1 and 2). In other words, the collective self was operationalized as a self-exclusive rather than inclusive category in the context of the experiment. The methodology adopted may thus have inadvertently diminished the psychological relevance and significance of this social category to the perceiver. In addition, Gaertner et al.'s operationalization of the collective self (Investigations 1 and 2) failed to evoke an outgroup, or intergroup comparison in terms of a comparative dimension that correlated with the relevant social categorization (cf. Brown & Turner, 1981). In short, the "threat" was uncorrelated with a division into social groups (cf. Spears, Doosje, et al., 1997; see also Oakes, 1987, in particular her discussion of the collective deviance condition). It is possible therefore that a strong interpersonal context was contrasted with a comparatively weak group context, which did not directly implicate the self. Under these conditions it may not be altogether surprising that the personal self was protected, at the expense of a relatively amorphous collective self.

In relation to the primacy issue, the position of self-categorization theory is clear. To reiterate the most crucial points of the analysis: First, this perspective is called "self-categorization theory" rather than "social identity theory" because it speaks as much of the personal as of the group level of identity (cf. Tajfel & Turner, 1979). The theory makes explicit that neither personal nor social identity represents the "basic" level of self-categorization. On the contrary, the theory asserts that the issue of which self will emerge as "figure" rather than "ground" cannot be decided in the abstract, apart from knowledge of relevant contextual parameters. Second, the theory states that self-perception is likely to occur at the midpoint of the interpersonal–intergroup continuum much of the time, such that individuals will tend to define themselves as "moderately different from ingroup members, who in turn will be perceived as moderately different from outgroup members" (Turner et al., 1987, p. 50). Third, self-categorization theory "asserts the interdependence of individuality and shared, collective identity" (Turner & Oakes, 1989, p. 270). That is, the collectivity is implicated in the emergence and experience of the personal self. From a theoretical point of view, therefore, tests that pit personal identity against social identity, as if to suppose that one (social identity) implicates a social psychological group while the other (personal identity) does not, can be criticized for setting up a false dichotomy, one that does not exist anywhere in the theory. Self-categorization theory does not interpret personal identification as "egocentric" in the sense implied by Simon (1993) or as "acontextual" in the sense implied by Gaertner et al. (1999). Rather, it argues that the collective self is a precursor to the emergence of a personal self; there would be no personal self in the absence of a higher order "we" that provides the context for self–other differentiation in terms of person-specific attributes. In other words, *the "me" implies the existence of the "us."* From this vantage point then, empirical paradigms that pit personal identity against social identity in the abstract are missing a crucial point about the psychological basis of the "individual" self; the individual self is interdependent with and derived (not divorced) from the collective. Along similar lines, if social identity is indeed "that part of an individual's self-concept which derives from his/her knowledge of his/her membership in a social group (or groups) together with the value and emotional significance attached to that membership" (Tajfel, 1981, p. 255), operationalizations of the "collective" that explicitly exclude "me" (as in Gaertner et al., 1999) or that define the individual as highly unprototypical of it are unlikely to evoke a strong sense of identification or to inspire collective action.

We have addressed the primacy issue in our own laboratory, within a modified version of Markus's (1977) information-processing paradigm. Previous investigators have argued that the self-concept comprises enduring personality structures that guide information processing when stimuli relevant to one's personality are encountered. Thus when strongly independent people are presented with independent and dependent traits, they should consistently and rapidly endorse self-congruent traits and reject conflicting traits. Tests of this hypothesis have, however, proceeded on the assumption that the word *self* in the previous sentence can be equated with *personal identity*. In contrast, in our research we have attempted to show that although self-conception may be consistent with a personality variable when individual self-aspects are salient, when a conflicting self-inclusive group identity is made salient the same individual may respond in a diametrically opposed way.

In two closely related studies (Onorato & Turner, 1996, 1997), we examined whether the information-processing consequences of personal self-schemata are attenuated or perhaps eliminated when a conflicting high-order identity is made salient. In Study 1, Markus's (1977) classification scheme was used to identify individuals who were schematic for independence, schematic for dependence, or aschematic for both traits. At a subsequent testing session, participants' social identities as men or women (respectively) and the corresponding norms of independence and dependence were initially "primed" in the laboratory. Individuals then participated in a modified version of Markus's (1977) information-processing paradigm. Her explicit "personal identity" focus was replaced by an explicit "social identity" focus. Instead of asking participants to judge traits in terms of a "me/not me" self-rating task, they used an "us/them" self-rating task, where "us" referred to the self-inclusive category "women" for female participants and "men" for male participants. Our methodology differed from Markus's (1977) in one more important respect: Although Markus discarded those participants who did not fall into one of her three a priori categories (independent schematic, dependent schematic, or aschematic), we retained these unclassified individuals in the main experiment. In past studies a large number of individuals were invariably excluded because they did not fall into the investigator's preconceived categories; it seemed useful to examine the responses of such individuals.

The stimulus words presented in the us/them self-rating task included schema-relevant traits (i.e., independent and dependent words) and social identity-relevant traits (i.e., masculine and feminine words). Dependent measures included the proportion of traits endorsed as self-descriptive and response latencies for self-description. Contrary to self-schema theory, participants did not display schematic processing for schema-relevant traits. Instead, a significant interaction emerged between social identity and stimulus word type. As shown in Table 7.1, social identity salience produced depersonalized self-conception. Irrespective of their personal self-schemata, male participants endorsed more independent than dependent traits as self-descriptive, whereas the opposite pattern emerged

TABLE 7.1
Mean Proportion of Independent, Dependent, Masculine
and Feminine Words Endorsed as Self-Descriptive as a Function
of Social Identity, Together With Mean Latencies Corresponding
to Various Patterns of Responding

	Stimulus Word Type			
Social Identity	Independent	Dependent	Masculine	Feminine
Male				
Proportions	.74 (.23)	.29 (.24)	.84 (.21)	.33 (.24)
Latencies	3.38 (1.27)	4.46 (2.29)	3.15 (1.29)	3.77 (1.96)
Female				
Proportions	.35 (.17)	.79 (.21)	.18 (.17)	.79 (.15)
Latencies	3.68 (1.97)	3.06 (1.30)	4.16 (3.19)	2.76 (1.25)

Note. Standard deviations in parentheses. Mean latencies are in seconds. Reading across the table, latencies indicate mean time taken to make consistent(independent) responses, consistent(dependent) responses, consistent(masculine) responses, and consistent(feminine) responses, respectively. Adapted from Onorato and Turner (1996), with permission.

for females. Males also endorsed more independent traits than females, and females endorsed more dependent traits than males. In addition, Table 7.1 shows that a very similar pattern emerged for the endorsement of masculine and feminine traits.

Response latencies for self-description were analysed by calculating two new measures. The first measure yields the mean latency for all responses that are consistent with an independent self-concept; it was obtained by averaging latencies for "us" responses to independent words and "them" responses to dependent words. This measure will be referred to as a *consistent(independent)* pattern of responding. The second measure yields the mean latency for all responses that are consistent with a dependent self-concept; this measure was obtained by averaging latencies for "us" responses to dependent words and "them" responses to independent words. This measure will be referred to as a *consistent(dependent)* pattern of responding. [For masculine and feminine words, indexes of a consistent(masculine) pattern of responding, and a consistent(feminine) pattern of responding, were similarly derived.] A three-way analysis of variance, with pattern of responding as a repeated measures factor, revealed a significant interaction between social identity and pattern of responding. Irrespective of their self-schemata, we observed that males were generally faster to respond in a manner that implied independence, whereas females were generally faster to respond in a manner that implied dependence. These results are presented in Table 7.1. In particular, Table 7.1 reveals that males were faster to make consistent(independent) than consistent(dependent) responses, and females were faster than males to make consistent(dependent) responses. Table 7.1 also shows that a very similar pattern emerged for latencies corresponding to consistent(masculine) and consistent(feminine) responses.

Interestingly, even participants left unclassified in terms of self-schema theory displayed a pattern of responding that mirrored the effects normally expected from schematic individuals. Specifically, under conditions of a salient social identity, unclassified female participants behaved as though they had a self-schema for dependence (and indeed, femininity), whereas unclassified male participants behaved as though they had a self-schema for independence (and indeed, masculinity). By definition, such individuals do not have self-schemata for independence or dependence, yet their performance on a range of cognitive tasks was suggestive of self-schemata. The results of this first study have at least two important implications: First, they indicate that social identities can function like personal self-schemata in that they have similar information-processing consequences, and second, they suggest that schema-type effects may be produced on the spot, rather than being the product of specific, stored knowledge structures.

A second study was designed to extend this line of inquiry (Onorato & Turner, 1997). Only women participated in Study 2. In the initial screening phase, two groups were identified: a group of Low Independent and a group of High Independent females. In keeping with previous research (Markus, 1977), our classification scheme took into account the extremity of self-ratings, importance ratings, and perceived consistency on the central dimension. The Low Independents were individuals who were relatively low on various independence scales; they said that this characteristic was not particularly important to them, and they reported that they varied from situation to situation on this trait. In contrast, the High Independents gave very high independence self-ratings, very high importance ratings, and perceived themselves as cross-situationally consistent on this trait. This personality variable thus represents the degree to which people are schematic independents. High Independents are schematic for independence in the traditional sense (Markus, 1977), while Low Independents are those who are low on the relevant criteria. This classification was empirically derived; it was used because it represented the most powerful measure of individual differences attainable for our sample. It has the advantage of capturing the natural variation in the sample, while retaining a clear conceptual link to the notion of schematicity (as defined by Markus).

In a second testing phase, self-ratings were elicited from the same participants in a context that tapped either their personalized self-concept as individuals, or their depersonalized self-concept as women in contrast to men. In the former "personal identity" condition, female participants rated themselves as individuals in contrast to other women, making a "me" versus "not me" judgment; in the latter "social identity" condition they rated themselves as women in contrast to men, making an "us" versus "them" judgement (as in Study 1). We predicted that individual differences would emerge between Low and High Independents in the personal identity condition. In this case, Low Independents should endorse more dependent than independent words, and High Independents should endorse more independent than dependent words. Between-group differences should also be consistent with the personality variable. Conversely, it was expected that, being female, both the Low and High groups would strongly endorse dependent words in the social identity condition, because their group's position on the central trait dimension (rather than their own personal position) should inform self-ratings here.

For the proportion of independent and dependent words endorsed, a significant interaction was obtained between personality, level of self-categorization, and stimulus word type. As expected, individual differences came to the fore in the personal identity condition but not in the social identity condition. The results are presented in Table 7.2. At the level of *personal identity*, High Independents endorsed more independent traits

TABLE 7.2

Mean Proportion of Independent and Dependent Traits Endorsed
as a Function of Personality and Level of Self-Categorization

Level of Self-Categorization	Independent Words		Dependent Words	
	Low Indep.	High Indep.	Low Indep.	High Indep.
Personal identity	.49 (.20)	.69 (.20)	.70 (.15)	.54 (.19)
Social identity	.33 (.20)	.41 (.22)	.78 (.18)	.74 (.17)

Note. Standard deviations in parentheses. Low Indep. = Low Independent females; High Indep. = High Independent females. Adapted from Onorato and Turner (1997), with permission.

than Low Independents, and Low Independents endorsed more dependent traits than High Independents. Low Independents also endorsed more dependent than independent traits, whereas High Independents endorsed more independent than dependent traits. Thus the effects of the personality variable emerged under appropriate conditions. In direct contrast, in the *social identity* condition both groups endorsed more dependent than independent words. Equally importantly, in this condition, Low and High Independent females did not differ in the number of independent words endorsed, or in the number of dependent words endorsed. Thus under conditions of a salient social identity, self-perception is depersonalized; it tends to reflect the attributes that one shares with other ingroup members, more so than interpersonal differences within the ingroup.

For response times to process independent and dependent words, we expected that participants would be faster to make personally-consistent responses in the personal identity condition, and faster to make group-consistent responses in the social identity condition. However, the expected three-way interaction between personality, level of self-categorization, and pattern of responding was not obtained; indeed, there were no significant main or interaction effects involving the personality variable. Instead, a significant interaction emerged between level of self-categorization and pattern of responding, yielding partial support for expectations. The means are presented in Table 7.3. Importantly, participants were faster to make consistent(dependent) than consistent(independent) responses in the social identity condition. They were also faster to make consistent(independent) responses in the personal identity than the social identity condition. Thus, both groups of women (Lows and Highs) were faster to respond in a manner that implied dependence rather than independence when responses were elicited in terms of the social categorical self—"us women in contrast to men."

We also expected to see effects of depersonalization on feminine relative to masculine traits. Feminine rather than masculine traits should be

TABLE 7.3

Mean Latency (Sec) for Consistent(independent) and
Consistent(dependent) Responses as a Function
of Level of Self-Categorization

Level of Self-Categorization	Pattern of Responding	
	Consistent(independent)	Consistent(dependent)
Personal identity	2.94 (1.03)	2.85 (1.08)
Social identity	3.63 (1.52)	2.94 (0.94)

Note. Standard deviations in parentheses. Adapted from Onorato and Turner (1997), with permission.

endorsed by both groups of women in the social identity condition. In addition, we anticipated that individual differences might emerge in the personal identity condition, given the conceptual link between independence–dependence and masculinity—femininity. In general, results supported expectations. The obtained three-way interaction is presented in Table 7.4. In contrast to the personal identity condition where individual differences emerged for the endorsement of masculine traits, in the social identity condition Low and High Independents endorsed masculine traits to the same degree. Moreover, an even stronger tendency to self-stereotype on feminine rather than masculine traits emerged in this condition, for both Low and High Independents.

In addition, the personal identity condition revealed differences in speed of processing between Low and High Independent females, whereas the social identity condition revealed an attenuation of these differences. Specifically, although Low Independents were faster to make consistent(feminine) than consistent(masculine) responses at the level of personal identity, High Independents were equally fast to make consistent(feminine) and consistent(masculine) responses in this condition. In addition, High Independents were faster than Low Independents in making consistent(masculine) responses in the personal identity condition. In contrast, in the social identity condition, both Low and High Independents were faster to make consistent(feminine) than consistent(masculine) responses. The relevant means are presented in Table 7.4. Again, the results illustrate the general tendency for both individual differences and depersonalization to emerge, in each case under appropriate conditions.

Self-categorization theory argues that either personal or social identification can come to the fore, depending on social context. In other words, it is not assumed that personal identity has privileged status in defining the self (cf. Gaertner et al., 1999; Simon, 1993), nor that social identity has privileged status (cf. Brewer, 1991). The relevant question, from this per-

TABLE 7.4

Mean Proportion of Masculine and Feminine Traits Endorsed as a
Function of Personality and Level of Self-Categorization

Level of Self-Categorization	Masculine Words		Feminine Words	
	Low Indep.	High Indep.	Low Indep.	High Indep.
Personal identity				
Proportions	.45 (.17)	.58 (.21)	.77 (.16)	.72 (.15)
Latencies	3.02 (1.47)	2.56 (0.94)	2.33 (0.66)	2.52 (0.88)
Social identity				
Proportions	.31 (.19)	.30 (.22)	.87 (.12)	.82 (.15)
Latencies	3.41 (1.66)	3.10 (1.44)	2.75 (1.00)	2.46 (0.74)

Note. Standard deviations in parentheses. Low Indep. = Low Independent females;
High Indep. = High Independent females. Mean latencies are in seconds. Reading across the
table, latencies indicate mean time taken by Low and High Independents, respectively, to
make consistent(masculine) responses, followed by time taken by Low and High Independents, respectively, to make consistent(feminine) responses. Adapted from Onorato and
Turner (1997), with permission.

spective, is not whether personal or social identification is more important
in an absolute sense; rather, the question is, "Under what conditions will
individuals come to define themselves as individuals, and under what conditions will individuals come to define themselves as group members?"
Importantly, self-categorization theory argues that much of the time, self-perception involves aspects of both individual and group identity (Turner
et al., 1987). Nevertheless, an examination of how self-category content
changes as the conditions either facilitate or inhibit the depersonalization
of the self remains a valid empirical strategy (for other illustrations, see
Onorato, 2001).

Despite the encouraging results, the second study could have been improved by specifying the comparative context at the time that pretest ratings were obtained. We would argue that the context was implicitly
intragroup at the time that pretest measures were collected, because participants were filling out the questionnaire with other women present in
the room, and were aware that only women were being recruited for the
study; by inference, therefore, participants' responses would only be compared to other women's responses. Despite the viability of this assumption, in future studies the ingroup should be made explicit at the time that
pretest measures are elicited. To facilitate the emergence of the personality variable under appropriate conditions, in future research an explicit
intragroup context should be established at the time that initial self-ratings are obtained (i.e., at pretest) and the same intragroup context
should subsequently be reinstated at Time 2 (i.e., at posttest). Under these
conditions, the personality variable should emerge even more consistently

under personal identity instructions. Insofar as the role of intragroup processes in personal self-definition can thus be illuminated, a new, more
contextualist understanding of personal identity may in time come to replace the currently popular self-schema metaphor.

CONCLUSION

The idea that self-conception is depersonalized in group contexts is central to the self-categorization analysis. This idea has important implications for the schema metaphor for the self. Specifically, the observation
that the self can come to be defined and experienced in terms of something other than individual differences is problematic for any perspective
that equates the self-concept with a central, personalized schema that
functions like a fixed reference point from which self-relevant judgements
emanate. Importantly, the self-categorization perspective does not reject
the idea that interpersonal comparisons can and in many contexts do provide a basis for self-definition, but it does offer an critical extension and
qualification to the currently popular schema model of the self. The extension is that group self-categories (like personal self-categories) are an
equally integral part of the self, and the qualification is that in accepting a
role for personality structures, one need not assume that these structures
are stable and enduring; personal self-categories (like social identity) can
be conceived as context-dependent properties.

REFERENCES

Abrams, D., Sparkes, K., & Hogg, M. A. (1985). Gender salience and social identity: The im-
    pact of sex of siblings on educational and occupational aspirations. *British Journal of Edu-
    cational Psychology, 55*, 224–232.
Baldwin, M. W., & Holmes, J. G. (1987). Salient private audiences and awareness of the self.
    Journal of Personality and Social Psychology, 52, 1087–1098.
Baumeister, R. F. (1998). The self. In D. T. Gilbert, S. T. Fiske, & G. Lindzey (Eds.), *The
    handbook of social psychology* (4th ed., Vol. 2, pp. 680–740). Boston: McGraw-Hill.
Bem, S. L. (1974). The measurement of psychological androgyny. *Journal of Consulting and
    Clinical Psychology, 42*, 155–162.
Biernat, M., Vescio, T. K., & Green, M. L. (1996). Selective depersonalization. *Journal of Per-
    sonality and Social Psychology, 71*, 1194–1209.
Branscombe, N. R., & Wann, D. L. (1994). Collective self-esteem consequences of outgroup
    derogation when a valued social identity is on trial. *European Journal of Social Psychology,
    24*, 641–658.
Brewer, M. B. (1991). The social self: On being the same and different at the same time. *Per-
    sonality and Social Psychology Bulletin, 17*, 475–482.
Brewer, M. B., & Gardner, W. (1996). Who is this "we"? Levels of collective identity and self
    representations. *Journal of Personality and Social Psychology, 71*, 83–93.

Brewer, M. B., & Weber, J. G. (1994). Self-evaluation effects of interpersonal versus intergroup social comparison. *Journal of Personality and Social Psychology, 66*, 268–275.

Brown, J. D. (1998). *The self.* Boston: McGraw-Hill.

Brown, P. M., & Turner, J. C. (1996, July). *How do intuitive theories influence perceptions of group variability?* Paper presented at the 11th general meeting of the European Association of Experimental Social Psychology, Gmunden Austria.

Brown, P. M., & Turner, J. C. (in press). The role of theories in the formation of stereotype content. In C. McGarty, V. Y. Yzerbyt, & R. Spears (Eds.), *Stereotypes as explanations: The formation of meaningful beliefs about social groups.* London: Sage.

Brown, R. J., & Turner, J. C. (1981). Interpersonal and intergroup behaviour. In J. C. Turner & H. Giles (Eds.), *Intergroup behaviour* (pp. 33–65). Oxford: Blackwell.

Bruner, J. S. (1957). On perceptual readiness. *Psychological Review, 64*, 123–152.

Charters, W. W., & Newcomb, T. M. (1952). Some attitudinal effects of experimentally increased salience of a membership group. In G. E. Swanson, T. M. Newcomb, & E. L. Hartley (Eds.), *Readings in social psychology* (pp. 415–420). New York: Holt, Rinehart & Winston.

Chen, Y.-R., Brockner, J., & Katz, T. (1998). Toward an explanation of cultural differences in ingroup favouritism: The role of individual versus collective primacy. *Journal of Personality and Social Psychology, 75*, 1490–1502.

Chiu, C., Hong, Y., Lam, C., Fu, H., Tong, Y., & Lee, S. (1998). Stereotyping and self-presentation: Effects of gender stereotype activation. *Group Processes and Intergroup Relations, 1*, 81–96.

David, B., & Turner, J. C. (1992, July). *Studies in self-categorization and minority conversion.* Paper presented at the joint European Association of Experimental Social Psychology/Society for Experimental Social Psychology meeting, Leuven/Louvain-La-Neuve, Belgium.

Deaux, K. (1996). Social identification. In E. T. Higgins & A. W. Kruglanski (Eds.), *Social psychology: Handbook of basic principles* (pp. 777–798). New York: Guilford Press.

Dion, K. L., Earn, B. M., & Yee, P. H. N. (1978). The experience of being a victim of prejudice: An experimental approach. *International Journal of Psychology, 13*, 197–214.

Doosje, B., & Ellemers, N. (1997). Stereotyping under threat: The role of group identification. In R. Spears, P. J. Oakes, N. Ellemers & S. A. Haslam (Eds.), *The social psychology of stereotyping and group life* (pp. 257–272). Oxford, England: Blackwell.

Doosje, B., Ellemers, N., & Spears, R. (1995). Perceived intragroup variability as a function of group status and identification. *Journal of Experimental Social Psychology, 31*, 410–436.

Ellemers, N., Spears, R., & Doosje, B. (1997). Sticking together or falling apart: Ingroup identification as a psychological determinant of group commitment versus individual mobility. *Journal of Personality and Social Psychology, 72*, 617–626.

Ellemers, N., Spears, R., & Doosje, B. (Eds.). (1999). *Social identity: Context, commitment, content.* Oxford, England: Blackwell.

Ellemers, N., & van Knippenberg, A. (1997). Stereotyping in social context. In R. Spears, P. J. Oakes, N. Ellemers & S. A. Haslam (Eds.), *The social psychology of stereotyping and group life* (pp. 208–235). Oxford, England: Blackwell.

Fiske, S. T., & Taylor, S. E. (1991). *Social cognition.* New York: McGraw-Hill.

Gaertner, L., Sedikides, C., & Graetz, K. (1999). In search of self-definition: Motivational primacy of the individual self, motivational primacy of the collective self, or contextual primacy? *Journal of Personality and Social Psychology, 76*, 5–18.

Greenwald, A. G., & Banaji, M. R. (1989). The self as a memory system: Powerful, but ordinary. *Journal of Personality and Social Psychology, 57*, 41–54.

Greenwald, A. G., & Pratkanis, A. R. (1984). The self. In R. S. Wyer & T. K. Srull (Eds.), *Handbook of social cognition* (Vol. 3, pp. 129–178). Hillsdale, NJ: Lawrence Erlbaum Associates.

Hardie, E. A., & McMurray, N. E. (1992). Depersonalization, sex role ideology and menstrual attitudes: A social identity approach. *Sex Roles, 27*, 17–37.

Hardin, C., & Higgins, E. T. (1996). Shared reality: How social verification makes the subjective objective. In R. M. Sorrentino & E. T. Higgins (Eds.), *Handbook of motivation and cognition. Volume 3: The interpersonal context* (pp. 28–84). New York: Guilford.

Haslam, S. A. (2001). *Psychology in organizations: The social identity approach.* London: Sage.

Haslam, S. A., Oakes, P. J., McGarty, C., Turner, J. C., Reynolds, K. J., & Eggins, R. A. (1996). Stereotyping and social influence: The mediation of stereotype applicability and sharedness by the views of ingroup and outgroup members. *British Journal of Social Psychology, 35*, 369–397.

Haslam, S. A., Oakes, P. J., Reynolds, K. J., & Mein, J. (1999). Rhetorical unity and social division: A longitudinal study of change in Australian self-stereotypes. *Asian Journal of Social Psychology, 2*, 265–280.

Haslam, S. A., Oakes, P. J., Reynolds, K. J., & Turner, J. C. (1999). Social identity salience and the emergence of stereotype consensus. *Personality and Social Psychology Bulletin, 25*, 809–818.

Haslam, S. A., Oakes, P. J., Turner, J. C., & McGarty, C. (1995). Social categorization and group homogeneity: Changes in the perceived applicability of stereotype content as a function of comparative context and trait favourableness. *British Journal of Social Psychology, 34*, 139–160.

Haslam, S. A., Oakes, P. J., Turner, J. C., & McGarty, C. (1996). Social identity, self-categorization, and the perceived homogeneity of ingroups and outgroups: The interaction between social motivation and cognition. In R. M. Sorrentino & E. T. Higgins (Eds.), *Handbook of motivation and cognition, Vol. 3: The interpersonal context* (pp. 182–222). New York: Guilford Press.

Haslam, S. A., & Turner, J. C. (1992). Context-dependent variation in social stereotyping 2: The relationship between frame of reference, self-categorization and accentuation. *European Journal of Social Psychology, 22*, 251–277.

Haslam, S. A., & Turner, J. C. (1995). Context-dependent variation in social stereotyping 3: Extremism as a self-categorical basis for polarized judgement. *European Journal of Social Psychology, 25*, 341–371.

Haslam, S. A., Turner, J. C., Oakes, P. J., McGarty, C., & Reynolds, K. J. (1998). The group as a basis for emergent stereotype consensus. *European Review of Social Psychology, 8*, 203–239.

Haslam, S. A., Turner, J. C., Oakes, P. J., Reynolds, K. J., Eggins, R. A., Nolan, M., & Tweedie, J. (1998). When do stereotypes become really consensual? Investigating the group-based dynamics of the consensualization process. *European Journal of Social Psychology, 28*, 755–776.

Hensley, V., & Duval, S. (1976). Some perceptual determinants of perceived similarity, liking and correctness. *Journal of Personality and Social Psychology, 34*, 159–168.

Higgins, E. T., & Bargh, J. A. (1987). Social cognition and social perception. *Annual Review of Psychology, 38*, 369–425.

Hogg, M. A. (1992). *The social psychology of group cohesiveness: From attraction to social identity.* London: Harvester-Wheatsheaf.

Hogg, M. A., & Turner, J. C. (1987). Intergroup behaviour, depersonalization and the salience of social categories. *British Journal of Social Psychology, 26*, 325–340.

Hormuth, S. E. (1990). *The ecology of the self: Relocation and self-concept change.* Cambridge, England: Cambridge University Press.

James, K. (1993). Conceptualizing self with in-group stereotypes: Context and esteem precursors. *Personality and Social Psychology Bulletin, 19*, 117–121.

Katz, D., & Braly, K. (1933). Racial stereotypes in one hundred college students. *Journal of Abnormal and Social Psychology, 28*, 280–290.

Kelly, C. (1989). Political identity and perceived intragroup homogeneity. *British Journal of Social Psychology, 28*, 239–250.

Kihlstrom, J. F., & Cantor, N. (1984). Mental representations of the self. In L. Berkowitz (Ed.), *Advances in experimental social psychology* (Vol. 17, pp. 1–47). New York: Academic Press.

Kihlstrom, J. F., Cantor, N., Albright, J. S., Chew, B. R., Klein, S. B., & Niedenthal, P. M. (1988). Information processing and the study of the self. In L. Berkowitz (Ed.), *Advances in experimental social psychology* (Vol. 21, pp. 145–178). New York: Academic Press.

Klein, S. B., & Kihlstrom, J. F. (1986). Elaboration, organization, and the self-reference effect in memory. *Journal of Experimental Psychology: General, 115*, 26–38.

Lau, R. R. (1989). Individual and contextual influences on group identification. *Social Psychology Quarterly, 52*, 220–231.

Levy, B. (1996). Improving memory in old age through implicit depersonalization. *Journal of Personality and Social Psychology, 71*, 1092–1107.

Linville, P. W., & Carlston, D. E. (1994). Social cognition of the self. In P. G. Devine, D. L. Hamilton, & T. M. Ostrom (Eds.), *Social cognition: Its impact on social psychology* (pp. 143–193). New York: Academic Press.

Lorenzi-Cioldi, F. (1991). Depersonalization and self-enhancement in gender groups. *European Journal of Social Psychology, 21*, 403–417.

Markus, H. (1977). Self-schemata and processing information about the self. *Journal of Personality and Social Psychology, 35*, 63–78.

Markus, H., & Kitayama, S. (1991). Culture and the self: Implications for cognition, emotion, and motivation. *Psychological Review, 98*, 224–253.

Markus, H., & Sentis, K. (1982). The self in social information processing. In J. Suls (Ed.), *Psychological perspectives on the self* (Vol. 1, pp. 41–70). Hillsdale, NJ: Lawrence Erlbaum Associates.

Markus, H., & Wurf, E. (1987). The dynamic self-concept: A social psychological perspective. *Annual Review of Psychology, 38*, 299–337.

Mellor, C. S. (1988). Depersonalization and self-perception: Second Leeds Psychopathology Symposium: The psychopathology of body image. *British Journal of Psychiatry, 153*, 15–19.

Oakes, P. J. (1987). The salience of social categories. In J. C. Turner, M. A. Hogg, P. J. Oakes, S. D. Reicher, & M. S. Wetherell, *Rediscovering the social group: A self-categorization theory* (pp. 117–141). Oxford, England: Blackwell.

Oakes, P. J., Haslam, S. A., & Turner, J. C. (1994). *Stereotyping and social reality*. Oxford, England: Blackwell.

Onorato, R. S. (2001). *Recasting the problem of self-concept change: A self-categorization perspective*. Unpublished PhD thesis, Australian National University, Canberra, Australia.

Onorato, R. S., & Turner, J. C. (1996, May). *Fluidity in the self-concept: A shift from personal to social identity*. Paper presented at the second meeting of the Society of Australasian Social Psychologists, 25th meeting of Australasian Social Psychologists, Canberra, Australia.

Onorato, R. S., & Turner, J. C. (1997, April). *Individual differences and social identity: A study of self-categorization processes in the Markus paradigm*. Paper presented at the third meeting of the Society of Australasian Social Psychologists, 26th meeting of Australasian Social Psychologists, Wollongong, New South Wales, Australia.

Onorato, R. S., & Turner, J. C. (2001). The "I", the "me" and the "us": The psychological group and self-concept maintenance and change. In C. Sedikides & M. B. Brewer (Eds.), *Individual self, relational self, and collective self* (pp. 147–170). Philadelphia: Psychology Press.

Reicher, S., Hopkins, N., & Condor, S. (1997). Stereotype construction as a strategy influence. In R. Spears, P. J. Oakes, N. Ellemers, & S. A. Haslam (Eds.), *The social psychology of stereotyping and group life* (pp. 94–118). Oxford, England: Blackwell.

Reynolds, K. J., & Oakes, P. J. (1999). Variability in impression formation: A self-categorization theory perspective. In T. Sugiman, M. Karasawa, J. Lui, & C. Ward (Eds.), *Progress in Asian social psychology* (Vol. 2, pp. 213–235). Seoul, Korea: Kyoyook-Kwahak-Sa.

Rogers, T. B. (1981). A model of the self as an aspect of the human information processing system. In N. Cantor & J. F. Kihlstrom (Eds.), *Personality, cognition, and social interaction* (pp. 193–214). Hillsdale, NJ: Lawrence Erlbaum Associates.

Rogers, T. B., Kuiper, N. A., & Kirker, W. S. (1977). Self-reference and the encoding of personal information. *Journal of Personality and Social Psychology, 35,* 677–688.

Rosenberg, M. (1987). Depersonalization: The loss of personal identity. In T. Honess & K. Yardley (Eds.), *Self and identity: Perspectives across the lifespan* (pp. 193–206). Boston: Routledge & Kegan Paul.

Rosenkrantz, P., Vogel, S., Bee, H., Broverman, I., & Broverman, D. M. (1968). Sex-role stereotypes and self-concepts in college students. *Journal of Consulting and Clinical Psychology, 32,* 287–295.

Rudolph, U. (1993). The self-reference effect: Methodological issues and implications from a schema-theoretical perspective. *European Journal of Social Psychology, 23,* 331–354.

Salancik, G. R., & Conway, M. (1975). Attitude inferences from salient and relevant cognitive content about behavior. *Journal of Personality and Social Psychology, 32,* 829–840.

Sedikides, C., & Brewer, M. B. (Eds.). (2001). *Individual self, relational self, and collective self.* Philadelphia: Psychology Press.

Sedikides, C., & Skowronski, J. J. (1997). The symbolic self in evolutionary context. *Personality and Social Psychology Review, 1,* 80–102.

Sherman, S. J., Judd, C. M., & Park, B. (1989). Social cognition. *Annual Review of Psychology, 40,* 281–326.

Simon, B. (1992). The perception of ingroup and outgroup homogeneity: Reintroducing the social context. In W. Stroebe & M. Hewstone (Eds.), *European Review of Social Psychology* (Vol. 3, pp. 1–30). Chichester, England: Wiley.

Simon, B. (1993). On the asymmetry in the cognitive construal of ingroup and outgroup: A model of egocentric social categorization. *European Journal of Social Psychology, 23,* 131–147.

Simon, B. (1999). A place in the world: Self and social categorization. In T. R. Tyler, R. M. Kramer, & O. P. John (Eds.), *The psychology of the social self* (pp. 47–69). Mahwah, NJ: Lawrence Erlbaum Associates.

Simon, B., & Brown, R. J. (1987). Perceived intragroup homogeneity in minority-majority contexts. *Journal of Personality and Social Psychology, 53,* 703–711.

Simon, B., Glassner-Bayerl, B., & Stratenwerth, I. (1991). Stereotyping and depersonalization in a natural intergroup context: The case of heterosexual and homosexual men. *Social Psychology Quarterly, 54,* 252–266.

Simon, B., & Hamilton, D. L. (1994). Depersonalization and social context: The effects of relative in-group size and in-group status. *Journal of Personality and Social Psychology, 66,* 699–711.

Simon, B., & Kampmeier, C. (2001). Revisiting the individual self: Towards a social psychological theory of the individual self and the collective self. In C. Sedikides & M. Brewer (Eds.), *Individual self, relational self, and collective self* (pp. 199–218). Philadelphia: Psychology Press.

Simon, B., Pantaleo, G., & Mummendey, A. (1995). Unique individual or interchangeable group member? The accentuation of intragroup differences versus similarities as an indicator of the individual self versus the collective self. *Journal of Personality and Social Psychology, 69,* 106–119.

Smith, E. R. (1984). Attributions and other inferences: Processing information about the self versus others. *Journal of Experimental Social Psychology, 20,* 97–115.

Smith, E. R., Coats, S., & Walling, D. (1999). Overlapping mental representations of self, in-group, and partner: Further response time evidence and a connectionist model. *Personality and Social Psychology Bulletin, 25,* 873–882.

Smith, E. R., & Henry, S. (1996). An in-group becomes part of the self: Response time evidence. *Personality and Social Psychology Bulletin, 22,* 635–642.

Spears, R. (2001). The interaction between the individual and the collective self: Self-categorization in context. In C. Sedikides & M. Brewer (Eds.), *Individual self, relational self, and collective self* (pp. 171–198). Philadelphia: Psychology Press.

Spears, R., Doosje, B., & Ellemers, N. (1997). Depersonalization in the face of threats to group status and distinctiveness: The role of group identification. *Personality and Social Psychology Bulletin, 23,* 538–533.

Spears, R., Oakes, P. J., Ellemers, N., & Haslam, S. A. (Eds.). (1997). *The social psychology of stereotyping and group life.* Oxford, England: Blackwell.

Tajfel, H. (1981). *Human groups and social categories.* Cambridge, England: Cambridge University Press.

Tajfel, H., & Turner, J. C. (1979). An integrative theory of intergroup conflict. In W. G. Austin & S. Worchel (Eds.), *The social psychology of intergroup relations* (pp. 33–47). Monterey, CA: Brooks/Cole.

Taylor, D. M., & Dube, L. (1986). Two faces of identity: The "I" and the "We." *Journal of Social Issues, 42,* 81–98.

Tice, D. M. (1992). Self-concept change and self-presentation: The looking glass self is also a magnifying glass. *Journal of Personality and Social Psychology, 63,* 435–451.

Trafimow, D., Triandis, H. C., & Goto, S. G. (1991). Some tests of the distinction between the private self and the collective self. *Journal of Personality and Social Psychology, 60,* 649–655.

Triandis, H. C. (1989). The self and social behavior in differing cultural contexts. *Psychological Review, 96,* 506–520.

Turner, J. C. (1975). Social comparison and social identity: Some prospects for intergroup behaviour. *European Journal of Social Psychology, 5,* 5–34.

Turner, J. C. (1978). Social categorization and social discrimination in the minimal group paradigm. In H. Tajfel (Ed.), *Differentiation between social groups: Studies in the social psychology of intergroup relations* (pp. 101–140). London: Academic Press.

Turner, J. C. (1982). Towards a cognitive redefinition of the social group. In H. Tajfel (Ed.), *Social identity and intergroup relations* (pp. 15–40). Cambridge, England: Cambridge University Press.

Turner, J. C. (1984). Social identification and psychological group formation. In H. Tajfel (Ed.), *The social dimension: European developments in social psychology* (Vol. 2, pp. 518–538). Cambridge, England: Cambridge University Press.

Turner, J. C. (1985). Social categorization and the self-concept: A social cognitive theory of group behavior. In E. J. Lawler (Ed.), *Advances in group processes: Theory and research* (Vol. 2, pp. 77–122). Greenwich, CT: JAI Press.

Turner, J. C. (1991). *Social influence.* Milton Keynes, UK: Open University Press.

Turner, J. C. (1999). Some current issues in research on social identity and self-categorization theories. In N. Ellemers, R. Spears, & B. Doosje (Eds.), *Social identity: Context, commitment, content* (pp. 6–34). Oxford, England: Blackwell.

Turner, J. C., Hogg, M. A., Oakes, P. J., Reicher, S. D., & Wetherell, M. S. (1987). *Rediscovering the social group: A self-categorization theory.* Oxford, England: Blackwell.

Turner, J. C., Hogg, M. A., Turner, P. J., & Smith, P. M. (1984). Failure and defeat as determinants of group cohesiveness. *British Journal of Social Psychology, 23,* 97–111.

Turner, J. C., & Oakes, P. J. (1989). Self-categorization theory and social influence. In P. B. Paulus (Ed.), *The psychology of group influence* (2nd ed., pp. 233–275). Hillsdale, NJ: Lawrence Erlbaum Associates.

Turner, J. C., Oakes, P. J., Haslam, S. A., & McGarty, C. (1994). Self and collective: Cognition and social context. *Personality and Social Psychology Bulletin, 20,* 454–463.

Turner, J. C., & Onorato, R. S. (1999). Social identity, personality, and the self-concept: A self-categorization perspective. In T. R. Tyler, R. M. Kramer, & O. P. John (Eds.), *The psychology of the social self* (pp. 11–46). Mahwah, NJ: Lawrence Lawrence Erlbaum Associates.

Tyler, T. R., Kramer, R. M., & John, O. P. (Eds.). (1999). *The psychology of the social self.* Mahwah, NJ: Lawrence Lawrence Erlbaum Associates.

Wilder, D. A. (1984). Predictions of belief homogeneity and similarity following social categorization. *British Journal of Social Psychology, 23,* 323–333.

Wilder, D. A., & Thompson, J. E. (1988). Assimilation and contrast effects in the judgments of groups. *Journal of Personality and Social Psychology, 54,* 62–73.

SYMBOLIC PROCESSES

Part IV highlights symbolic processes associated with the self. Meaningful symbols make up the cultural world, which constitutes and is constructed by human activities; cultural processes over time make up human history, which in turn shapes contemporary culture. When a symbolic perspective is taken within a period of time, it tends to emphasize culture. In contrast, when viewed across time, it takes a historical perspective. When viewed in a symbolic perspective, the issue of self and identity centers on how the experience of self, or selfhood, is symbolically understood by people around the world and people in the past. In particular, what is the meaning attributed to selfhood in the form of a conception of the person, and how do people construct their understandings of themselves based on the symbolic resources provided by history and culture?

In chapter 8, Kashima and Foddy traverse the historical emergence of the Western individualist self. In contrasting traditional and modern social systems, they make the point that much of the decontextualized, agentic self is a historical product of economic and social changes in Western society. Whether these historical forces will now bring in a new "Postmodern" era with attendant qualitative changes of the self or are simply magnifying the features of the "Modern" self is not possible to answer at this stage. Nonetheless, they suggest that the same socioeconomic conditions, which are claimed to be associated with globalization, may not necessarily produce the same "Modern" self in non-Western cultures. Contrary to what is often argued, non-Western societies cannot necessarily be simply equated with traditional Western societies.

Kashima's chapter 9 continues this theme of parallel and different cultural–historical trajectories stemming from socioeconomic change. To do this, he introduces a cultural dynamical perspective, which treats cultural and psychological processes as mutually constitutive and dynamically evolving over time. In particular, he describes the micro–macro linkage between situated symbolic activities on the one hand and the cultural symbolic system on the other, and sheds light on the contemporary cross-cultural literature on culture and self. In particular, he argues that accumulating evidence suggests cultural differences in self-conception cannot be understood within the same conceptual framework as that used to discuss the historical changes outlined in chapter 8.

Time and Self: The Historical Construction of the Self

Yoshihisa Kashima
University of Melbourne

Margaret Foddy
La Trobe University

"The past is a foreign country: they do things differently there."
—L. P. Hartley, *The Go-Between*, 1953, Prologue

That self-conceptions are socially constituted is perhaps an accepted wisdom in social psychology. In this perspective, the claim that people's conceptions of themselves have varied from one historical period to another may seem trivially true. If one accepts the view that self-conceptions are significantly affected by social institutional constraints and their associated normative expectations, significant changes in socioeconomic conditions should produce corresponding shifts in self-conceptions. Nonetheless, an historical analysis of self and identity points to the possibility that not only are self-conceptions affected by changes in socioeconomic conditions, but they may also participate in producing these changes in socioeconomic conditions over historical time. We contend that the view postulating a dynamic interaction between socioeconomic conditions and self-conceptions should be taken seriously, and that the links between macro socioeconomic conditions and micro self-conceptions are symbolically mediated. Both the socioeconomic conditions and the symbolic meanings that are attributed to them significantly shape people's understandings of themselves. In turn, symbolically constituted self-conceptions may provide significant constraints as well as opportunities for individual social action (e.g., Hacking, 1986; Novas & Rose, 2000; Rose, 1996).

The first part of this chapter sketches a Western history of self-conceptions. The main source of this exposition is the current literature on history and self from psychological perspectives, as urged by Smith (1978), and carried out by Baumeister (1986, 1987) and others (e.g., Cushman, 1990, 1995; Danziger, 1990, 1997; Gergen, 1991; Rose, 1996). This shows that prevalent self-conceptions changed in the course of Western European and North American history from the medieval to the modern period. The second part examines major theoretical explanations of the historical changes. Some theories emphasize the effect of socioeconomic conditions on self-conceptions. Here, a particular form of social structural and economic conditions is assumed to produce a particular kind of conception of the person (e.g., Schooler, 1996, 1998). However, there is a class of theories that accord a greater significance to symbolic processes in their capacity to shape the course of human history. In this type of historical analysis, symbolically constituted self-conceptions are assumed to contribute to the emergence of new socioeconomic conditions in history. Finally, we examine the contemporary sociocultural change associated with the developments in global mobility, information technology (especially the Internet), and genetic technology, and consider implications of these changes for social psychology of self and identity.

HISTORY OF WESTERN SELF-CONCEPTIONS

The current view of history and self generally accepted in social psychology suggests that self-conceptions in Western Europe and North America have undergone significant changes over time roughly from the medieval period (up to 15th century) to the 20th century. According to the accepted view, self-conceptions changed from one embedded in a group (e.g., family, community) to another that emphasizes individuality, from a collectivist conception to an individualist one. Clearly, this summary is an inadequate schematization of the scholarly work, let alone of historical records. Nevertheless, this generalization reflects the narrative of the historical evolution of self-conceptions, which often underlies discussions about self and identity in contemporary Western Europe and North America.

Baumeister (1986, 1987) characterized the medieval self as unproblematically situated in the Christian social order. One understood oneself as located in St Augustine's hierarchical structure, whose primary life objective was salvation and eternal life. The questions such as choice of one's occupation, ways to actualize the self and to maximize the quality of one's life—all too familiar to us in the 21st century—did not arise in this worldview. One was what one was to be; one did what one was to do. In this way, one fulfilled one's destiny. Roles (e.g., occupational, familial) were tightly organized in the hierarchical structure and functioned within the collectives to which they belonged. The meaning of roles was provided by Christianity as stations in one's life. In short, one's self was largely coextensive with the social role that one occupied.

As the medieval social order crumbled, self-conceptions changed as well. According to Baumeister, when physical and social mobility increased, and the social hierarchy was no longer fixed, the separation between the visible social role and the invisible "true" person became an issue. First of all, it became difficult for people to discern others' "true" locations in the social hierarchy (Trilling, 1971). The problem of perceiving others was then transferred to one's self-perception. One's "true" self now also became a problem, and was in need of being discovered and actualized. In particular, the need for discovering the "true" self was made acute by the Protestant doctrine of predestination. That is, although it was predestined whether one was to be saved or not, and there was no way of knowing, a person wished to find some positive sign of personal salvation. This resulted in relentless self-scrutiny and self-search. So, the individual, both self and other, was now conceptualized as consisting of an outer mask and an inner self.

In the late 17th and 18th centuries, the self-conception inspired by Enlightenment thought began its ascent in Britain and Western Europe. British empiricists such as Locke conducted philosophical inquiries into consciousness and the inner self (see Danziger, 1997). Their emphasis on evidence and rational reason was backed by the spectacular success of natural science, especially Newtonian mechanics. Simmel (1950) noted that this gave rise to a conception of the person as a locus of causal processes governed by natural law, something akin to the universal law of gravity. In other words, the Enlightenment self was conceptualized as an individuated agent, endowed with the universal capacity for reason. This self-conception was closely aligned with the conception of society as an aggregate of isolated, rational individuals as in Locke's social contract (Danziger, 1997). Enlightenment thought challenged Christianity with its new emphasis on skepticism, reasoning based on observable evidence, and overall rationality.

Somewhat later in the late 18th and early 19th centuries, the Romantic conception of the person emerged in part due to the decline of Christianity, according to Baumeister (1986). Christianity once provided not only the destination of one's life (i.e., salvation), but also the methods by which to reach the destination (i.e., following moral and religious precepts). With the decline of Christianity as the dominant way of life, people began to seek the meaning of their lives not in an afterlife, but in this world. In search of worldly fulfillment, people sought to cultivate the "true" and unique inner self, which distinguished oneself from everyone else. This self was, however, not readily available, but had to be discovered and actualized.

As Simmel (1950) noted, if the Enlightenment self was an instance of universal reason, with each person being essentially equal according to natural law, the Romantic self was located in the deep invisible interior, whose core was profound emotionality and differentiated personality. The essence of the Enlightenment self was on the verge of a cool calculating machine, whose rationality is undermined by the environment in which it is situated. With education and proper guidance, universally shared reason should emerge under optimal conditions. In contrast, the Romantic self was a kind of reaction to this image of the person, and it emphasized uniqueness, creativity, and human potential for growth. When the constraining environment is removed, the unique individuality of each person should emerge with his or her striving for the actualization of the "true" inner self.

Against this backdrop of the Enlightenment and Romantic conceptions of the person, two of the most prevalent and contrasting clusters of ideas and practices about what it means to be human, theorists have traced somewhat different trajectories of self-conceptions during the 20th century. First, Baumeister (1986, 1987) charted the descent of the Romantic self-conception. The conception of the self as a being separate from the social environment enabled self and society to be considered in relation to each other. Especially, the Romantic "true" self was valorized as the source of goodness and legitimacy, whereas society and culture were increasingly depicted as corrupting the self's virtue and frustrating its actualization. The Romantic self was now in conflict with society.

In search of fulfillment, the Romantic self struggled for social change and sought further freedom of the self from the social. Society became more flexible, but as a consequence offered even less guidance for self-actualization. The unfulfilled Romantic self sought its actualization in privacy and escape from society. However, the 20th century saw a further increase in the circumstances of social connectedness through improved communication and a greater economic interdependence. Recognizing the inevitability of social connectedness, the Romantic self became helpless and bitter; a stage of alienation and social criticism ensued. According to Baumeister, the self in the contemporary world (late 20th century) faces the predicament of no escape from society and no foreseeable fulfillment. This human condition may have given rise to what Cushman (1990, 1995) called the *empty self*; when one sought meaning in one's inner self, one could no longer find a promising self-potential, but saw only a void.

In contrast, Gergen (1991) regarded the trajectory of the 20th-century self-conception as a gradual swaying of the pendulum back in the direction of the Enlightenment self, and a rise of its contemporary heir, the

Modernist self. According to Gergen, the Modernist self is the rational optimist, whose integrity is maintained in words and deeds. Everyone is seen to be equipped with reason, and therefore created equal; with education and scientific technologies, democratic society consisting of such rational agents is believed to continue to progress. The optimism about the future and trust of reason provided by Modernist thought may have made a more alluring alternative to the Romantic self. Nonetheless, despite Modernism's dominance, Gergen contends that both the Modernist and Romanticist self-conceptions are available in the current symbolic culture of Western Europe and North America (also see Taylor, 1989).

In the late 20th century, the question of identity, that is, the process of defining who one is, has become a critical question in both everyday discourse and academic writings. One reason for this, according to Baumeister (1986, 1987), was that social conditions required a process of self-definition that is more psychologically demanding. Although self-definition can be attained by assignment (e.g., family lineage, gender), achievement (e.g., wealth, motherhood), or choice (e.g., religious affiliation, mate, work), defining oneself by choice would be more problematic than doing so by assignment. In Baumeister's analysis, as the sociocultural system became more flexible and complex, and one did not simply follow one's parents' footsteps in work and marriages were no longer arranged, it became obligatory that one make a choice about one's own career and spouse. With this, the establishment of an identity through self-definition by choice became a significant psychological issue.

History thus may have contributed to the emergence of self and identity as a critical issue in contemporary discourse. On one account, this is due to the decline of the Romantic self. As Baumeister noted, contemporary society no longer provided a viable method of fulfilling one's life project of self-discovery and actualization in one's worldly pursuit. As we suggest later, this view that the individual has been "detached" from society is not accepted uncritically by all analysts. The idea of the independent, responsible, and calculating individual can be seen as being just as embedded in a historical context, and as providing a solution to the problem of social order (e.g., Rose, 1996).

MODELS OF SOCIOCULTURAL CHANGE

Underlying the accepted view of historical changes in self-conception is a model of sociocultural conditions and their change over time. Given that self is affected, if not derived, from the social environment, major changes in social and economic conditions should produce related changes in conceptions of the self and the person. The model outlined in the late 19th century by social scientists such as Tönnies (1887/1955) and Durkheim (1893/1964), and developed and refined since then, will serve to illustrate this point. According to this analysis, the Western sociocultural system evolved from a traditional one to a modern one. We first schematically describe the traditional and the modern social conditions as postulated in these models, and point out how these differing social conditions were argued to produce the Medieval, as compared with Romantic and Modernist, self-conceptions. We then briefly describe the most significant mechanisms postulated to account for the change from the traditional to the modern society.

Traditional Social Condition. The traditional social condition had general characteristics of what Tönnies called *Gemeinschaft* (usually translated as community), which may be regarded as a schematic abstraction of Medieval society. People here are said to have lived in a tightly knit network of social relationships, which were generally bound by the necessity to produce agricultural goods, with people working cooperatively on cultivated land. People produced goods and services in a household, a village, or a town for their own consumption. Trading of these was limited by the boundary of the village and township, and therefore there were few direct material connections beyond them. The household, village, and township were regarded as one's material and psychological world, the community.

It was a world populated by "peasants," whose mode of production and consumption of goods and services was closely tied up with their family household and their land (see, e.g., Macfarlane, 1978). A majority of the population engaged in agriculture mainly to provide physical labor with some technological aids (e.g., plough, hoe), sometimes powered by large animals. What differentiates this type of society from hunter–gatherer societies is the presence of an external political organization (e.g., empire, kingdom). That is, these peasant households resided within a sovereign state, which held political and judicial power over particular households, villages, and towns. The external ruling hierarchy of governance therefore provided a socioeconomic framework within which some market trading could take place. Trading was done in marketplaces in towns, which acted as a center for collecting and distributing goods and services. In this limited network of exchanges, family households were units of production and consumption.

Members of these communities participated in their activities together (e.g., religious, ceremonial, agricultural–economic), and hence relationships among them were *multiplex*. That is, one would engage in multiple activities with another in the community, rather than an individual being connected to another only through a specific activity such as a hobby and a pastime (this is often called a *simplex* relationship). All community members performed activities that served their individual needs, including the production and consumption of food, clothing, and shelter. However, this was done together as a group, as a collective endeavor. Such patterns of activities made for a denser social network, which means that individuals in the network were more likely to have some social relationships among themselves or one's "friends" were likely to be "friends" with each other. The participation in communal activities as well as the fact of dense interpersonal connections enhanced the sense of community belonging.

Furthermore, these factors strengthened the social pressure for conformity, in both thought and action. Deviation from the norm of the community, the point of convergence, would be punished in some form (e.g., corporal punishment, confinement, ostracism), and sanctioned by repressive laws such as criminal laws (Durkheim). Or, because the circumstances of their lives were similar, people may have "naturally" thought, felt, and acted in a similar manner (Tönnies), and to use Durkheim's term, the collective consciousness and individual consciousness were largely coextensive. The symbolic content of people's activities was dominated by religion, and largely in the realm beyond discussion and individual control, and to this extent superhuman and transcendental. In other words, the legitimacy of a religious worldview was unquestioned, and uncontested. At the same time, the content of the self was said to be largely concrete, very much constrained by and tied to the concrete circumstances of the community in space and time.

Tönnies took the traditional social condition to be a collective expression of *natural will*, a "natural" expression of human volition, almost implying its origin in biological evolution. In contrast, in direct criticism of Tönnies's somewhat nostalgic characterization of traditional homeliness (Durkheim, 1889/1972, pp. 146–147), Durkheim called it *mechanical solidarity*, underlining the mechanical enforcement of the sameness within the collective. Despite the difference in evaluation, in Tönnies and Durkehim's views the ideal typical traditional society was homogeneous in thought and action. In its extreme, everyone thought the same, felt the same, and acted the same; all members of the community participated in most activities that served their biological, psychological, and socioeconomic needs, including the production and consumption of goods and services. The homogenizing force in this sociality would make for an unproblematic sense of belonging on the one hand, and the mechanical conformity on the other.

It is plausible that the Medieval self might emerge from this social condition. Provided that Christianity was in full force as an all-encompassing worldview, questions about one's selfhood, and meaning of life, could have been immediately answered. Being a serf or a king is justified as a station in life; one's salvation, the main objective in life, is linked to living in accordance with religious precepts. The fact of being a serf or a king, which contemporary social psychologists would regard as a social role, then would be understood as what one is; one's self would be largely coextensive with the social role one occupied in life. The Christian worldview was reinforced by the constant presence of the church in community life and the constant involvement of the community in not only religious but also other activities as a collective. This is not to say that individuals never contested the self-definitions that were available, or that governments never exploited them in the process of producing social order.

Modern Social Condition.   The modern social condition is characterized by heterogeneity and complexity. Tönnies called it *Gesellschaft* (translated as society or association). Various activities necessary for a person to survive, or *social functions* in Durkheim's term, are performed by different people, groups, and institutions. A division of labor (Durkheim) is a hallmark of this social condition. People, who perform only a subset of the totality of social functions, enter into a variety of exchange relationships with others to obtain goods and services for their consumption. In turn, goods and services are produced by industries, whose capital, labor, and technology draw on a wide range of sources. This is in contrast to traditional society, where a single social unit such as a family household engages in both the production and consumption of goods and services, but production and consumption are separated and situated in different social domains of activities, industry and family. Trade and exchange of goods and services are therefore an integral part of this social condition, without which its very existence is jeopardized. Furthermore, a network of exchange of goods and services is not necessarily confined to any particular sociopolitical unit or a community, but tends to extend across a number of such units.

Tönnies regarded this as a collective expression of *rational will*, human volition resulting from calculated means–ends analyses and maximization of one's profit. To him, it was a cognitively driven motivation, which was distinguished from the emotionally driven motivation that was natural will. He saw modern society as an artificial collection of goal-oriented separate individuals, who allow others to enter into their own sphere of activity only to the extent that those others are willing to give some equivalent goods and services for exchange. In sharp contrast, Durkheim regarded this type of social relationship as no less natural than that in the traditional society. He called the modern sociality *organic solidarity*, emphasizing the dynamic interdependence among people who perform social functions that are dependent on each other's performance of other relevant social functions. According to Durkheim, the necessity for cooperative collaboration facilitates the emergence of a nonmechanical, organic relationship among individuals.

At an extreme, this is a society populated by "traders" in a broad sense of the term (Tönnies). A majority of people exchange their labor (white collar or blue collar, intellectual or physical) for monetary rewards, which then act as a medium of exchange for other goods and services. Some of the monetary rewards may be used for capital investment, which may then finance the very industries that employ these people. The exchange of goods and services is done through contracts, and some principle of equivalence of exchanged commodities regulates the exchange. In addition, many goods and services are exchanged through a market mechanism, including labor, capital, information, and any other items insofar as there are others who are willing to enter into exchange relationships. The market mechanism tends to diversify the types of goods and services on offer, which then further enhances the heterogeneity of the society.

In this type of society, one tends to have simplex relationships. That is, a person tends to engage in one activity with another person, but not in many other activities. So one may exchange one type of good or service with another, but not other types. This is a correlate of the division of labor and specialization of social functions. When different people perform different social functions, they develop specialized expertises. When obtaining experts' services and their products, one would not be interested in other goods and services, nor in obtaining knowledge of their relationships with others. Furthermore, simplex relationships tend to make for more sparse social networks. One gets to know others through different activities, but there is no reason why those acquaintances should know each other or have any direct exchange relationships. Sparse social networks imply more limited pressure to conform to any overarching view, although there are expectations of conformity to the relevant norms of the specific exchange relationship. A consequence for self-concept and identity is that there are possibilities for multiple self-representations.

Durkheim maintained that this is nonetheless a type of solidarity. When there is a great deal of interdependence among those who perform interdependent social functions, there must emerge a spirit of collaboration and cooperation. Otherwise, a society cannot function as an organic whole, and would fall into anomie. To maintain the cooperative functioning among individuals in the society, those who do not cooperate would not be punished, but would be told to restore troubled interdependent relationships. Durkheim referred to restitutive laws such as civil codes and administrative laws. They ensure social order, but their more impersonal nature allows for greater flexibility and individual choice. Individual consciousness is no longer coextensive with collective consciousness, but is permitted to deviate from the latter. In short, the individuation of a person is seen as emergent from modern sociocultural conditions (see also Schooler, 1996).

It is interesting to note that Durkheim's model of modern sociality is congruent with both the Romanticist and Modernist views of self and identity. First of all, as a person engages in specialized social functions and a unique set of social roles, the person is seen to be quite different from others. The conception of the individual as a unique being is congruent with the Romanticist self (Simmel, 1950). Second, as people engage in exchanges of commodities in an increasingly wider geographical area that includes a number of different communities, a more abstract (less context-bound) conceptualization becomes necessary and desirable. When peoples of different cultural backgrounds are to communicate with each other, they can no longer rely on concrete shared realities, but must use more abstract concepts with which to reach a mutual understanding. The Modernist conception of the self as a rational autonomous agent is one such abstraction, which endows a universal quality to the individual.

As Giddens (1972) noted, Durkheim insisted that the emancipation of people from their mechanical solidarity, with the generation of a particular individual as a differentiated personality, was accompanied by what he called "the cult of the individual" as a kind of shared moral worldview that emphasizes human rights and capacities as a human universal in abstraction. This moral individualism that celebrates individuality was to replace the coercive collective consciousness dominated by religion as transcendental sources of truth and goodness. Paradoxically, moral individualism is nonetheless a shared collective ideal that provides a moral underpinning to the division of labor and organic solidarity. In psychology, however, individualism has often been regarded as an empirical truth, rather than a socially and historically constituted conception of the person.

Mechanisms of Sociocultural Change

Various of theories have been proposed to explain the transition from traditional to modern society. Some theories explained it in terms of macro-level socioeconomic processes, largely playing down the importance of symbolic processes. As we show, they typically employ two general classes of ideas, industrialization or more generally technological development, and capitalism. However, there exist other theories that accord a greater role to symbolic processes in the shaping of Western history and self. Although they acknowledge the significance of socioeconomic conditions, these theories typically argue that symbolically represented meanings shaped people's self-understandings, which in turn contributed to the historical changes in socioeconomic conditions in a significant way. We briefly examine these positions next.

Theories That Highlight Socioeconomic Processes. Generally two classes of ideas have been called upon to explain the process of modernization of the Western society. One class emphasizes industrialization, or more generally, technological development, as a major force behind this change. Spencer (1896), a clear example, took the basic principle of sociocultural evolution to be one of increasing complexity, and specialization of social functions. Spencer regarded the division of labor as a concomitant characteristic of industrial society. Lukes (1973a) suggested that, by modifying Spencerian social evolution, Durkheim nominated the increased density of human population especially in urban areas, and a resultant increased competition among individuals and groups, as a mechanism for increasing division of labor, and therefore an engine of sociocultural evolution. When individuals and groups that perform similar social functions vie with each other, some may find it more profitable to specialize in other functions. This then leads to greater division of labor and greater specialization of occupational groups.

The other class of theories emphasizes capitalism as a mechanism of sociocultural change from the traditional to the modern. As is well known, Marx (1867/1976) was the most significant theorist to formulate this thesis. In the thesis's classical form, the cumulation of sufficient wealth in a society enables the emergence of a class of people who have capital (i.e., private ownership of resources) to run large-scale industries and another class of people who do not. Those who have the capital employ those who do not and produce goods and services (i.e., commodities). Commodities are exchanged in markets. Those who do not have the capital exchange their labor in the labor market; that is, human resources become a commodity. The struggle between the haves and the have-nots necessarily accompanies the capitalist mode of production. Marx's central claim was that the cumulation of private wealth, and the capitalist mode of material production and exchange, is the engine of sociocultural transformation.

Marx's classical analysis of capitalism has been criticized on several grounds (e.g., Dahrendorf, 1959; Lipset, 1960). For instance, in recent times, ownership and management of industries, which Marx assumed to be performed by the same people, are now performed by different people. In typical Western European and North American companies, the owners of stocks do not manage the companies. In fact, those who are employed by companies can own the companies too (i.e., via the purchase of stocks). The division between owner/employer and labor/employee is blurred, and class struggle seems a distant cry of the past.

Nonetheless, Wallerstein's (1974) analysis of the capitalist world system recasts the capitalist mode of production as an engine of the transformation of traditional societies. According to him, the capitalist system is characterized by a division between the private ownership of resources, and the economic division of labor between the core and the periphery. Wealth is cumulated in the core, while the periphery provides material and human resources for capitalist production. What marks the capitalist world system apart from the previous agrarian empires is the use of economic power of the core over the periphery, rather than that of politico-military power. From the phase of merchant capitalism in the 16th and 17th century, through colonization of Americas, Africa, and Asia, and to the postcolonial era of the world today, the capitalist world system transformed the traditional agrarian society into the modern one. Although the capitalist world system divided the industrialist and working classes at its beginning, this structure was expanded to cover the globe to differentiate the affluent First World and the exploited Third World.

Theories That Highlight the Role of Symbolic Processes.   Although the capitalist industrialization models of sociocultural change from the traditional to the modern tend to describe the changes in sociocultural conditions at a macro level, some models paid closer attention to psychological mechanisms underlying the human action that carried through such sociocultural changes. In these theories, symbolically mediated self-conceptions play a constitutive role in the process of sociocultural change. According to these views, people's self-conceptions, which were influenced by the then prevalent conceptions of the person, in part brought about the sociocultural changes that transformed the traditional condition into the modern social condition.

Weber's (1958) theory of capitalism is a case in point. He sought motivational underpinnings for capitalist material production in the Protestant ethic, which was closely associated with the emergence of the Enlightenment self. According to Protestant, especially Calvinist, doctrine, salvation is predetermined and a person's personal deeds cannot influence whether he or she is saved. Nevertheless, a person's material success in this world is an indication of whether he or she may have been preselected for salvation . It then behooves one to find one's calling, the occupation given by God, and to work hard in one's occupational role. Weber argued that when this Protestant ethic of ascetic diligence lost its otherworld significance and was secularized through the Reformation and the Enlightenment, the ascetic lifestyle for worldly success became morally sanctioned in and of itself. This is the spirit of capitalism, according to which hard work is morally sanctioned for both capitalists and workers. Weber argued that the ethic of hard work then motivated both capitalists' and workers' activities of production.

Nevertheless, as Campbell (1987) noted, the division of labor that is so much a characteristic of modern capitalist industrial society, and the expansion of production and consumption that goes with it, cannot be fully explained by the ethos of work and production alone. The other side of production, that is, consumption, needs to be explained as well. According to Campbell, a strand of Protestantism called Pietism gave rise to Romanticism, whose moral commitment lay in the passionate longing for the absolute ideal. In parallel with the development of the spirit of capitalism, he argued that the spirit of consumerism emerged from this Romantic ethic. Campbell suggests that the characteristic of modern consumerism is its insatiable longing for novel products, and continuous creation of desire. In his analysis, the cyclical process of creation of desire follows the following four steps: imagining using or obtaining the object of desire, actually using or obtaining it, subsequently recognizing a discrepancy between the imagined ideal and the reality of the object of desire, and experiencing a lack of satisfaction. This last step then leads on to a further imagining of another object of desire, and so on ad infinitum. Campbell suggested that it was this spirit of consumerism that complemented the spirit of capitalism.

According to these analyses of capitalist industrialization, individuals who populated the industrializing Western Europe were influenced by the historically constituted meaning systems such as Protestantism and Pietism, and their more general patterns such as the Enlightenment and Romanticism. In these analyses, people were assumed to construct their own self-conceptions in line with the prevailing conceptions of the person, and these symbolically mediated self-conceptions are said to have contributed to the production of the modern industrial society. The expansion of consumption prepared for enhanced productivity; the growth of production catered to greater desire. According to this view, the Enlightenment–Modernist and the Romanticist conceptions of the self then fueled the development of the first capitalist industrial society in 18th-century England.

The historical shift in self-conception from the Medieval self to the Enlightenment–Modernist and Romanticist selves appears to have occurred hand in hand with the change in economic and sociocultural conditions from traditional to modern sociality. The Medieval self-conception is congruent with the traditional social condition, whereas the individualistic Modernist–Romanticist conceptions seem coherent with the modern social condition of increasing division of labor and expanding capitalist production and consumption. Although some theories emphasize evolutionary changes of sociocultural conditions, there exists a perspective that allocates a significant causal role to psychological processes motivated by prevalent self-conceptions at the time. Once self-conceptions that provide moral and motivational underpinnings and also suitable sociocultural conditions are present, they would form a positive feedback loop that pushed each other along the path toward the modernization of England originally and elsewhere in Continental Europe and North America.

More recently, some sociologists (e.g., O'Malley, 1996; Rose, 1996) have argued that, at least in the industrialized Western societies today, we are in a "neo-liberal" sociocultural condition. In this political environment, the responsible, self-governing and self-regulating individual fits well with an approach to government that stresses innovation and enterprise, and espouses minimal interference with its citizens. Freedom of choice is not only a statement of the autonomy of the individual, but also a political doctrine. The autonomous individual retains elements of the 19th-century person, especially its emphasis on autonomy and self-control. However, the normative environment surrounding the neo-liberal person is one that stresses self-fulfillment rather than denial (as in the Protestant ethic of asceticism), and individual responsibility for outcomes that might once have been the domain of God, the Church, or the state.

A key point in this form of analysis is that new ways of thinking about individuals regularly arise through technological and social inventions; these are taken up by various authorities and used to govern people, but they are also taken up by individuals to govern and to imagine themselves. An extensive example of this is provided by Rose's (1996) account of how psychology emerged as an individualizing technology in the neo-liberal sociocultural environment and became linked with other political and social events. In a sense, Rose argued, psychologists are responsible for the "invention" of this form of the self, which then became the subject of psychological measurement and intervention. Further, people have adopted many of the images and metaphors produced by psychologists, as well as techniques of self-improvement and self-cure. Indeed, the image of self-regulating autonomous individual portrayed in the current social psychology of self and identity (see Foddy & Kashima, chap. 1, this volume) strongly reminds us of the neo-liberal self. Might it be a coincidence that social psychology "discovered" the neo-liberal self, or is it contributing to or influenced by the current symbolic sociocultural milieu?

Is the Model of Self-Conceptions and Sociocultural Change Universally Applicable?

The models of sociocultural change and self-conceptions have been developed mainly on the basis of the history of England and continental Europe, as well as North America. Are they then applicable to the understanding of transformations of the sociocultural conditions and self-conceptions elsewhere? Some sociological theorists have taken industrialization to be a universal mechanism that increases the wealth of a society and its general affluence everywhere. For instance, Kerr, Dunlop, Harbison, and Myers (1960) regarded this process to be a universal march toward the industrial society, a convergence of sociocultural conditions because of what they called "the internal logic" of industrialization. A related argument (Schooler, 1996, 1998) is that the increasing environmental complexity and opportunities for self-directed work brought about by economic development lead to growth in individualism. As its psychological correlates, individual modernity as postulated by Inkeles and Smith (1974) would imply that the psychological makeup would modernize as the universal process of industrialization continues.

Other theorists (e.g., Bendix, 1964) postulated that the trajectory and final form of industrialization of a particular society would depend on its culture and tradition, although liberal democracy has often been considered to be a necessary political correlate of the process. To the extent that liberal democracy implies an individualist conception of the person equipped with the capacity for rational calculation of self-interest (Lukes, 1973b), these theories too seem to imply a convergence of self-conceptions to a version of the Enlightenment–Modernist self.

In personality and social psychology as well, Triandis (1989) postulated that as a society becomes more complex and affluent, it tends to become more individualistic, and therefore individualist self-conceptions would become more prevalent and more accessible. If capitalist industrialization involves a division of labor as Durkheim emphasized (Triandis suggested that the number of occupational groups can be used to measure cultural complexity), and if industrialization tends to bring about greater affluence in society, Triandis's theory implies that individualist self-conceptions should become more prevalent. This argument is similar to that proposed by Schooler (1994) and others, who describe an inexorable effect of social structural change on individual self-conceptions. These theories are intended to describe processes of the development of self-conception over time at a more abstract level than the history of Western self-conceptions described before. The implication is that self-conceptions around the world will converge to a more individualist one if all societies industrialize.

Nevertheless, it is premature to suggest that worldwide industrialization necessarily leads to a convergence of self-conceptions to an individualist one around the globe. First of all, the functionalist argument that a person's psychological makeup converges to a single type under the same socioeconomic conditions, and therefore that self-conceptions converge as a result of industrialization, underestimates the range of possibilities that afford comparable levels of functioning under the same condition. This objection is in line with the argument of equifinality (Gould & Lewontin, 1979; Heider, 1958; Hempel, 1966), according to which the same objective can be attained by a variety of different courses of action. Similar levels of adaptation to industrial socioeconomic conditions can be obtained by a variety of psychological mechanisms. If self-conceptions constitute an aspect of psychological adaptations to the environment, they can be quite variable even if the capitalist industrial society is assumed to produce similar socioeconomic conditions. Even the individualistic self can take a range of forms.

Second, it is possible that the current model of a capitalist industrial society is peculiarly English, one that may or may not be similar to other indigenous sociocultural conditions in other parts of the world. In a monograph examining the sociocultural condition of the 13th-century England, Macfarlane (1978) noted this:

> There were already a developed market and mobility of labour, land was treated as a commodity and full private ownership was established, there was very considerable geographical and social mobility, a complete distinction between farm and family existed, and rational accounting and the profit motive were widespread. . . . We could describe thirteenth century England as a capitalist-market economy without factories. (pp. 195–196)

He contended that this sociocultural pattern was not found anywhere in Eastern Europe, Russia, or Asia, and was even different from the 13th-century Celtic or continental Western European sociocultural systems. As Macfarlane noted, this implies that individualist conceptions of the person prevalent in the modern industrial society may have derived from indigenous cultural ideas and practices of preindustrial England in the 13th century or earlier.

There are some contemporary data that may be interpreted as supporting his thesis. Hofstede (1980, p. 232) reported that the country score of his individualism index was well predicted by 1970 per capita gross national product (GNP) of each country using linear multiple regression ($r = .82$), pointing to the possibility that industrialization leads to individualism. What is informative is the list of the countries that deviated from this regression prediction. Seven countries more individualistic than expected included Australia, South Africa, New Zealand, Ireland, Great Britain, India, and Italy. Note that with the exception of Italy, all countries are either English-speaking countries or countries that were strongly influenced by English culture either by proximity or by colonial rule. None of the seven countries that were less individualistic than expected included countries that were strongly influenced by English culture: Yugoslavia, Venezuela, Chile, Portugal, Sweden, Japan, and Germany. In line with this, Kashima (1998) reported that Englishness is a reliable predictor of Hofstede's individualism index even when per capita GNP is controlled for; being an English-speaking country gives a large 24-point increase in Hofstede's individualism index.

Third, the history of Japanese industrialization provides a counterpoint to the universal convergence hypothesis. In Japanese manufacturing industries, the division of labor, postulated by Durkheim to drive the process of modernization, did occur; however, specialized activities of industrial production, which Durkheim assumed would be assigned to individuals, were assigned not to individuals but to work groups. Kashima and Callan (1994) argued that Japanese companies often used work groups as a functional unit in industrial settings. A work group was typically given a clear set of objectives, whereas individual workers' job descriptions were relatively unclear in Japanese companies when compared to their U.S. counterparts (e.g., Clark, 1979; Lincoln, Hanada, & McBride, 1986; Lincoln & Kalleberg, 1990).

In fact, both the individualist self-conceptions of Western Europe and North America and the contemporary Japanese organizational behavior could be viewed as different forms of cultural adaptation to the necessity of the modern capitalist industrial society (but see Schooler, 1998, for a contrasting point of view). Divisions of labor and specialization of industrial functions may indeed be a necessity. In England, those specialized functions were performed by individuals, who were after all culturally available functional units, as Macfarlane pointed out. In Japan, it may have been the case that these specialized functions were performed by work groups. Kashima and Callan argued that *ie* households were functional units that were available in the 19th century Japan. *Ie* is a family unit with a strong connotation of living and working together. Japanese organizations may have been structured using this unit as a metaphor. At the height of Japanese industrialization in the late 20th century, Japanese companies continued to use work groups as functional units in their organizational structure. Whether these characteristics of Japanese industry will persist in the 21st century is a matter that requires future investigation. Nonetheless, the sustaining causal effect of continuing industrialization in the 21st century on the individualist self-conceptions of the Modernist or the Romanticist form even in Western Europe and North America is a matter of considerable debate, as we discuss in the next section.

WHITHER SELF AND IDENTITY?

On its own logic, the argument that social and economic conditions shape the form and content of self-conceptualizations implies that further change in the former should produce ongoing changes in the latter. Despite the picture already painted of the move to capitalism and global economies, there are further major developments that may turn out to be significant. We consider two technological innovations as examples. In the first, we concentrate on the effect of computer technology on patterns of interaction, and in the second, on the way in which new genetic technology creates "mutations" in the ways people imagine or conceive of themselves.

The Emergence of Cyberspace.   Among technological innovations, the development of electronic communication and the interactions it provides must be regarded as one of the most significant. In less than two decades, the World Wide Web has become part of the everyday life of the majority of people in Western countries, and is rapidly becoming available globally. Commentators declare it to be bigger than the industrial revolution, the advent of the printing press, even the invention of the wheel (Smith & Kollock, 1999). However, many researchers argue that the emergence of virtual communities, or "cyberspace," can be analyzed as a variation on, or an extension of, prior social changes that altered the distribution of people and resources. The industrial revolution moved large populations from traditional communities to new communities, where they had opportunities for interaction with a wider range of people, and experienced greater anonymity. We noted earlier that this put more emphasis on individuals' responsibility for their own fates, and changed the way people thought about their relationships with others. Similarly, the Internet has altered the number and type of contacts one can have, has increased the opportunity for both anonymous and multiple identities, and has created new forms of commerce (Kollock & Smith, 1996). Will this make any difference to the way that people think of themselves and their relations with others? Are we looking at another fundamental transformation of the self-concept?

In the introduction of any innovation, there are usually prophets of doom as well as euphoric advocates of a brave new world. This is true of the developments in electronic communication and commerce, and was true of earlier innovations such as electricity, the telephone, and so on. Putting aside the more emotive responses, it is possible to detect two main assessments of the potential effects of the Web on self, identity and community. One, represented by McKenna and Bargh (2000), is that the Web is just another medium in which people may interact. It has the potential to produce new opportunities for the construction of selves unencumbered by the details of one's physical being and economic position. If this is so, these developments may signal a major change in concepts of identity, if in fact the sorts of people one may meet and exchange goods and services with are now a matter of choice. In this view, people's impressions of others (and self) will be less affected by irrelevant biasing features such as physical appearance, socioeconomic status, ethnicity, and so on, and there will be more opportunity to control the nature of interaction with others. The Internet is also viewed as a means by which large-scale cooperation among distant individuals can take place, resulting in greater ease of production of public goods, and the building of communities of people with shared interests (Kollock, 1999; Kollock & Smith, 1999). Some see this as an opportunity to overcome the inequality of opportunity that characterizes capitalist societies, with corresponding implications for the development of identities.

Against this optimistic interpretation is the claim that this technological change will accelerate the alienation of people from one another, leading to a society in which people are disembodied and isolated (McKenna & Bargh, 2000). There is also a concern that, because the Web represents a new and unstructured environment, people will deal with its uncertainty by reproducing simplistic and repressive social institutions. Many authors have documented the tendency for controllers of web sites (chatrooms as well as more elaborated virtual worlds) to create elaborate systems of social control that closely resemble existing, and perhaps more authoritarian, systems (e.g., Smith & Kollock, 1999; Suler, 1997). Thus, rather than liberating individuals to realize their "true selves" freed of historical prejudices, the virtual world of the Internet may simply spread existing forms of control and their accompanying stereotypes more quickly over a wider domain.

Donath (1999) noted that the technology of the Internet, built initially for the exchange of scientific data among academics, has produced a range of unexpected and unintended consequences for the establishment of identity. One is the creation of a virtual or symbolic world, in which all the usual processes of social bonding, communication, influence, control, and so on continue. Although the new medium provides unprecedented choice of the identity, a major point of discussion in scholarly papers, as well as on the Web, is authenticity of the self and the possibility of deception (e.g., Donath, 1999; McKenna & Bargh, 2000). In many web sites, it is completely acceptable to build "virtual" identities, so that the meaning of the "true" self has altered. This concern recalls the sociocultural condition of the post–Industrial Revolution era, in which people's "true" identities (whether a "real" nobility or not) became an issue. Nevertheless, there appear to be strong demands for consistency within an identity, and for orderly behavior. Suler (1997) asserted: "No one wants to be completely anonymous. No one wants to be totally invisible, with no name or identity or presence or interpersonal impact at all. Everyone wants . . . others to acknowledge and react to some aspect of their identity." Thus, despite the seemingly total decontextualization of individuals online, some issues such as the social realization of the self seem to remain.

Perhaps Gergen (1991) has made the most vocal case for a dramatic emergence of a new form of self and identity due to these technological developments. He argued that these sociotechnological conditions lead to the production of the Postmodern self, which departs significantly from both the Romanticist and Modernist selves. The Romanticist and Modernist conceptions of the person, despite their differences, have a significant commonality. First, both regard the human individual as an autonomous agent. The difference lies in what is taken to be the desired goal. The Romantic self seeks for the ideal self, and its Modernist counterpart, happiness and worldly success. Second, both the Romantic and Modernist conceptions locate the "true" self as existing internal to the person. This essence inside the person is the source of creativity and emotionality in the case of the Romantic self, but an instantiation of universal human rationality in the Modernist self.

Nevertheless, the array of technologies available now (e.g., e-mail, Internet) allows us to be in communication with others in all corners of the world. These, which Gergen calls technologies of social saturation, provide us with a level of social connectedness unprecedented in human history. According to Gergen's analysis, as an individual forms a greater number of relationships with others, it becomes increasingly more difficult to experience the unified essential self that is supposed to exist inside each person. Gergen also argued that the concept of "truth" that presupposes the existence of a single objective reality is increasingly questioned in contemporary academic circles. With the concept of truth in doubt, the presupposition of the true essentialist self was brought into question as well. In combination, the conception of the self as a unified individual agent became both experientially and conceptually untenable. In response to this contemporary social situation, Gergen argued that a new form of self-conception emerged, which may be called Postmodern. The Postmodern self is nonindividualist, but relational, almost like a terminal connected with others through a number of communication networks. It is also nonessentialist in that the self is not regarded as a unified entity defined by the presence of some essence such as emotionality or rationality, but as a nexus of relationships (see also Hall & Du Gay, 1996).

As Smith (1994) credited, Gergen's analysis of the contemporary experience of the increasingly connected world, and of its potential threat to the unified, integral self of the Romanticist or Modernist vein, aptly captures the current sociocultural condition of the industrialized part of the world. However, Smith also criticized Gergen's characterization of the current status of the truth concept in academia for overestimating the prevalence of Postmodern discourse. Further, Rose (1996, p. 177) noted that Gergen's own analysis is itself imbued with a view of the individual as a privileged source of self-narratives, "that comforting 'I' of humanist philosophy, . . . with all the attached assumptions concerning singularity and cumlativeness in the lived time of consciousness."

Furthermore, it has been debated whether Gergen's technologies of social saturation, and the resultant expansion of social relatedness, have ushered in a new sociocultural condition that deserves the label of *Post-*

modern. For instance, Giddens (1991) labeled the current sociocultural condition *high modernity*, implying that the current sociocultural circumstance is still Modern. According to Giddens, one of the characteristics of modernity is the separation of time and space. In traditional society, most forms of social relationships were localized in a particular place, the community; in contrast, in Modern society, social relationships span a space that encompasses a number of localities, and the immediacy of communication transcends the confines of the here and now in connecting spatially distant relationships. Indeed, this type of social relationship was characterized by both Durkheim and Tönnies as a feature of Modern society, although they would not have foreseen the current degree of immediate connectivity among people via such electronic media as e-mail and the Internet. If Giddens's argument is taken seriously, we are still in the Modern society. What Gergen called the Postmodern self may indeed be a final shape that the Modernist self has taken.

It will no doubt take some time for a clear picture to emerge as to whether developments in electronic media and communications have produced a major change in how people conceive of themselves, and how they relate to others. The relevant point is that social psychologists may learn from the history of the present as well as from the history of the past. Changes in technology bring about changes in the distribution of social networks and resources, and in the identities that people have access to. This most recent technological change is one that promises to be important to social psychologists as a place to test theories about the development and maintenance of identity and self.

The Development of Genetic Technologies.   According to Novas and Rose (2000), unanticipated events can precipitate the emergence of new identities (see also Howard, 2000), and these may in turn force a rethinking of our more general conception of the self. Their case example deals with the way in which developments in genetic research and technology have contributed to a move to a more embodied or "corporeal" view of the self. With advances in genetics, it is now possible to ascertain a person's genetic risk for a variety of disorders such as fragile X, Huntington's disease, and others. Novas and Rose argued that these developments do not herald a return to a fatalistic view that one is helpless in the face of biological determinism, but rather, that the neo-liberal person starts to think of how he or she can plan or arrange life to take various biological risks into account. People can seek genetic counseling as well as genetic information, to assist their decisions about whether to marry, to have children, and other self-defining actions. Presumably we are not too far from being able to choose to alter the genetic structure, if not of ourselves, of our offspring.

What will be the consequences of these developments? On the one hand, they create new ways of thinking about the self, and new opportunities as well as obligations for the person. On the other, they also create the concomitant possibility of genetic discrimination: Should you hire a person with a high probability of a debilitating disease? Should you insure that person? Should people be prevented from having children who may be a burden to the state? Further down the track, should we discriminate against people who refuse to intervene genetically to perfect their off-spring? These developments in turn create new categories of people, who may adopt an identity defined by the category (e.g., AIDS sufferers).

The analysis of the type just carried out can be repeated for a range of technological developments—drug therapies of various sorts; psychological tests that predict risk for a range of disorders and potentials; brain scans that identify abnormalities. In more general terms, these create the possibility of a major change in cultural metaphors of the self, which in turn will be modified as some people improve on them and others resist them. The idea that this constitutes change is more obvious if we contrast the genetically malleable persons in charge of their own fates, with the members of traditional society whose fate was believed to be in the hands of God. However, the technological developments do not in themselves explain the changes; these are interpreted through the symbolic resources provided by the existing social and cultural context. Gene technology in traditional religious society in the middle ages might have produced different results, as it might, say, in a country where the locus of cause and responsibility lies more with the group than with the individual. And although the trend to see the individual in terms of his or her physical and molecular makeup seems in contrast to the creation of a nonphysical self in cyberspace, these two share a similar ethos of being mechanisms by which the responsible and self-actualizing person can craft an identity.

CONCLUDING COMMENTS

The current view of history and self generally accepted in social psychology suggests that self-conceptions in Western Europe and North America have undergone significant changes over time as traditional societies changed into modern ones. According to the accepted view, self-conceptions changed from the kind embedded in a group (e.g., family, community) to another that emphasizes individuality, from a collectivist conception to an individualist one. The currently accepted conception of the self in social psychology, which Foddy and Kashima (chap. 1, this volume) outlined as the social cognitive self, coincides in many ways with the "neo-liberal" self, which regards the self as a self-regulating and responsible person. It departs in many ways from how the self has been conceptualized in the past, and yet it may be seen as a product of the Western socio-historical tradition.

To trace historical changes of self and identity, one needs a conceptual framework in which to conduct transhistorical comparisons. Thus, to map the concomitant changes in social structure and available conceptualizations of self and identity, one needs to have a set of variables to characterize each of these. Historical and sociological analyses of changes to social structure in the West refer to changes in technology and modes of production, and the nature of work. The changing distribution of people, the number and types of relations available, and the distribution of resources are all abstract dimensions along which societies can be compared transhistorically. Can the same be said for the self-concept? At one level, yes. Using the existing literature, we have identified the dimensions on which historical variation occurs, including those of degree and locus of autonomy and responsibility, abstraction or decontextualization, and uniqueness. Although self-conceptualizations may differ in the degree of independence, contextualization, uniqueness, and multiplicity/singularity, these concepts nevertheless provide a multidimensional framework for comparison. We have attempted to show how these dimensions of self can be related to features of social structure.

However, it should be kept in mind that these dimensions and the framework for comparison have been developed in order to compare the current Western sociocultural conditions to those of the past, to gain an understanding about the contemporary situation of self and identity. The same framework may or may not be useful for an inquiry with other analytical purposes. A careful analysis is required for comparing self-conceptions across different sociocultural traditions, for instance. We have offered several reasons for this caution. In general, certain socioeconomic conditions may enable and constrain people's symbolic activities to some extent, and some forms of self-conceptions may turn out to be more or less adaptive. Nonetheless, to argue that only certain self-conceptions are adaptive under given socioeconomic conditions, is to commit a fallacy of adaptationism, a disregard of the principle of equifinality, the possibility that there may be multiple ways to attain a similar end result. More specifically, there does exist a viewpoint that Western capitalist industrialization is a historical development that is peculiar to English sociocultural conditions, and there may be a different mode of symbolic solution to the problem of social order in the contemporary industrial society.

Recent technological developments have also presented a number of possibilities and constraints for symbolic activities associated with self and identity. On the one hand, the developments in information technology have afforded people a greater flexibility in symbolically constructing themselves. Yet a number of procedures have been instituted to ensure trust and personal responsibilities in cyberspace. On the other hand, biological and medical technologies (especially genetic technologies), although providing people with possibilities of medically reconstituting themselves and genetically engineering their offspring, may have had an effect of generating other societal concerns about discrimination and other forms of inequality, and may further influence how we understand ourselves as an embodied being. These new technologies may work within the symbolic environment of the neo-liberal, self-regulating individual. Although technologies and socioeconomic conditions do provide the environment with which people are required to cope, their coping with and adaptation to the environment may indeed be mediated by their symbolic activities. In so doing, symbolically constituted self-conceptions may participate in the construction of historical processes.

REFERENCES

Baumeister, R. F. (1986). *Identity: Cultural change and the struggle for self.* New York: Oxford University Press.

Baumeister, R. F. (1987). How the self became a problem: A psychological review of historical research. *Journal of Personality and Social Psychology, 52,* 163–176.

Baumeister, R. F. (1997). The self and society: Changes, problems, and opportunities. In R. D. Ashmore & L. Jussim (Eds.), *Self and identity: Fundamental issues* (pp. 191–217). New York: Oxford University Press.

Bendix, R. (1964). *Nation-building and citizenship.* New York: Wiley. [Also see this as a critique of the Kerr et al. convergence theory.]

Campbell, C. (1987). *The Romantic ethic and the spirit of modern consumerism.* Oxford, UK: Blackwell.

Clark, R. (1979). *The Japanese company.* New Haven, CT: Yale University Press.

Cushman, P. (1990). Why the self is empty: Towards a historically situated psychology. *American Psychologist, 45,* 599–611.

Cushman, P. (1995). *Constructing the self, constructing America.* Reading, MA: Addison-Wesley.

Dahrendorf, R. (1959). *Class and class conflict in industrial society.* Stanford, CA: Stanford University Press.

Danziger, K. (1990). *Constructing the subject: Historical origins of psychological research.* Cambridge, UK: Cambridge University Press.

Danziger, K. (1997). The historical formation of selves. In R. D. Ashmore & L. Jussim (Eds.), *Self and identity: Fundamental issues* (pp. 137–159). New York: Oxford University Press.

Donath, J. (1999). Identity and deception. In M. A. Smith, & P. Kollock (Eds.), *Communities in cyberspace* (pp. 29–59). London: Routledge.

Durkheim, E. (1964). *The division of labor in society* (G. Simpson, Trans.). New York: Free Press. (Original work published 1893)

Durkheim, E. (1972). Review of Tonnies: Gemeinschaft und Gesellschaft. In A. Giddens (Ed., Trans.), *Emile Durkheim: Selected writings* (pp. 146–147). Cambridge, UK: Cambridge University Press. (Original work published 1889)

Gergen, K. J. (1991). *The saturated self.* New York: Basic Books.

Giddens, A. (1972). Introduction: Durkheim's writings in sociology and social philosophy. In A. Giddens (Ed.), *Emile Durkheim: Selected writings* (pp. 1–50). Cambridge, UK: Cambridge University Press.

Giddens, A. (1991). *Modernity and self-identity.* Stanford, CA: Stanford University Press.

Gould, S. J., & Lewontin, R. (1979). The spandrels of San Marco and the Panglossian paradigm: A critique of the adaptationist programme. *Proceedings of the Royal Society, B205,* 581–598.

Hacking, I. (1986). Making up people. In T. C. Heller, M. Sosna, & D. E. Wellbery (Eds.), *Reconstructing individualism: Autonomy, individuality and the self in Western thought* (pp. 222–236). Stanford, CA: Stanford University Press.

Hall, S., & Du Gay, P. (1996). *Questions of cultural identity.* London: Sage.

Heider, F. (1958). *The psychology of interpersonal relations.* New York: Wiley.

Hempel, C. G. (1966). *Philosophy of natural science.* Englewood Cliffs, NJ: Prentice Hall.

Hofstede, G. (1980). *Culture's consequences.* Beverly Hills, CA: Sage.

Howard, J. A. (2000). Social psychology of identities. *Annual Review of Sociology, 26,* 367–93.

Iukeles, A., & Smith, D. H. (1974). *Becoming modern: Individual changes in six developing countries.* Cambridge, MA: Harvard University Press.

Kashima, Y. (1998, January). *Relativizing individualism, or Hofstede's individualism as a measure of Englishness.* Paper presented at the Emerging Themes in Psychology Conference, Osmania, India.

Kashima, Y., & Callan, V. (1994). The Japanese work group. In H. C. Triandis, M. D. Dunnette, & L. M. Hough (Eds.), *Handbook of industrial/organizational psychology* (Vol. 4, pp. 610–646). Palo Alto, CA: Consulting Psychologists Press.

Kerr, C., Dunlop, J. T., Harbison, F. H., & Myers, C. A. (1960). *Industrialism and industrial man.* Hammondsworth, UK: Penguin.

Kollock, P. (1999). The production of trust in online markets. *Advances in Group Processes, 16,* 99–123.

Kollock, P., & Smith, M. (1996). Managing the virtual commons: Cooperation and conflict in computer communities. In S. Herring (Ed.), *Computer-mediated communication* (pp. 109–128). Amsterdam: John Benjamins.

Kollock, P., & Smith, M. A. (1999). Communities in cyberspace. In M. A. Smith & P. Kollock (Eds.), *Communities in cyberspace* (pp. 4–25). London: Routledge.

Lincoln, J. R., Hanada, M., & McBride, K. (1986). Organizational structures in Japanese and U.S. manufacturing. *Admnistrative Science Quarterly, 26,* 93–115.

Lincoln, J. R., & Kalleberg, A. L. (1990). *Culture, control, and commitment.* Cambridge, UK: Cambridge University Press.

Lipset, S. M. (1960). *Political man.* New York: Doubleday.

Lukes, S. (1973a). *Emile Durkheim: His life and work.* Stanford, CA: Stanford University Press.

Lukes, S. (1973b). *Individualism.* Oxford, UK: Blackwell.

Macfarlane, A. (1978). *The origins of English individualism: The family, property and social transformation.* Oxford, UK: Blackwell.

Marx, K. (1867/1976). *Capital. Volume 1.* (E. Mandel, Ed.). Hammondsworth, UK: Penguin.

McKenna, K. Y. A., & Bargh, J. A. (2000). Plan 9 from cyberspace: The implications of the internet for personality and social psychology. *Personality and Social Psychology Review, 4,* 57–75.

Novas, C., & Rose, N. (2000). Genetic risk and the birth of the somatic individual. *Economy and Society, 29,* 485–513.

O'Malley, P. T. (1996). Risk and responsibility. In A. Barry & N. Rose (Eds.), *Foucault and political reason* (pp. 189–208). London: UCL Press.

O'Malley, P. T. (1999). Imagining insurance: Risk, thrift and industrial life insurance. *Connecticut Insurance Law Journal, 5,* 675–705.

Rose, N. (1996). *Inventing ourselves: Psychology, power, and personhood*. Cambridge: Cambridge University Press.

Schooler, C. (1994). A working conceptualization of social structure: Mertonian roots and psychological and sociocultural relationships. *Social Psychology Quarterly, 57*, 262–273.

Schooler, C. (1996). Cultural and social structural explanations of cross-national psychological differences. *Annual Review of Sociology, 22*, 323–349.

Schooler, C. (1998). History, social stucture and individualism: A cross-cultural perspective on Japan. *International Journal of Comparative Sociology, 1998*, 32–51.

Simmel, G. (1950). *The sociology of Georg Simmel* (K. H. Wolff, Ed., Trans.). New York: Free Press.

Smith, M. A. & Kollock, P. (Eds.). (1999). *Communities in cyberspace*. London: Routledge.

Smith, M. B. (1978). Perspectives on selfhood. *American Psychologist, 33*, 1053–1063.

Smith, M. B. (1994). Selfhood at risk: Postmodern perils and the perils of postmodernism. *American Psychologist, 49*, 405–411.

Spencer, H. (1896). *The principles of sociology*. London.

Suler, J. (1997). *The bad boys of cyberspace: Deviant behaior in online mutimedia communities and strategies for managing it* [Online]. Available: http://www.rider.edu/users/suler/psycyber/badboys.html

Taylor, C. (1989). *Sources of the self*. Cambridge, MA: Harvard University Press.

Tönnies, F. (1955). *Community and association* (C. P. Loomis, Trans.). London, UK: Routledge & Kegan Paul. (Original work published 1887)

Triandis, H. C. (1989). The self and social behavior in differing cultural contexts. *Psychological Review, 96*, 506–520.

Trilling, L. (1971). *Sincerity and authenticity*. Cambridge, MA: Harvard University Press.

Wallerstein, I. (1974). *The modern world system* (Vols. 1–3). New York: Academic Press.

Weber, M. (1958). *The Protestant ethic and the spirit of capitalism* (T. Parsons, Trans.). New York: Scribner. (Original work published 1904–1905)

Chapter 9

Culture and Self:
A Cultural Dynamical Analysis

Yoshihisa Kashima
University of Melbourne

Culture is a concept that has been out in the cold for quite some time in psychology. Despite strong interests of its founding fathers (e.g., Wundt's Völkerpsychologie, Bartlett's cultural psychology), much of the 20th-century academic psychology shunned the concept of culture. Perhaps it is not too surprising given that even the concept of meaning, and with it the concept of culture, was largely bypassed in psychology. Most notably, behaviorism banned the concept of thought and meaning from academic psychological discourse. Its epistemological counterpart, logical positivism, too narrowly defined the concept of meaning as verifiability; unverifiable concepts (these would include concepts like liberty, equality, and fraternity) were rendered meaningless. The 1960s cognitive revolution was to bring human meanings back into psychology (Bruner, 1990). But it was more than a quarter century later that psychology in general and social psychology in particular began to embrace the concept of meaning and culture as central to the definition of human mind.

It is intriguing to note that the entry point for the culture concept in contemporary social psychology was "self" (Markus & Kitayama, 1991; Triandis, 1989), that is, a term with some of the richest meaning of all psychological phenomena. As Smith (1991; also see chap. 10, this volume) noted some time ago, a person's experience of him- or herself, or selfhood, is not exhausted by publicly observable aspects of the person. In other words, unlike many other objects and events in the world, it is impossible to define oneself by ostensive definition, by pointing. This state of affairs makes it inevitable that selfhood can only be understood within a web of meaningful concepts, using a metaphor or a story, or what may be loosely called a theory (e.g., Epstein, 1973), without a requirement that it be of a formal scientific kind. From this perspective, culture becomes a central source of the metaphors and narratives in which self-conceptions are embedded (see Bruner, 1990; Smith, 1991). When conceptualized as a repository of symbolically coded meanings to which people in the present and past have contributed, and which are publicly available, culture can be thought of as a pool from which various self-conceptions can be drawn and used for private consumption. It becomes a rich symbolic resource for self-understanding.

As Foddy and Kashima (chap. 1, this volume) noted, social psychology adopted a metaphor of the von Neumann-type serial computer. The central processing unit (CPU) provided a unique and powerful metaphor for the social cognitive self. Although it is still a useful model for investigating some phenomena and conceptualizing some issues, it fails to take note of two significant insights that the current cultural perspective presents. First, the central processing unit is an invariant structure that transcends the symbols that it processes. This metaphor precludes the possibility that culture affects human psychology so deeply that it may transform the very mind that enabled humans to have the kind of culture we do. Second, the central processing unit is itself a cultural metaphor, which may have become prevalent at a particular point of time and space. The social cognitive self constitutes one part of the symbolic resource that is human culture.

In this chapter there are two major objectives. First of all, I develop a metatheoretical argument about the importance of *cultural dynamics*. By cultural dynamics, I mean the stability and change of culture over time. I argue that this requires an attempt to integrate two different conceptualizations of culture. Second, I give an illustrative example about how an approach that takes cultural dynamics seriously may shed new light on the interplay between culture and self. This cultural dynamical analysis of culture and self will be shown to point to the utility of considering the social embeddedness of the social cognitive self and the importance of examining seriously the symbolic meaning of self-conceptualizations.

CULTURAL DYNAMICS

In the contemporary literature on culture and mind, there are two general images of culture (see Kashima, 2000). One image regards culture as a relatively enduring *system* of meaning, a structured set of symbolic meanings that are shared by a group of people. It is seen as a repository of meanings that provide an organization to people's shared experiences. Examples of this image come from a number of cross-cultural researchers such as

Triandis (1972, 1994) in psychology and Geertz (1973) in anthropology. Another image presents culture as a *process* of meaning making, a stream of symbolically mediated activities by concrete individuals in particular contexts. This latter image derives mainly from researchers influenced by Vygotsky and Luria's Russian sociocultural tradition, including Cole (1996), Lave and Wenger (1991), Rogoff (1990), and Greenfield (1997).

A good example of research that adopts a systems view is the research on individualism and collectivism. Hofstede (1980) conducted a large-scale survey of work values of IBM employees around the world. He computed country means of the item responses, and constructed an index of individualism by aggregating some of these country means. In this study, the unit of analysis was a country (or a national culture), and the differences in the country index were regarded as reflecting meaningful cultural differences in the extent to which an individual employee was embedded in his or her company. Subsequent cross-cultural comparisons typically sought cultural differences in social behaviors (see Triandis, 1996, for an extensive review) between two or sometimes more countries that are assumed to have enduring and pervasive cultural differences in individualism and collectivism. In this research, culture becomes an independent variable in a quasi-experiment.

Although most research involving culture in personality and social psychology has taken the culture-as-meaning-system view so far, researchers interested in children's enculturation processes have adopted a view of culture as meaning making processes. For instance, Cole (1996) viewed schooling as a collection of context-specific and domain-specific cognitive and motor activities (e.g., reading and writing, remembering a list of words), which influence children's cognitive task performance such as recall and syllogistic reasoning. In other words, instead of explaining cultural differences in syllogistic reasoning performance in terms of differences in cognitive style (e.g., logical vs. prelogical reasoning), this approach suggests that people from Western cultures tend to perform syllogistic reasoning tasks better than illiterate people because the reasoning tasks resemble activities that the former are used to at school.

First of all, the two views are different in time perspective. The system view of culture takes a long-term perspective, and looks for a common pattern in a group within a relatively long historical period. This view strategically freezes culture in time as if it is stable during a historical period. In a way, this is a necessity for cross-cultural comparisons. Here, time slices of cultural traditions are treated as showing some uniform patterns, and these time slices are compared with a view to identifying characteristics that mark cultural similarities and differences. Unless some stability is assumed in cultures, this research strategy may end up finding cultural differences that are merely transient fads.

By contrast, the process view of culture adopts a short-term perspective, and seeks fluctuating and yet recurrent patterns displayed by concrete individuals engaging in specific activities in particular contexts. This view regards culture as constantly in flux, and continuously produced and reproduced over time. People engage themselves in this continuous flow in interaction with others, and they are regarded as possessing psychological mechanisms that enable them to participate in cultural practices of the community. Cultural activities are, then, skilled mental and behavioral performances, which people acquire through enculturation. It is no coincidence that developmental psychologists with interest in culture adopt the process view of culture. After all, children must learn their culture from their concrete experiences, not by osmosis or other magical means. Here, researchers identify recurrent patterns of activities, and examine the process by which these activities are first displayed in interpersonal contexts and then eventually internalized by the participating children.

The systems and process views of culture differ in context specificity and domain specificity. The systems view is generally concerned with culture seen as a whole, as a context-general and domain-general meaning system that is carried and realized by a group of individuals. Culture, then, is abstracted from specific contexts of social activities. Culture is often regarded as present, although it may lie dormant, in all contexts of social activities and all domains of life. The process view, on the other hand, is interested in culture as particular activities using particular artifacts (i.e., tools and other material objects) in particular contexts. This is a view of culture as a collection of context-specific signification activities. To the extent that a domain of meaning is often associated with a particular context (e.g., things to do at school or at home), this image of culture tends towards a view that cultural meanings are domain specific.

Finally, the systems and process views of culture are different in unit of analysis. The systems-view takes a group of individuals as a unit of analysis, and culture is a phenomenon closely associated with the collectivity. In a way, culture is regarded as a property of the group. In contrast, the process view takes a practice (a pattern of activities carried out by people) as a unit of analysis. In this perspective, culture is a property of situated activities, that is, people acting in context. It should be noted that this notion of practice and situated activities includes not only individuals, but also routinized activities taking place in space and time.

Although differences between the two images of culture are not yet widely known to social psychologists (the systems view is often assumed), the division runs deep and could result in not only differences in method and subject matter, but also disagreements in epistemology and metaphysics (see Kashima, 2000, for a more detailed discussion). Nevertheless, these two images of culture present complementary vantage points from which to approach culture–mind relations. The complementary nature of the systems and process views becomes clear when considering cultural dynamics, or the stability and change of culture over time. One view's strength is the other's weakness. On the one hand, the systems view takes the stability of a culture for granted and, as a result, often looks for factors external to culture as engines of cultural change (e.g., technology, material wealth, and ecology). Creative activities within a culture as a basis for cultural change tend to fall outside the scope of this perspective. On the other hand, the process view takes culture as constantly produced and reproduced. As such, both stability and change are part and parcel of culture. However, it is unclear in this view how one can theoretically determine which aspects of situated activities are to persist and which are to change. Furthermore, although this view provides detailed analyses of particular activities, it fails to shed light on a general pattern, a cultural theme, or something like a context-general meaning system that seems to cut across a number of domains of activities (e.g., see Jahoda's 1980 criticism of Cole's approach).

Thus, the systems and process views of culture provide complementary perspectives on cultural dynamics. The culture-as-system view highlights the persistence of culture over time, whereas the culture-as-process view focuses on the fluctuation of cultural meaning across contexts and over time. Nonetheless, both local fluctuations and global stability characterize culture. My contention is that we must investigate how both can be true. From the present perspective, the central question of cultural dynamics is how individuals' context-specific signification activities can generate, under some circumstances, something stable that may be called a context-general meaning system and, under other circumstances, a rapid and even chaotic change.

CULTURE AND CONCEPTIONS
OF THE PERSON AND SELF

How should one approach the interplay between culture and self from a cultural dynamics perspective? There are two fundamental questions. First of all, what are culturally constituted parts of self-conceptions, and how do world cultures differ from each other? Second, how are cultural differences acquired and maintained over time? To begin to answer the first question, it is best to start with Clifford Geertz's (1984) well-known characterization of the Western conception of the person,

> as a bounded, unique, more or less integrated motivational and cognitive universe, a dynamic center of awareness, emotion, judgment, and action or-

ganized into a distinctive whole and set contrastively both against other such
wholes and against its social and natural background. (p. 126)

This passage contains at least three meaning units. One is the claim of
uniqueness, that the Western conception regards a person as a unique being. A second is that the Western conception takes a person as an agent
equipped with cognition, emotion, and motivation, that is, a person as a
mental agent. A third claim is one of a person as a decontextualized distinctiveness, namely, "a distictive whole . . . set contrastively both against
other such wholes and against its social and cultural background."

It is probably safe to say that the uniqueness aspect of the Western conception of the person may have come from the Romantic era, in which
each individual was thought of as possessing and seeking the true inner
self, which is unique to each individual (see Baumeister, 1986; also see
Kashima & Foddy, chap. 8, this volume). This conception gained prominence and became prevalent in 19th-century Western Europe and North
America. The claims of mental agency and decontextualized distinctiveness may have possibly persisted longer than that of uniqueness in the
Western conception of the person as Geertz described it. These ideas may
be traced back at least to the Enlightenment conception of the person that
became widely available in the 18th century. In this view, a person was a
being endowed with universal reason, which was regarded as a locus of
natural law and as a reflection of the clockwork Newtonian universe in hu-
manity (see Simmel, 1950; also see Kashima & Foddy, chap. 8, this volume). This conception decontextualized a person to the extent that his or
her capacity to reason was seen as universal, and that cultural and historical contexts only function to mask this universal capacity. Because reason
can guide each individual to make rational decisions for him- or herself,
this conception treats a person as a mental agent with clear sense of self-
interest.

So far, we have established that Geertz's characterization of the Western
conception of the person includes at least three meanings: a person as a
unique being, as a decontextualized entity, and as a mental agent. I have
also suggested that the use of personality traits in describing a person may
reflect two of the three components of the Western conception of the person, that is, a person as a decontextualized entity and as a mental agent.
Do we have sufficient psychological evidence to suggest that Geertz's characterization correctly describes the Western conception in contradistinc-
tion to conceptions of the person in other parts of the world?

In the early 1980s, Hofstede's (1980) work on individualism and
Shweder and Bourne's (1982) paper on conceptions of the person appeared. Together they formed a significant basis from which to launch the
active research program of culture and self. Although their differences are

numerous (for a detailed discussion, see Kashima, in press), it suffices here to comment on two. Hofstede's and Shweder and Bourne's contributions highlighted cultural differences in self and person conceptions, respectively. That is, Hofstede's research on individualism highlighted participants' responses about themselves, that is, their own work values, whereas Shweder and Bourne were concerned with conceptions of the person in general, particularly examining North Americans' and Indians' free descriptions of their acquaintances. Another difference between them has to do with meanings of cultural differences. Hofstede's conception of individualism emphasized the extent to which people valued the pursuit of individual goals, or mental agency; in contrast, Shweder and Bourne's egocentric conception of the person picked out decontextualization and the extent to which North Americans use personality trait terms in describing their acquaintances as a central respect in which North American and Indian cultures differ. In other words, these two studies inadvertently selected two of Geertz's characterization of the Western conception of the person, namely, mental agency and decontextualization.

These cultural differences were subsequently explained in terms of cultural conceptions of the self by Triandis (1989) and Markus and Kitayama (1991). Triandis argued that there are three kinds of self-conceptions: private, public, and collective selves. Private selves are the aspect of self-conceptions that are shown and known to oneself; public selves are those aspects that are presented to others; and collective selves represent the self as members of various groups. Markus and Kitayama's influential formulation postulated independent and interdependent self-construals as ways of construing one's self as an independent, unique, and distinctive being and a social being suspended in a web of interpersonal relationships. Basically, the concept of interdependent self-construal conflates Triandis's public and collective selves into one type of conception of the self that emphasizes its social and contextual embeddedness. The argument has been that public and collective selves in Triandis's terms and interdependent self-construal in Markus and Kitayama's conceptualization are more prevalent and emphasized in collectivist cultures such as East Asia and Latin America, whereas public selves and independent self-construals are predominant in Western European-based cultures including North America and Australia.

Cultural Differences in Conceptions of the Person and Self

Careful examination of cross-cultural research on self-conception shows that the cultural differences postulated by theorists are not supported as clearly as often assumed. I examine the research in two steps. First,

Triandis's and Markus and Kitayama's models of self-conception are considered, and evidence for their postulate regarding cross-cultural differences is examined. This consideration further refines our understanding about the Western conception of the person. Next, cross-cultural evidence is examined. What evidence there is does suggest that Geertz's anthropological insights about the Western conception of the person are generally consistent with psychological evidence. Yet, as we show later, there is no strong evidence to show that non-Western cultures, in particular, Japanese and other East Asian cultures, are particularly collectivistic or characterized by interdependent or collectivistic conceptions of the self.

Tripartite Model of Cultural Selves. In considering cross-cultural differences, it is important to conduct a careful analysis of the meaning of various concepts. What I propose here is a tripartite model of cultural self (see Kashima, Kashima, & Aldridge, 2001; Kashima et al., 1995), which permits a clear delineation of different components of meaning in conceptions of the person and self. First of all, it is assumed that the individual person as an embodied being is universally recognized as an entity. However, this embodied being may be conceptualized differently in relation to other entities. It is postulated that a self is conceptualized in relation to at least three major classes of other entities: goals, individuals, and groups (other entities such as spiritual or supernatural beings may also be included). A self in relation to a goal is an *agentic* self; a self in relation to another individual is a *relational* self; and a self in relation to a group is a *collective* self. These three aspects constitute three components of the meaning of a self. Similar divisions of self-conceptions have been postulated by Brewer and Gardner (1996) and others.

This model implies that some of the meaning components that have been confounded in the past cross-cultural research may need to be conceptually differentiated further. One is the extent to which a self is abstracted from its context, or *decontextualization* of the self (see Rhee, Uleman, Lee, & Roman, 1995). It has often been assumed that an abstract representation of a self implies that the self is individualistically represented. However, it should be noted that a self in relation to another individual or a self in relation to a group can be abstracted from its context as much as a self in relation to a goal. Another component that is often confounded in the past research is the extent to which a self is believed to be *unique*. Note that a self in relation to a goal may be unique in that the goal is unique. It is in this sense that belief in a unique self is regarded as individualistic. However, it should be obvious that a self in relation to another individual can be equally unique in that the kind of interpersonal relationship a self has with this particular other is unique. Uniqueness of a self is a matter of how one description of a self in relation to something is different and distinctive from another description of a self in relation to something else. Thus, both decontextualization and uniqueness of a self are conceptually orthogonal to the tripartite division of self-conceptions into agentic, relational, and collective aspects.

Viewed from this perspective, Geertz's Western conception of the person is that a person is described as agentic, unique, and decontextualized. However, it does not imply that a person is not relationally or collectively conceptualized. Triandis's model of private, public, and collective selves is similar to the current tripartite division. However, although both conceptions of collective selves are analogous, the other two aspects are somewhat different. Triandis's distinction between private and public selves is based on whether a self is presented to some other people (public) or not (private), whereas the current model emphasizes the distinction between a self conceptualized in relation to a goal (agentic) and an individual (relational). Clearly, there is some overlap between these conceptions. However, it should be noted that a self in relation to another person may be publicly presented to the person or held privately, being hidden from the person. Imagine a boy who pretends to be uninterested in a girl he likes, trying to hide his "self" in relation to her. A self presented in public may or may not be a self in relation to another individual. Finally, Markus and Kitayama's independent self-construal is similar to the current agentic self (although they confound decontextualization and uniqueness as well); however, their interdependent self-construal conflates relational and collective selves.

There are both theoretical and empirical reasons for postulating the current tripartite model. Theoretically, there exists a psychological model that can learn to distinguish agentic, relational, and collective aspects of the self. Kashima, Kashima, and Aldridge (2001; also see Kashima & Kashima, 1999) used a connectionist model to simulate the learning of input sequences similar to English sentences involving *I* or *We* as the subject of each sentence. First, We-sentences were clearly differentiated from I-sentences, implying that collective selves (that is, "We") are represented distinctively from other aspects of the self. Furthermore, I-sentences that followed another sentence that described a different person's action directed to the self (i.e., I-sentences that described relational actions) were distinguished from the other I-sentences. This implies that relational selves are regarded as distinct from agentic selves that define the self in relation to objects. In total, the results suggest that self-representations that signify agentic, relational, and collective selves may be distinguished as people learn to represent their actions symbolically (see Humphreys & Kashima, chap. 2, this volume, for a more detailed description).

There is some empirical evidence for the tripartite division among agentic, relational, and collective selves. Kashima et al. (1995) administered measures that tap different aspects of the self in five locations (Australia, Hawaii, Japan, Korea, and the United States), and found that the measures of agentic, relational, and collective selves formed separate factors in a factor analysis of the entire sample. Kashima and Hardie (2000) administered a battery of measures of self-conception including the ones used by Kashima et al. to a sample of Australian participants, and examined their relationships by multidimensional scaling. They reported that measures of agentic, relational, and collective selves appeared in three separate areas within a two-dimensional space, implying that these self-aspects are empirically distinguishable. Brewer and Gardner (1996) provided some preliminary evidence for the separation of the three aspects using more cognitive measures of self-conception.

Cross-Cultural Differences in Agentic, Relational, and Collective Self. First of all, a handful of studies have examined cross-cultural differences in terms of the tripartite model of cultural self. Kashima et al. (1995) provided clear evidence for cultural differences in self-conception in two East Asian countries (Japan and Korea), two Western countries (Australia and the United States), and Hawaii. Australian and American students were higher on the measure of agentic self than Japanese and Korean students, with the Hawaiian sample in between. Although there was a small cultural differences on the collective aspect of the self, cultural differences in relational self showed an unexpected pattern with the Korean and Japanese samples marking the highest and lowest scores, respectively. Instead, there was a stronger gender difference on relational self: women were more relational than men in most samples.

Singelis (1994) compiled items used in a number of preexisting measures of individualism and collectivism, and showed that Asian Americans scored higher on the interdependent and lower on the independent self-construal factor than European Americans. Examination of the Singelis's items suggests that his independent self-construal items were primarily concerned with individual agency whereas his interdependent self-construal items were mostly to do with self–ingroup relationships. Taken together, the studies by Singelis and by Kashima et al. studies suggest that differences in cultural self-conceptions may be primarily localized in individualist self, and secondarily in collective self. That is, the key difference may be the extent to which the self is conceptualized as a goal-directed agent, or embedded in an ingroup, rather than whether the self is conceptualized in relation to other individuals.

Nevertheless, it is important to consider regional differences within each culture: The urban environment may foster agentic self and decrease the strength of collective or relational self. To examine this, Kashima, Kokubo, Kashima, Boxall, Yamaguchi, and Macrae (submitted) conducted a study in which samples taken from metropolitan cities and regional centers in Australia and Japan (Melbourne vs. Wodonga in Australia; Tokyo versus Kagoshima in Japan) were administered measures of agentic, relational, and collective selves. The results showed that only the agentic self differed between Australia and Japan; urban versus regional differences were localized in collective self in both cultures. As in Kashima et al. (1995), men and women differed on relational self.

There are a number of studies that examined open-ended descriptions of the self typically using the Twenty Statements Test (TST; Kuhn & McPartland, 1954) or its variants, in which people are asked to answer the question "Who am I?" by completing 20 sentences that start with "I am . . ." (e.g., Bond & Cheung, 1983). However, most of them did not differentiate agentic self from decontextualization, and regarded self-descriptions using personality trait terms as indicating individualist self-conceptions. Rhee et al. (1995) were probably the first to clearly distinguish these two aspects of self-conception, and showed that European Americans' self-conceptions are more agentic and abstract than those of Koreans and Asian Americans. They examined self-descriptions of Koreans, Asian Americans, and European Americans on TST, and showed that the percentage of abstract self-descriptions increased from Koreans, to Asian Americans, to European Americans. Likewise, the percentage of agentic (they called it "autonomous") self-descriptions followed the exact same pattern as that of abstract ones. In line with this, most studies using a similar technique showed that both in Malaysia (Bochner, 1994) and India (Dhawan, Roseman, Naidu, Thapa, & Rettek, 1995), self-descriptions tended to have lower percentages of abstract, personality trait-like descriptions than in English-speaking countries (Australia and Britain for Bochner; the United States for Dhawan et al.). It is interesting to note, however, that English-speaking Indian participants showed a level of personality trait use similar to British and Bulgarian participants (Lalljee & Angelova, 1995).

Finally, support for belief in the uniqueness of the self in Western European-based cultures may be found in the work of Heine, Lehman, and their colleagues on self-regard. Heine, Lehman, Markus, and Kitayama (1999) argued that East Asians and Japanese in particular do not have a strong need for positive self-regard as it is usually conceived within contemporary social psychology. According to them, North Americans are *self-enhancing* whereas Japanese are *self-improving*. North Americans seek to identify positive attributes of the self (positive abilities in particular), and attempt to maintain and enhance self-esteem by affirming those positive attributes when their self-esteem is under threat (e.g., failing in a task). In contrast, Japanese seek to identify discrepancies between what is ideally required of them and what they perceive themselves to be, and attempt to improve those failings (e.g., failing in a task). In other words, both North Americans and Japanese try to reach the ideal, but the former focus on positives and try to move toward the ideal, whereas the latter focus on negatives and try not to fall behind. Heine et al. (in press) showed that Japanese samples have consistently revealed lower levels of self-esteem than their North American counterparts as gauged by Rosenberg's (1965) self-esteem measure. Corroborating this is the finding that the self-esteem of Japanese visiting North America tends to increase, while the self-esteem of North Americans visiting Japan tends to decline. One instance of the North American tendency for believing positive uniqueness is the so-called unrealistic optimism bias (for reviews, see Greenwald, 1980; Taylor & Brown, 1988). Heine and Lehman (1995) showed that European Canadian students exhibited a greater degree of optimism relative to Japanese students. The Canadian students showed an optimism bias. That is they estimated the likelihood of their enjoying positive events to be greater, and that of their suffering from negative events to be smaller, than the average students. Their Japanese counterparts, however, did not exhibit this pattern.

Kitayama, Markus, Matsumoto, and Norasakkunkit (1997) provided evidence that such cultural differences may be in part sustained by the kind of social situations available in North America and in Japan. They had their American and Japanese participants generate situations that would affect their self-esteem upward or downward, and had another set of participants in the United States and Japan rate the extent to which the American-made and Japanese-made situations influence their self-esteem. A majority of American participants showed a positivity bias: Regardless of whether the situations were generated in Japan or the United States, they estimated that their self-esteem would be enhanced overall. A majority of Japanese students in Japan showed the opposite tendency, estimating that their self-esteem would be negatively affected overall. However, Japanese students studying in the United States exhibited a self-enhancing tendency similar to their American peers for the situations generated in the United States, but a self-critical tendency similar to their Japanese peers for situations generated in Japan. Furthermore, American-made situations were overall evaluated to be more self-enhancing and less self-critical than Japanese-made situations by all participants. All in all, the results suggest that cultures provide culture-specific situations that tend to afford certain psychological activities. Clearly, members of a given culture react to their own cultural situations more strongly, but members of other cultures may react to those situations in a like manner. Nonetheless, as members of a culture become enculturated into another host culture, they begin to acquire a bicultural tendency to react to the host cultural situations as the members of the host culture would, while still retaining the behavioral pattern prevalent in their culture of origin.

Summary. Overall, cross-cultural research on self-conception has mainly examined Western European-based cultures such as North America and Australia on the one hand, and East Asian cultures such as Hong Kong, Japan, and Korea. Cultural differences in self-conception are not as clearly documented as often assumed. There is no strong evidence that East Asian culture (as opposed to urban–rural differences) emphasizes relational or collective selves when compared to Western European-based cultures. Yet there is strong evidence for Geertz's anthropological insight that the Western conception of the person is unique, agentic, and decontextualized. Nonetheless, from a cultural dynamical perspective, the next central question is how these cultural differences are acquired and maintained, the question to which I turn next.

CULTURAL PRACTICE OF THE SELF

From a cultural dynamical perspective, it is best to look for situated social activities that may contribute to the maintenance of the cultural differences in conceptions of the self. I suggest that the cultural practice of describing oneself and others in personality trait terms is the central mechanism that helps to maintain the Western conception of the person. I call this the cultural practice of trait ascription, by which I mean the verbal practice of describing oneself using trait adjectives such as intelligent, sensitive, and considerate and stating that "I am kind and sociable," for instance, in conversation and written communication. In concrete terms, I am postulating that there is a cultural practice in which when one asks oneself who one is, one is to answer by saying "I am kind and sociable" in European-based cultures.

It is important to note several aspects of the cultural practice of trait ascription when asked, "Who am I?" First of all, it is implicitly a communicative practice that takes the form of a question–answer pair. There is assumed to be a person who asks a question, "Who am I?"; the self is to answer this question in a specific way. In a sense, this is a practice of coordination between two parts of the self, Subject and Object. Second, it is an internalization of a publicly observable communication. That is, this type of exchange can be learned from an activity in which adults engage socializing children by asking "Who are you?" and providing an answer for the children by saying "You are a clever child!" When this type of exchange is internalized, it may become the psychological process in which a person ascribes a personality trait to him- or herself. In other words, the acquisition of this cultural practice by the process that Vygotsky (1978) postulated is possible.

The cultural practice of trait ascription is also related to the Western conception of the person as a mental agent. To put it simply, to ascribe a personality trait to oneself typically means to attribute agency to the self in English at least. In this sense, personality trait dispositions such as sociable and shy may combine the two conceptions of the person (a person as a mental agent and as a decontextualized abstract entity) as a meaningful concept. In fact, Rhee et al. (1995) found that the extent to which people's self-descriptions were agentic and the degree of decontextualization in their self-descriptions were more strongly correlated among European Americans than among Koreans. Perhaps it is also instructive to recall that a conceptual distinction between the two meanings, agency and decontextualization, was clarified in attribution theory only recently (Hilton, Smith, & Kin, 1995: Semin & Marsman, 1994). Perhaps it took scientific psychology some time to go beyond the implicit cultural assumption that confounds traits and agency, that is, the view that to characterize someone by a personality trait disposition means to attribute agency to the person.

Figure 9.1 describes a model that sets the cultural practice of trait ascription as a central mechanism that maintains the cultural difference. Ac-

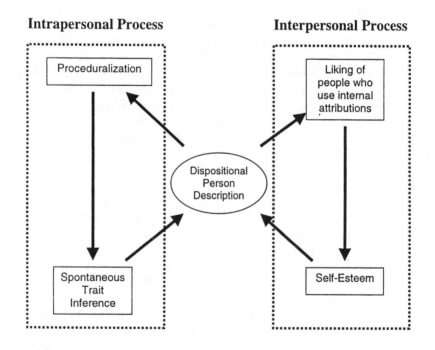

FIG. 9.1. A schematic representation of intrapersonal and interpersonal processes that help maintain the cultural practice of dispositional person description.

cording to this model, intrapersonal and interpersonal processes form positive feedback loops, which may causally promote the cultural practice of trait ascription. To describe the model, let us start from the cultural practice of trait ascription, and assume that a person describes him- or herself in personality trait terms. In the intrapersonal arena, it is well known that when an activity is repeated, people tend to become efficient in carrying out the activity. Likewise, when people repeatedly describe a person dispositionally, this activity can become so well learned that it can become automatic (e.g., Schneider & Shiffrin, 1977; Shiffrin & Schneider, 1977). Once learned, repeated activation of the process of trait ascription would make the activation of the process easier, and the practice effect (repetition priming) tends to generalize from a specific dispositional inference to general dispositional inferences (Smith, 1989; Smith, Branscombe, & Bormann, 1988). This process further facilitates the tendency to make spontaneous trait inferences (Uleman, Newman, & Moskowitz, 1996), which in turn help carry out the practice of trait ascription.

There is also an interpersonal loop that may contribute to the maintenance of the cultural practice of trait ascription. First, North Americans tend to like those who give agentic self-descriptions. Jellison and Green (1981) presented a fictitious college student's responses to Rotter's (1966) locus of control scale. This well-known scale measures the extent to which people believe that human action is determined by the actor's internal characteristics (internal locus) or factors outside the actor's control (external locus). Jellison and Green created four response patterns that indicated four levels of locus of control, varying from external to internal. Each response pattern was attributed to a fictitious college student, and American participants rated the extent to which this fictitious respondent was seen to possess various personality characteristics. The results showed that the more internal was the response pattern, the more socially approved was the target person. If attributing dispositions to oneself also implies the self-attribution of internal locus of control as discussed before, the results may suggest that North Americans are fond of those who ascribe personality dispositions. Given that there is a North American tendency to ascribe positive characteristics to oneself, this practice is likely to lead to the liking of these people.

Those who are liked by others tend to have a high level of self-esteem and positive self-regard (reflected appraisals; e.g., Rosenberg, 1981). Clearly, those who describe themselves as internally driven are liked, and therefore likely to like themselves. In fact, there is a robust relationship between internal locus of control and high self-esteem at least in North America. Intriguingly, Block and Funder (1986) found that self-esteem correlated positively with the extent to which people made a correspondent inference. That is, those who are high in self-esteem tended to describe others in dispositional terms. Although this correlational evidence cannot imply a direct causal effect of self-esteem on dispositional inference, it is an intriguing possibility that may deserve further investigation.

In combination, the cultural practice of trait ascription may become self-perpetuating. Both the intrapersonal process of proceduralization and spontaneous trait inference and the interpersonal process involving positive self-regard may push this cultural practice along and make it more likely to happen within each individual. When this practice is learned by others through socialization and verbal learning, or even by sheer imitation, it could not only maintain but also enlarge the cultural difference in the extent to which a person description is decontextualized. The model also implicates the cultural difference in self-esteem maintenance as part of the interpersonal mechanism that may contribute to the cultural maintenance. In continuing to engage in the cultural practice of trait ascription, the practitioner may continue to feel positive about him- or herself, thus helping to maintain and possibly enhance the level of self-esteem. Thus, the two cultural practices, trait ascription and self-esteem maintenance, may proceed in tandem as mutually reinforcing processes.

The current perspective sheds light on Cousins's (1989) findings about American and Japanese self-descriptions using different test formats. He first used the TST, and examined all the self-descriptions. U.S. students' self-descriptions included a greater proportion of personality trait-like descriptions (58%) than their Japanese counterparts (19%). Immediately after the typical TST, Cousins asked his participants to "Describe yourself in the following situations" followed by the phrases *at home, at school,* and *with close friends* (p. 126). Although the exact format of this "contextualized" version of self-description task is unclear from his writing, Cousins reported the reversal of the TST finding: that is, the Japanese participants mentioned pure attributes more (41%) than the Americans did (26%). In this contextualized version, the Americans qualified their trait-like self-descriptions more (35%; e.g., "I am usually open with my brother," p. 129) than the Japanese did (22%).

Cousins (1989) interpreted these findings as showing that the Japanese conception of the self is more situated and contextualized. However, it is not immediately clear how to interpret the meaning of trait ascription. On the one hand, the use of personality trait adjectives in self-description cannot be directly interpreted as the extent of abstraction of the self. It does not make sense to say the Japanese self is abstracted when TST-like questions are asked with concrete contexts like "at school" and "at home," but not abstracted when the typical TST format is used. Rather, North Americans' trait ascription to the self when the question "Who am I?" (or "Who are you?") is asked in the TST may be understood simply as a cultural practice. When the slightly different question "Who am I at school?" is asked, for instance, this cultural routine may not help them answer the question, and people in North America may need to construct an answer on the spot. This may lead to the use of verbal hedges such as "I am usually like X."

CONCLUDING REMARKS

This chapter proposed a perspective that I called cultural dynamics elsewhere. The central question in this perspective is the process by which culture as an enduring meaning system can be generated from and maintained by concrete individuals' meaning-making activities. I speculated that the cultural practice of ascribing personality traits to oneself in an implicitly communicative context of asking "Who am I?" is a central mechanism in European-based cultures, which may contribute to the maintenance of what Geertz called the Western conception of the person as an agentic, unique, and decontextualized being.

To make this case, I first reviewed the cross-cultural research on self-conception, and showed that, despite the widespread assumption, there is no strong evidence that East Asian self-conceptions are relational or collective relative to Western European self-conceptions. But what evidence there is suggests that Western European self-conceptions are more agentic, unique, and decontextualized. I then extracted from the literature on social cognitive processes in North America a model that postulates the double positive feedback loops of intrapersonal and interpersonal processes that may perpetuate the enactment of the cultural practice of trait ascription. According to the model, the cultural practice of trait ascription to oneself is promoted by the intrapersonal cognitive dynamics as well as the interpersonal self-esteem enhancement. Although it is hard to ascertain how these double positive feedback loops began, once they got going, the process may have become self-perpetuating. Eventually, this cultural practice may have stabilized and become prevalent in European based cultures through cultural transmission and socialization practices.

It is interesting that thus reproduced cultural practice then can be taken metaphorically as a text as Ricoeur suggested (1981). As a text, it can be interpreted as a signature of the individualist conception of the person (Geertz, 1984), which appears to be embedded in the individualist meaning system that became a strong political and social ideology institutionalized in Western Europe in the 18th century and onward. The cultural practice of trait ascription then came to contribute to the reproduction of the individualist conception of the person. Interestingly, this cultural dynamical analysis suggests, by implication, that the individualist conception of the person could change over time when this cultural practice is not performed as frequently. At this stage, however, it is hard to say what may put a stop to this self-perpetuating process.

REFERENCES

Baumeister, R. F. (1986). *Identity: Cultural change and the struggle for self.* New York: Oxford University Press.

Block, J., & Funder, D. C. (1986). Social roles and social perception: Individual differences in attribution and error. *Journal of Personality and Social Psychology, 51,* 1200–1207.

Bond, M. H., & Cheung, T.-S. (1983). College students' spontaneous self-concept: The effect of culture among respondents in Hong Kong, Japan, and the United States. *Journal of Cross-Cultural Psychology, 14,* 153–171.

Brewer, M. B., & Gardner, W. (1996). Who is this "we"? Levels of collective identity and self representations. *Journal of Personality and Social Psychology, 71,* 83–93.

Bruner, J. (1990). *Acts of meaning.* Cambridge, MA: Harvard University Press.

Cole, M. (1996). *Cultural psychology.* Cambridge, MA: Belknap Press.

Cousins, S. D. (1989). Culture and self-perception in Japan and the United States. *Journal of Personality and Social Psychology, 56,* 124–131.

Dhawan, N., Roseman, I. J., Naidu, R. K., Thapa, K., & Rettek, S. I. (1995). Self-concepts across two cultures: India and the United States. *Journal of Cross-Cultural Psychology, 26,* 606–621.

Epstein, S. (1973). The self-concept revisited, or a theory of a theory. *American Psychologist, 28,* 404–416.

Geertz, C. (1973). *The interpretation of cultures.* New York: Basic Books.

Geertz, C. (1984). "From the native's point of view": On the nature of anthropological understanding. In R. A. Shweder & R. A. LeVine (Eds.), *Culture theory* (pp. 123–136). Cambridge, UK: Cambridge University Press.

Greenfield, P. M. (1997). Culture as process: Empirical methods for cultural psychology. In J. W. Berry, Y. H. Poortinga, & J. Pandey (Eds.), *Handbook of cross-cultural psychology* (Vol. 1, pp. 301–346). Boston: Allyn & Bacon.

Greenwald, A. G. (1980). The totalitarian ego: Fabrication and revision of personal history. *American Psychologist, 35,* 603–618.

Heine, S. J., & Lehman, D. R. (1995). Cultural variation in unrealistic optimism: Does the West feel more invulnerable than the East? *Journal of Personality and Social Psychology, 68,* 595–607.

Heine, S. J., Lehman, D. R., Markus, H. R., & Kitayama, S. (1999). Is there a universal need for positive self-regard? *Psychological Review, 106,* 766–794.

Hilton, D. J., Smith, R. H., & Kin, S. H. (1995). Processes of causal explanation and dispositional attribution. *Journal of Personality and Social Psychology, 68,* 377–387.

Hofstede, G. (1980). *Culture's consequences.* Beverly Hills, CA: Sage.

Jahoda, G. (1980). Thoretical and systematic approaches in cross-cultural psychology. In H. C. Triandis & W. W. Lambert, (Eds.), *Handbook of cross-cultural psychology* (Vol. 1, pp. 69–141). Boston: Allyn & Bacon.

Jellison, J. M., & Green, J. (1981). A self-presentation approach to the fundamental attribution error: The norm of internality. *Journal of Personality and Social, 40,* 643–649.

Kashima, E. S., & Hardie, E. A. (2000). Development and validation of the relational, individual, and collective self-aspects (RIC) scale. *Asian Journal of Social Psychology, 3,* 19–48.

Kashima, Y. (in press). Culture and social cognition: Towards a social psychology of cultural dynamics. In D. Matsumoto (Ed.), *Handbook of culture and psychology*. New York: Oxford University Press.

Kashima, Y. (2000). Conceptions of culture and person for psychology. *Journal of Cross-Cultural Psychology, 31*, 14–32.

Kashima, Y., & Kashima, E. S. (1999). Culture, connectionism, and the self. In J. Adamopoulos & Y. Kashima (Eds.), *Social behavior in cultural contexts* (pp. 77–92). London, UK: Sage.

Kashima, Y., Kashima, E., & Aldridge, J. (2001). Towards cultural dynamics of self-conceptions. In C. Sedikides & M. B. Brewer (Eds.), *Individual self, relational self, and collective self: Partners, opponents, or strangers* (pp. 277–298). Philadelphia, PA: Psychology Press.

Kashima, Y., Kokubo, T., Kashima, E., Yamaguchi, S., Boxall, D., & Macrae, K. (2001). *Culture and a tripartite model of self: Are East Asians individualistic, more collectivistic, or more relational than Westerners?* Manuscript submitted for publication.

Kashima, Y., Yamaguchi, S., Kim, U., Choi, S.-C., Gelfand, J. M., & Yuki, M. (1995). Culture, gender, and self: A perspective from individualism-collectivism research. *Journal of Personality and Social Psychology, 69*, 925–937.

Kitayama, S., Markus, H. R., Matsumoto, H., & Norasakkunkit, V. (1997). Individual and collective processes in the construction of the self: Self-enhancement in the United States and self-criticism in Japan. *Journal of Personality and Social Psychology, 72*, 1245–1267.

Kuhn, M. H., & McPartland, T. S. (1954). An empirical investigation of self-attitudes. *American Sociological Review, 19*, 68–76.

Lalljee, M., & Angelova, R. (1995). Person description in India, Britain, and Bulgaria. *Journal of Cross-Cultural Psychology, 26*, 645–657.

Lave, J., & Wenger, E. (1991). *Situated learning*. Cambridge, UK: Cambridge University Press.

Markus, H., & Kitayama, S. (1991). Culture and the self. *Psychological Review, 98*, 224–253.

Rhee, E., Uleman, J., Lee, H. K., & Roman, R. J. (1995). Spontaneous self-descriptions and ethnic identities in individualistic and collectivistic cultures. *Journal of Personality and Social Psychology, 69*, 142–152.

Ricoeur, P. (1981). *Hermeneutics and the human sciences* (J. B. Thompson, Ed., Trans.). Cambridge, UK: Cambridge University Press.

Rogoff, B. (1990). *Apprenticeship in thinking*. Oxford, UK: Oxford University Press.

Rosenberg, M. (1965). *Society and the adolescent self-image*. Princeton, N.J.: Princeton University Press.

Rosenberg, M. (1981). The self-concept: Social product and social force. In M. Rosenberg & R. H. Turner (Eds.), *Social psychology: Sociological perspectives* (pp. 593–624). New York: Basic Books.

Rotter, J. B. (1966). Generalized expectancies for internal versus external control of reinforcement. *Psychological Monographs, 80* (1, Whole No. 609).

Schneider, W., & Shiffrin, R. M. (1977). Controlled and automatic human informaton processing: I. Detection, search, and attention. *Psychological Review, 84*, 1–66.

Semin, G. R., & Marsman, J. G. (1994). "Multiple inference-inviting properties" of interpersonal verbs: Event instigation, dispositional inference, and implicit causality. *Journal of Personality and Social Psychology, 67*, 836–849.

Shiffrin, R. M., & Schneider, W. (1977). Controlled and automatic human information processing: II. Perceptual learning, automatic attending, and general theory. *Psychological Review, 84*, 127–190.

Shweder, R. A., & Bourne, E. J. (1982). Does the concept of the person vary cross-culturally? In R. A. Shweder & R. A. LeVine (Eds.), *Culture theory* (pp. 158–199). Cambridge, UK: Cambridge University Press.

Simmel, G. (1950). *The sociology of Georg Simmel* (K. H. Wolff, Ed., Trans.). New York: Free Press.

Singelis, T. M. (1994). The measurement of independent and interdependent self-construals. *Personality and Social Psychology Bulletin, 20,* 580–591.

Smith, E. R. (1989). Procedural efficiency: General and specific components and effects on social judgment. *Journal of Experimental Social Psychology, 25,* 500–523.

Smith, E. R., Branscombe, N. R., & Bormann, C. (1988). Generality of the effects of practice on social judgment tasks. *Journal of Personality and Social Psychology, 54,* 385–395.

Smith, M. B. (1991). *Values, self and society.* New Brunswick, NJ: Transaction.

Taylor, S. E., & Brown, J. D. (1988). Illusion and well-being: A social psychological perspective on mental health. *Psychological Bulletin, 103,* 193–210.

Triandis, H. C. (1972). *The analysis of subjective culture.* New York: Wiley.

Triandis, H. C. (1989). The self and social behavior in differing cultural contexts. *Psychological Review, 96,* 506–520.

Triandis, H. C. (1994). *Culture and social behavior.* New York: McGraw-Hill.

Uleman, J. S., Newman, L. S., & Moskowitz, G. B. (1996). People as flexible interpreters: Evidence and issues from spontaneous trait inference. *Advances in Experimental Social Psychology, 28,* 211–279.

Vygotsky, L. S. (1978). *Mind in society: The development of higher psychological processes* (M. Cole, V. John-Steiner, S. Scribner, & E. Souberman, Eds., Trans.). Cambridge, MA: Harvard University Press.

CONCLUSION

Part V pays tribute to Brewster Smith's early insights into the self and identity as an intersection of personal, social, and symbolic processes. In chapter 10, Smith revisits his "Perspectives on Selfhood," which predated much of the contemporary research on the social self. While providing a personal overview of the intellectual landscape of both social and personality psychology's investigation of the self in the past, he reflects on selfhood in the contemporary socio-historical context. His chapter acts as a reminder of the tendency of social psychologists to repeat debates that have occurred before, a possible consequence of ignoring our own intellectual history.

Chapter 10

Self and Identity in Historical/Sociocultural Context: "Perspectives on Selfhood" Revisited

M. Brewster Smith
University of California, Santa Cruz

I am an oldtimer identified with the older conception of personality and social psychology, who at present identifies more with personality than with contemporary cognitive social psychology—already I have to speak of identity! So I cannot aspire to be in close touch with the forefront of treatment of self and identity in current social psychology, although I try to keep up, and this chapter is a splendid occasion in which to do so. I can best contribute here by making a virtue of these limitations, bringing to bear my oldtimer's perspective on the issues. I am concerned with how our social psychological conceptions of selfhood may be enriched from a perspective that is mainly rooted in personality psychology.

My baseline consists of three papers I wrote two decades ago (Smith, 1978a, 1978b, 1980). These papers came rather early in the continuing surge of psychological interest in self and identity. Sober judgment leads me to conclude that they have had virtually no influence on what subsequently got published—metaphorically, I was a relatively early surfer on the tide of self and identity but didn't make or shape the waves. Looking at the agenda of this volume, however, I am pleased to see that some of the ideas I thought were good then continue to be interesting—and that some deserve to be revived, as I hope to do here. I refer to these papers in the light of subsequent developments.

A BIT OF HISTORY

Another role I can play, as a personality-oriented oldtimer, is to reinstate some relevant history that I think gets neglected from the current cognitive-social perspective. Everyone interested in self and identity is well aware of James's (1890) treatment of "The Consciousness of Self," with its distinction between *I* and *Me*—and many will remember its positivistically resolute reduction of the I to the passing thought that integrates recollection of the person's past and anticipation of the person's future. The title of his chapter as I have quoted it from his full-length *Psychology* fits his basically phenomenological approach better than "The Self," as he captioned the corresponding chapter in his *Briefer Course* (1892). We are also likely to cite G. H. Mead (1934), although not always with as full acquaintance, for his emphasis on the social origins of reflexive self-consciousness, its dependence on symbolic communication, and its importance for *Mind, Self, and Society*. But we are likely to neglect Helen Lynd's (1938) *On Shame and the Search for Identity*, which connects better with current thought now that we are less frozen on the psychoanalytic formulations of shame and guilt. We may also need to be reminded how Erich Fromm's (1941) *Escape From Freedom* gave a powerful account of the burdens imposed on selfhood in modern times by liberation from feudal social connectedness.

Most psychologists have completely forgotten the contribution of Gardner Murphy, a leading psychologist at midcentury and coauthor of the early text *Experimental Social Psychology* (Murphy & Murphy, 1931; Murphy, Murphy, & Newcomb, 1937), which featured socialization research, not experimentation. Murphy (1947) devoted a major section of his remarkably comprehensive postwar textbook on personality to the self as a thing perceived and conceived, giving an account of its origins and development and making the self the focus of his treatment of psychoanalytic defense mechanisms. For Murphy, "a large part of the behavior that constitutes personality is self-oriented behavior" (p. 479). He stands close to the origin of the tide of self psychology in which we are immersed.

And there is Erikson (e.g., 1959), whose symphonic treatment of identity resists cleanly defined conceptualization but has been very influential on the present intellectual climate concerning self and identity. In his recent definitive biography, the historian Lawrence Friedman (1999) examined the retrievable details of Erikson's life with psychologically sophisticated concern for their relevance to his developing ideas. It became very clear that Erikson had dramatic lifelong unresolved problems about his own identity. Erik Homberger was conceived out of wedlock and raised as the son of a Danish Jewish mother and a German Jewish stepfather, who were not honest with him about his origins. He fantasized that his biological father was from Danish gentility, nobility, or artistic circles, and he managed not to pursue his true parentage to a conclusion until the people who might have been able to inform him were deceased. Living with ambiguities as to whether he was or was not a Jew and whether he was inside or outside the Freudian inner circle, he adopted the name Erikson, making himself symbolically his own progenitor when he resolved another identity problem by becoming an American citizen. His conceptualization of identity may be symphonic and fuzzy, but his own problems with it seem to have concerned very basic uncertainties and ambivalences.

Other contributors to theorizing about selfhood from a psychodynamic standpoint should not be entirely neglected by social psychologists. There was Harry Stack Sullivan (1953), whose view of the "self system" was entirely defensive, and Heinz Kohut (1971), whose version of psychoanalysis as "self psychology" increasingly converged on positions similar to those of the emphatically nonpsychoanalytic Carl Rogers (1961).

Another bit of history to be noted, this time for its conspicuous lack of central relevance to today's concerns, is Wylie's (1961, 1974, 1979) thorough reviews of the major literature on the self-concept. At the time of her reviews, which then were central to psychological treatment of selfhood, empirical research on the self-concept was mainly concerned with the measurement of self-esteem, which seemed to have important links with psychodynamic views of personality then in fashion. Neither the self-concept nor its evaluation as self-esteem is lost in the dustbin of faded concepts and issues, of course, but it is clearly a gain from cognitive social psychology that our present conceptions of self-cognition are much more complex, and that, to a considerable extent, measures of self-efficacy (Bandura, 1997) appropriately get more attention than pencil-and-paper measures of self-esteem, which have always seemed to me very vulnerable to effects of self-presentation to self and others.

SOME MATTERS OF DEFINITION

Because their use in common speech touches central human interests to the quick, the terms *self* and *identity* give rise to substantial definitional problems as psychologists and others employ them in theoretical discourse. I don't think there is much point in fussing about definitions as long as we try individually to make as clear as we can what we intend by our terms—definitions have to follow our gains in understanding. All the same, I'd like to try once more to promote a convention that I proposed in 1980. I take *selfhood* as labeling criterial features of the human condition that center on reflexive self-awareness—a historical, cultural, creative project in symbolization. For me, selfhood involves much the same features that Sedikides and Skowronski (1997) ascribed to symbolic self-awareness, although I would add some additional ones that seem to me to have important existential implications (which I discuss later).

> There are a number of terms in the domain of selfhood that give me no trouble, or seem potentially useful. There is the *person*, the actual, concrete

participant in symbolically construed and governed social relations. There is *personality*, the psychologist's formulation or construction of the person, a construction of organized processes, states, and dispositions. . . . There is Erikson's (1959) rich but slippery concept of *identity*—some trouble, here, to disentangle and pin down the meanings. There is a set of terms in the reflexive mode—*self-perceptions, self-attributions, self-concepts, self-theories* (Epstein, 1973)—in which the prefix *self-* implies reflexive reference but does not imply a surgically or conceptually separable object of reference, other than *the person*. People—persons—may reify "I" and "Me," but psychologists shouldn't, except as they recognize the causal–functional importance of people's own reifications. . . . I don't see a place for *the self* in such a list. It is not a term that designates an entity or agency, except in usages that treat it as synonymous with the *person* in which case one or the other term is superfluous.

Yet there are contexts in which *self* is employed in near synonymy with person that seem to me more justifiable. We may talk about transformations of the Greek self from Homer to Euripides, or of the Western self from Shakespeare to Proust, Pynchon, or R. D. Laing. When we use such locutions, we are emphasizing the symbolic *self-referential* aspect of being a person (with the reflexive prefix having its usual sense as interpreted above), with the implied reminder that self-referential features in which we are interested are somehow constitutive of the person as social actor. We are not talking about an entity, conceptual or otherwise, that is distinguishable from the person. If it makes sense to talk about a fragmented or divided self, the fragmentation or division is a metaphor of metaphors: a characteristic of the metaphoric symbol system that partly constitutes us as persons. (Smith, 1980, pp. 69–70)

The *person*, that is, has aspects of both *I* and *Me*, of both agent and self-object, but it seems to me confusing to use the term *self* to refer to both. The deepest problem, how the reflexive structures of meaning that make up the *Me* or "symbolic self" participate in constituting the person's structures of motivation, intention, and agency, is obscured if we simply say that they are input and output aspects of the same Self. As I see it, it is a problem for personality theory—of psychological conceptualization of the organization and functioning of the human person, now seen more clearly in sociocultural context, a problem to which the considerable resources of cognitive social psychology can be expected to contribute.

PERSPECTIVES ON SELFHOOD THEN AND NOW

Two decades ago, I sorted out three major perspectives on selfhood along lines much like those underlying Foddy and Kashima (chap. 1, this volume): the evolutionary phylogenetic perspective, the cross-cultural or transhistorical perspective, and the developmental or ontogenetic perspective. I felt some originality in asserting that historical change and cross-cultural variation pose the same conceptual and methodological problems for our formulations of selfhood.

The Evolutionary Perspective. My attempt to speculate responsibly about the emergence of selfhood in human evolution could have benefited substantially from the more recent information about human origins interpreted by Sedikides and Skowronski (1997), but I think it continues to stand up pretty well. It included a further speculative idea that seems to me to go beyond their evolutionary account in a way that is very consequential. As they proposed, the symbolic selfhood that emerged with the attainment of fully elaborated language competence had obvious adaptive features that favored human survival and proliferation, especially in regard to planful and socially coordinated intentional behavior and the cultural retention and transmission of problem-solving tactics. But it also had side effects that could only create problems for people. To quote what I wrote for an Australian publication that I imagine is now lost to sight:

> Yet there are heavy costs in the side-effects of attaining symbolic selfhood. Human self-consciousness breaks the unity of Man [sic] and Nature and, when forethought and afterthought are added as gifts of language, the ingredients of the human existential predicament emerge. As speaking self-conscious human beings, we and our forebears for more than 50,000 years have faced the cognitive puzzle of whence we came into the world, why we are here and what happens when we die. . . . Primarily through language, we have become *persons*, linked to other persons whom we love and care for in a web of "inter-subjective" meaning (Schutz, 1967). The inevitability of the eventual death of self and loved ones and the arbitrary unpredictability of death from famine, disease, accident, predation or human assault become the occasion not for momentary animal terror but for what is potentially unremitting human anguish. So the quest for meaning, for meanings compatible with a human life of self-conscious mortality, becomes a matter of life and death urgency. I don't think Ernest Becker (1973) exaggerated the importance of this theme in the history of human culture. [Greenberg, Pyszczynski, and Solomon (1986) and Solomon, Greenberg, and Pyszczynski (1991) recently resurrected Becker's ideas in their theory of terror management.]
>   Of course, this mainly familiar account is wrong in one obvious respect. Contrary to the old myth, our forebears cannot have been cast out of Nature's Garden of Eden in one sudden tragic event of "birth trauma." . . . Self-conscious selfhood, with its peremptory challenge to find supportive meaning in the face of creature mortality, must have been a gradual emergent.
>   If so, the symbolic resources of language-bearing human communities could meet the need for meaning as it arose. Thus emerged the many cultural worlds of myth, ritual and religion, which provided the traditional answers to the question of what it means to be human. They were good answers, proclaiming to each communicating tribal group its value as The

People; legitimizing the group's way of life as ordained by their ancestors; giving intelligible meaning to the exigencies of life and death; providing appropriate ways in which individual and community could participate in the encouragement of auspicious outcomes and the avoidance of ominous ones. These traditional mythic answers could not fully eliminate occasions for anguish and terror, but they could give intelligible shape to formless terror; and they could make the blows of fate more bearable to the victim and certainly more endurable to the fellow members of the victim's kindred and community. (Smith, 1978a, pp. 9–11)

It is important to our enterprise, I think, to see cultural evolution in close connection with biological evolution in some such way. Donald Campbell (1991) has made a similar suggestion in regard to the emergence of culturally established moral sanctions, especially religious ones, against selfish, socially destructive behaviors that biological evolution may have selected, a consideration that is relevant to current concerns about sociocultural challenges to moral values as constitutive ingredients of selfhood.

The Cross-Cultural and Transhistorical Perspectives. These two perspectives raise essentially the same serious problem for the culture-bound views of selfhood that had been prevalent in the United States and Western Europe. Once this contextual point is grasped, we are still left with the question raised by Foddy and Kashima (chap. 1, this volume) as to whether the underlying psychological processes are appropriately regarded as human universals with the "content" provided historically and culturally, or whether aspects of even these processes are subject to historical and cultural influence. The perspectives are similar in their conceptual and methodological significance, but they point in different directions in regard to the research required to give them substance.

For an historical approach to selfhood, I relied on humanistic scholarship such as that of Snell (1953) and Onians (1951/1973) on the emergence of the self-conscious European mind in the centuries that followed the Homeric epics, and of Lionel Trilling's *Sincerity and Authenticity* (1972) for apparent transformations of selfhood revealed in the European literature of modern times. Baumeister (1986) meanwhile provided us with a well-focused treatment of the historical vicissitudes of Euro-American selfhood since the Middle Ages. From immersal in the philosophical history of ideas, Taylor (1989) gave us a rich account of "the making of the modern identity." The British sociologist Giddens (1991) carried historical analysis forward to challenging conceptual vistas in his treatment of "self and society in the late modern age." It seems to me that the case for major historical changes in the content and organization of selfhood in the Western tradition has been made beyond reasonable doubt. Because of the nature of historical data and historical scholarship, however, we cannot expect to understand these changes with much scientific firmness or precision—and of course, Euro-American psychologists have not explored whatever literature may be relevant to changes in selfhood in other historical traditions.

The situation is different with the cross-cultural approach, because in spite of the homogenizing effect of global communication, living examples of considerably diverse cultures can be studied by our most sophisticated ethnographic and psychological methods, and the multicultural network of psychologists interested in such research and competent to do it keeps expanding. Two decades ago I relied heavily on the work of Geertz (1973, 1975) to make the now obvious point that culture matters to selfhood. More recently, I was captured by the "anthropology of the self" presented by Heelas and Lock (1981), which also served mainly to illustrate the variety of cultural influence. And I got glimmerings of the processes involved in how culture enters the constitution of selfhood in Lakoff and Johnson's *Metaphors We Live By* (Lakoff & Johnson, 1980; see also Lakoff, 1987; Smith, 1985). The recent ground-breaking work by Kitayama, Markus, and their collaborators (Kitayama, Markus, Matsumoto, & Norasakkunkit, 1997; Markus & Kitayama, 1991) seems to me to open a new era. It is no longer important just to illustrate the obvious fact that culture affects selfhood. We can now accept the challenge to understand what is invariant transculturally and what is culture specific in selfhood, and to understand the processes by which environing symbolic culture has its influence. This ambitious objective is beyond the resources of a narrowly conceived cognitive social psychology. Affect and emotion, motivation, and action are involved. Cognitive social psychology needs not only interdisciplinary collaboration as with anthropology and sociology, which it is ready to accept, but also collaboration with other subdisciplines of psychology, which may be more difficult.

The recent substantive focus on individualism and collectivism as cultural orientations (e.g., Triandis, 1989) has special relevance to the psychology of self and identity, because the very emphasis on self and identity as interesting topics may be a reflection of Euro-American individualism. Bandura's (1997) masterwork on self-efficacy is certainly a comprehensive exploration of the agency pole of Bakan's (1966) dimension of agency vs. communion, where agency is the conventionally individualistic (and also masculine) pole. Perhaps we may be ready to go beyond the controversies involved in these polarities. I am impressed that Kağitçibasi (1996), in her recent examination of early child development from a "Majority World" perspective influenced by her path-breaking Turkish research, suggested that developing countries might well reaffirm their commitment to values of relatedness while adopting the Western value of autonomy. Her position goes beyond the conventional relativism of multiculturalism at the same time that it rejects the necessity of cultural choice in terms of the polarity.

The Ontogenetic or Developmental Perspective. Two decades ago I was able to take note of the emerging empirical work on early child development that was refining and partly replacing G. H. Mead's (1934) schematic account of the development of reflexive self-reference and its accompaniments. Developmental psychologists have continued to contribute to an enriched picture of the roots of selfhood in individual development, which social psychological theorizing must take into account. As Foddy and Kashima (chap. 1, this volume) observe, Higgins (1996) provides a coherent version for social psychologists in his "self-digest" theory of self-knowledge. The present challenge, as they also note, is whether this individually focused theory can be made to deal adequately with the self-constituting role of participation in cultural symbol systems and practices, and in the stratification and role differentiation of the social order.

In the 1970s, developmental psychologists were still mainly responding to the Piagetian challenge. In the recent decades, the social–historical school with roots in the Marxist work of Lev Vygotsky has gained in visibility and importance, linked with the increasing prominence of "cultural psychology" (Cole, 1996) as a metatheoretical alternative to cross-cultural psychology that takes a more fluid dialectical or transactional approach to the development of selfhood in the context of social participation. Rogoff's (1990) work on *Apprenticeship in Thinking* is an especially challenging recent example, as Foddy and Kashima (chap. 1, this volume) note, with strong transcultural foundations.

WHY THE SURGE OF INTEREST
IN SELFHOOD AND IDENTITY?

It may be productive to consider possible reasons that underlie the recent surge of interest in self and identity and why social psychologists in particular have joined in it enthusiastically. The long-term tide of general interest has sources that have been much discussed by Baumeister (1986), Giddens (1991), and many others. Modern society with its geographical and social mobility and loosened social bonds highlights individual choice in the lives of its more fortunate members, and both the goals intentionally chosen and the anxieties exposed by the waning of traditional social supports make self-conscious selfhood salient. The diminishing role of traditional religion in a society featuring science and technology is a special case of waning sociocultural support, felt so keenly by many that religious fundamentalism is on the rise. My speculations earlier about the cultural-evolutionary basis of religion suggest grounds for taking this loss seriously. In earlier modern times, faith in earthly progress (Nisbet, 1980) compensated for the fading prospect of heavenly reward (and punishment)—whether via the ascending dialectics of Hegel's romantic view of history or of Marx's materialistic equivalent or via the mundane progressivism of modern bourgeois democracies. The century's calamities have shaken belief in progress and led to skepticism about the prospect that science and technology can solve the looming, potentially catastrophic problems. Rather than fin-de-siècle malaise, also, we were recently experiencing end-of-the-millenium heeby-jeebies. This unease makes people, at least people in the Western individualistic tradition, more saliently aware of their vulnerably exposed selfhood.

I return shortly to considering some features of the immediate scene that make selfhood especially problematic and therefore of research interest, but I first note a matter of subdisciplinary politics that seems to me to have played a part in social psychologists' special interest in identity and selfhood in recent years. The partnership of personality and social psychology reflected in Division 8 of the American Psychological Association (now the Society for Personality and Social Psychology) and embodied in the dual leadership roles of pioneers like Gardner Murphy and Gordon Allport came under great strain in the expansive days of post-Festingerian experimental social psychology. In my own department at the University of California at Santa Cruz, for example, I found it desirable to maneuver to link our graduate program in personality with developmental psychology, not with social as in the original arrangement—the tendency of my social psychological colleagues was so strong to regard any reference to personality as exemplifying Lee Ross's (1977) "fundamental attribution error." Under these circumstances, selfhood and identity became attractive emblems under which social psychology could establish its own claims to territory otherwise occupied by a personality psychology that it had come to regard as hardly legitimate.

Reinforcing this attraction was the amenability of self-related concepts to treatment in cultural and historical context, with which we have been centrally concerned. One could address *Culture and Self* (Marsella, DeVos, & Hsu, 1985) without being encumbered by the mistakes and blind alleys of the failed culture-and-personality movement. "Culture and self" allowed a fresh start, with the option of salvaging much that remained valuable in the earlier tradition.

I would not put much stress on these by-products of academic intellectual politics. More important, it seems to me, are some recent historical developments that inherently focus attention on selfhood and identity, and give human urgency to the attempt to bring social psychology to bear on them. I highlight two: disorientation with respect to moral values as anchors of identity (Baumeister, 1986), which I will label De-Moralization, and heightened in-group identification (Us vs. Them), as involved in the current plague of ethnic, tribal, religious, or national conflict. Having these concrete sets of human problems in mind should reduce the danger that our theoretical examinations of selfhood and identity remain at a level of empty abstractions.

De-Moralization

The firm anchoring of traditional moral values in consensual religious belief has been under attack in Western societies for a long time. But there have been recent changes that must be quite disorienting, especially to the young. With worldwide intercommunication and worldwide sharing of the pop culture of which the United States is a leader and primary source, the changes are by no means limited to the United States or Western Europe. I am thinking about the results of lifting the old moral taboos about sexuality after the "sexual revolution" of the 1960s, the prevalence of corrosive relativism in academic/intellectual circles and its ethical promotion in the name of multiculturalism, the inescapable invitation to recreational sex in the mass media of entertainment, the pervasive cynicism about government and purported idealistic motivation, the weakening of ties that hold families together—this is beginning to sound like a litany of those of the Religious Right who feel they have a monopoly on "Family Values." I would be among the first to recognize that there have been major human gains in getting beyond the stifling restrictions of Main Street. But it seems indubitable to me that insofar as moral values have been a stabilizing anchor in personal identity and a link binding people together in a livable society, we are in trouble.

The immediacy of our problem was brought home to me by Mary Pipher's (1995) popular best-seller, *Reviving Ophelia*. Her account displays the predicament of adolescent girls in school settings characterized by the pervasive presence of alcohol and drugs, sexual pressures from boys, gender-linked academic expectations, peer pressures, and cultural pressures from immersion in the synthetic youth culture of the mass media, including its stress on physical beauty of a biologically improbable kind. These current features of the early adolescent world combine with the biological stirrings of puberty and its sequels to make the adolescent passage of teenage girls riskier and more disturbing to their selfhood and identity than girls of earlier generations mostly experienced. Similar qualitative accounts about other segments of the population would enrich our consideration of selfhood in historical context.

As an old Liberal, I am troubled that I am troubled about the lifting of older cultural constraints. But we are becoming aware of human costs in the reformulations of human nature partly brought about by Sigmund Freud's campaign against Victorian restrictiveness. The Superego, such a cruel bugbear to the Freudian generations, is no longer much of a problem. Indeed, the cases that seem to get the most psychoanalytic attention today, "borderline" states and the like, draw therapists to the self-and-other intricacies of self-psychology and object relations theory, rather than to the compromises negotiated by a coherent Ego between Id and Superego that Freudians used to be concerned with.

One current response to our loss of the old anchors—not only loss of moral values but, more generally, loss of our previous conviction that truthful conceptions of the nature of reality and of people's place in it are at least approachable if not finally attainable, and can help people make a better life—is the fashion of "postmodernism" originating in the humanities and spreading in the softer side of psychology and the social sciences. Gergen (1991) has been a conspicuous spokesperson for the postmodern position in regard to the conceptualization of contemporary selfhood. I am not persuaded by his argument that the coherence of our symbolic selfhood is challenged primarily by relational overload, resulting in what he calls the "saturated self": It seems to me that the loss of anchors just noted and warranted loss of hope, are more important factors. I agree with him that the integral selfhood that Romantic and early Modern thought could regard as a worthy human achievement is in deep trouble. I do not share his sense of playful delight in the new freedom he values in the postmodern situation.

Our present historical/cultural situation strikes me as pathological, and because of the existential strains produced by the withdrawal of traditional sources of meaning (Baumeister, 1991), I think it is intrinsically unstable and cannot last for long. Because the religious answers that pull many toward a new fundamentalism make no sense to me, I look ahead with doubt and misgiving. Perhaps the "communitarians" (Etzioni, 2001) have a sense of direction that is relevant to our common predicament. In any case, a social psychology of selfhood and identity should be attending to these problems, which are now embedded in a worldwide multicultural context.

Problematic Ingroup Identification: Us Versus Them

Social psychologists shared in the general surprise and dismay that the end of Cold War polarization and latent terror about a prospective nuclear Doomsday has been followed not by peace but by a state of world affairs featuring tribal, ethnic, and religious conflict with little regard for national boundaries. In Ireland, the Middle East, Ruanda and the Congo, and the countries of the former Soviet Union, virulent internal conflicts erupted, seen by each side as between virtuous Us and diabolical Them, thus having genocidal potential (see Smith, 1999). Within the United States and several European countries, racial or ethnic antagonisms were also conspicuous. Multiculturalism became a widespread ideal replacing that of the "melting pot." These developments made salient the phenomena of ingroup identification and its role in intergroup conflict.

Fortunately, Tajfel (1978) and Turner (1987) provided social psychology with conceptual tools to deal with such conflicts in their social identity and self-categorization theories, to which Brewer (1991) and Deaux (1993) contributed, along with various others. These need to be elaborated in relation to processes by which historical/cultural factors enter into the constitution of social identity. I see an interesting possibility in the plausible interrelation between the challenges to selfhood already considered under De-Moralization and the pathological exaggeration of ingroup identification just noted. Sensed meaninglessness or hopeless impotence—intolerable states of selfhood—may be dispelled by identification with a group and commitment to its cause. The correlation between right-wing authoritarianism and both religious fundamentalism and trigger-happy superpatriotism (cf. Altemeyer, 1996) is in accord with this suggestion.

SOME CONSIDERATIONS OF CONCEPTUAL STRATEGY

To be adequate to the problems I have just been calling attention to, I think a systems/process view of selfhood is required, one that takes into account the whole person in his or her embeddedness in culture and social relationships. In the terminology borrowed from Dewey and Bentley (1949), the approach should be transactional, not just interactional or unidirectionally causal. People construct their social and cultural worlds at the same time that they themselves are being shaped by them. As social psychologists, we cannot be content with a conceptual world populated by independent and dependent variables.

Because reflexive self-reference, which is the central feature of selfhood, is a matter of the attribution or creation of meanings, I find the recent approaches that draw on self-narratives (McAdams, 1996; Sarbin, 1986) or multivocal dialogue (Hermans, 1996; Hermans & Kempen, 1993) especially attractive. But, given what I think we now know about the historical/cultural malleability of how self-reference as well as its contents are organized, whatever conceptualization we employ should not assume the privileged status of particular historically or culturally given models of selfhood. Thus, I wondered whether Hermans's view of selfhood as dispersed multivocal dialogue might not be viewed as a good metaphor for people's present response to the predicaments of "postmodern" times rather than as a general, transhistorical and pancultural model.

Meanings and values are at the heart of the humanities, the *Geisteswissenschaften* in Dilthey's old distinction between interpretative and explanatory (*Naturwissenschaftlich*) scholarship (Rickman, 1979). Advocates of a narrative approach to selfhood, especially those identified with the postmodern revolt against "positivism," often take a stand opposed to scientific concern with causal explanation. I think that is a mistake. It has long seemed to me that reflexive self-reference and self-awareness—that is, human selfhood—is the one natural phenomenon that requires by its very nature both causal and interpretative analysis. We can work productively on either side of this street, but it seems to me the most interesting challenge is how to coordinate explanatory and interpretative approaches. Modern experimental social psychology has been committed to the causal/explanatory vein, but it should be recognized that the research tradition beginning with Rotter's (1966) research on locus of control and including Seligman's work on explanatory styles (1990) is an excellent example of successful causal analysis of the attribution of meaning in regard to matters very relevant to self-conception. Bandura's (1997) impressive treatment of self-efficacy is closely related example. I think the chapters in this volume point constructively toward new directions for this scientific/humanistic pursuit of human self-understanding.

REFERENCES

Altemeyer, B. (1996). *The authoritarian spector*. Cambridge, MA: Harvard University Press.

Bakan, D. (1966). *The duality of human existence*. Chicago: Rand McNally.

Bandura, A. (1997). *Self-efficacy: The exercise of control*. New York: Freeman.

Baumeister, R. F. (1986). *Identity: Culture change and the struggle for self*. New York: Oxford University Press.

Baumeister, R. F. (1991). *Meanings of life*. New York: Guilford.

Becker, E. (1973). *The denial of death*. New York: Free Press.

Brewer, M. B. (1991). The social self: On being the same and different at the same time. *Personality and Social Psychology Bulletin, 17*, 475–482.

Campbell, D. T. (1991). A naturalistic theory of archaic moral orders. *Zygon, 26*, 91–114.

Cole, M. (1996). *Cultural psychology: A once and future discipline*. Cambridge, MA: Belknap/Harvard University Press.

Dewey, J., & Bentley, A. F. (1949). *Knowing and the known*. Boston: Beacon.

Deaux, K. (1993). Reconstructing social identity. *Personality and Social Psychology Bulletin, 19*, 4–12.

Epstein, S. (1973). The self-concept revisited: Or a theory of a theory. *American Psychologist, 28*, 404–416.

Erikson, E. H. (1959). Identity and the life cycle. *Psychological Issues, 1*(1).

Etzioni, A. (2001). *Next: The road to the good society*. New York: Basic Books.

Friedman, L. J. (1999). *Identity's architect: A biography of Erik H. Erikson*. New York: Scribner.

Fromm, E. (1941). *Escape from freedom*. New York: Farrar & Rinehart.

Geertz, C. (1973). *The interpretation of cultures*. New York: Basic Books.

Geertz, C. (1975). On the nature of anthropological understanding. *American Scientist, 63*, 47–53.

Gergen, K. J. (1991). *The saturated self: Dilemmas of identity in contemporary life*. New York: Basic Books.

Giddens, A. (1991). *Modernity and self-identity: Self and society in the late modern age*. Stanford, CA: Stanford University Press.

Greenberg, J., Pyszczynski, T., & Solomon, S. (1986). A terror management theory of the role of the need for self-esteem in social behavior. In R. F. Baumeister (Ed.), *Public self and private self* (pp.   ). New York: Springer Verlag.

Heelas, P. L. F., & Lock, A. J. (Eds.). (1981). *Indigenous psychologies: The anthropology of the self*. New York: Academic Press.

Hermans, H. J. M. (1996). Voicing the self: From information processing to dialogical interchange. *Psychological Bulletin, 119*, 31–50.

Hermans, H. J. M., & Kempen, H. J. G. (1993). *The dialogical self: Meaning as movement*. San Diego, CA: Academic Press.

Higgins, E. T. (1996). The "self-digest": Self-knowledge serving self-regulating functions. *Journal of Personality and Social Psychology, 71*, 1062–1083.

James, W. (1890). The consciousness of self. In *Principles of psychology, Vol. l*. New York: Holt.

James, W. (1892). *Psychology: Briefer course*. New York: Holt.

Kağitçibasi, C. (1996). The autonomous-relational self: A new synthesis. *European Psychologist, 1*, 180–186.

Kitayama, S., Markus, H. R., Matsumoto, H., & Norasakkunkit, V. (1997). *Journal of Personality and Social Psychology, 72*, 1245–1267.

Kohut, H. (1971). *The analysis of self*. New York: International Universities Press.

Lakoff, G. (1987). *Women, fire, and dangerous things: What categories reveal about the mind*. Chicago: University of Chicago Press.

Lakoff, G., & Johnson, M. (1980). *Metaphors we live by*. Chicago: University of Chicago Press.

Lynd, H. M. (1958). *On shame and the search for identity*. New York: Harcourt Brace.

Markus, H. R., & Kitayama, S. (1991). Culture and the self: Implications for cognition, emotion, and motivation. *Psychological Review, 98*, 224–253.

Marsella, A. J., DeVos, G., & Hsu, F. L. K. (Eds.). (1985). *Culture and self: Asian and western perspectives*. New York: Tavistock.

McAdams, D. P. (1996). Personality, modernity, and the storied self. *Psychological Inquiry, 7*, 295–321.

Mead, G. H. (1934). *Mind, self, and society*. Chicago: University of Chicago Press.

Murphy, G. (1947). *Personality: A biosocial approach to origins and structure*. New York: Harper.

Murphy, G., & Murphy, L. B. (1931). *Experimental social psychology*. New York: Harper.

Murphy, G., Murphy, L. B., & Newcomb, T. M. (1937). *Experimental social psychology* (rev. ed.). New York: Harper.

Nisbet, R. (1980). *History of the idea of progress*. New York: Basic Books.

Onians, R. B. (1973). *The origins of European thought*. New York: Arno. (Original work published 1951)

Pipher, M. (1994). *Reviving Ophelia: Saving the selves of adolescent girls*. New York: Putnam.

Rickman, H. P. (1979). *Wilhelm Dilthey: Pioneer of the human studies*. Berkeley, CA: University of California Press.

Rogers, C. (1961). *On becoming a person*. Boston: Houghton-Mifflin.

Rogoff, B. (1990). *Apprenticeship in thinking: Cognitive development in social context*. New York: Oxford University Press.

Ross, L. (1977). The intuitive psychologist and his shortcomings: Distortions in the attribution process. In L. Berkowitz (Ed.), *Advances in experimental social psychology* (pp. 173–220). New York: Academic Press.

Rotter, J. R. (1966). Generalized expectations for internal versus external control of reinforcement. *Psychological Monographs 80* (1, Whole No. 609).

Sarbin, T. (Ed.) (1986). *Narrative psychology: The storied nature of human conduct*. New York: Praeger.

Schutz, A. (1967). *The phenomenology of the social world*. Evanston, IL: Northwestern University Press.

Sedikides, C., & Skowronski, J. J. (1997). The symbolic self in evolutionary context. *Personality and Social Psychology Review, 1*, 80–102.

Seligman, M. E. P. (1990). *Learned optimism*. New York: Knopf.

Smith, M. B. (1978a). Essay 1. In R. Fitzgerald (Ed.), *What it means to be human: Essays in philosophical anthropology, political philosophy, and social psychology* (pp. 3–24). Rushcutters Bay, New South Wales: Pergamon.

Smith, M. B. (1978b). Perspectives on selfhood. *American Psychologist, 33*, 1053–1063. [Reprinted in M. B. Smith (1991). *Values, self, and society*. New Brunswick, NJ: Transaction.]

Smith, M. B. (1980). Attitudes, values, and selfhood. In H. E. Howe & M. M. Page (Eds.), *Nebraska Symposium on Motivation 1979* (pp. 305–350). Lincoln: University of Nebraska Press. [Reprinted in M. B. Smith (1991). *Values, self, and society*. New Brunswick, NJ: Transaction.]

Smith, M. B. (1985). The metaphorical basis of selfhood. In A. J. Marsella, G. DeVos, & F. L. K. Hsu (Eds.), *Culture and self: Asian and western perspectives* (pp. 56–88). New York: Tavistock. [Reprinted in M. B. Smith. (1991). *Values, self, and society*. New Brunswick, NJ: Transaction.]

Smith, M. B. (1999). Political psychology and peace: A half century perspective. *Peace and Conflict: Journal of Peace Psychology, 5*, 1–16.

Snell, B. (1953). *The discovery of mind: The Greek origins of European thought*. Oxford: Blackwell.

Solomon, S., Greenberg, J., & Pyszczynski, T. (1991). A terror management theory of social behavior: The psychological functions of self-esteem and cultural world views. *Advances in Experimental Social Psychology, 34*, 93–159.

Sullivan, H. S. (1953). *Conceptions of modern psychiatry*. New York: Norton.

Tajfel, H. (1978). *Differentiation between social groups: Studies in the social psychology of intergroup relations*. London: Academic Press.

Taylor, C. (1989). *Sources of the self: The making of modern identity*. Cambridge, MA: Harvard University Press.

Triandis, H. C. (1989). The self and social behavior in differing cultural contexts. *Psychological Review, 96*, 506–520.

Trilling, L. (1972). *Sincerity and authenticity*. Cambridge, MA: Harvard University Press.

Turner, J. C. (1987). *Rediscovering the social group: A self-categorization theory*. Oxford: Blackwell.

Wylie, R. C. (1961). *The self-concept*. Lincoln: University of Nebraska Press.

Wylie, R. C. (1974). *The self-concept* (Vol. 1). Lincoln: University of Nebraska Press.

Wylie, R. C. (1979). *The self-concept* (Vol. 2). Lincoln: University of Nebraska Press.

Concluding Comments

Yoshihisa Kashima
University of Melbourne

Margaret Foddy
Michael J. Platow
La Trobe University

In closing, it is appropriate to provide our own self-reflection on the content of the volume. After all, concern about self and identity is, itself, a phenomenon that has arisen out of the human capacity for self-reflection. Self-reflexivity is the point of convergence for social psychology as a discipline that *investigates* as well as *provides* self-conceptions. The central question here is this: While investigating self-processes, what are the conceptions of the person provided by these theoretical perspectives? Two themes have appeared in this volume.

One theme turns on the question of unitary self versus multiple selves. This contrast emerged in the form of two different conceptions of the person that are embodied by the two general theories of the mind, the serial computer and connectionist metatheories. The former (Foddy & Kashima, chap. 1) typically postulates the central processing unit, a unitary control mechanism, whereas the latter posits multiple processing units (Humphreys & Kashima, chap. 2), the interaction among which generates cognitive processes and, possibly, an emergent unitary self.

An analogous contrast emerged among the theoretical research programs represented in this volume. Although diverse in their specific claims and contents, they generally cluster around two contrasting viewpoints. One cluster takes the presence of a unitary self as a starting point, and makes significant moves toward mending the disembodied computer metaphor by contextualizing it in a variety of directions. This move is well represented by Twenge and Baumeister's attempt (chap. 3) at humanizing and embodying the capacity to self-regulate by bringing in the "muscle" metaphor, and by the Sedikides et al. program (chap. 5) of investigating the self-evaluative process within interpersonal contexts. The other cluster centers around the view that multiple selves emerge in different social contexts; a self in this perspective is a thoroughly contextualized existence that is continuously in flux. This view is most evident in Hermans's (chap. 4) multivoiced and dialogic self, Smith-Lovin's treatment of role identities (chap. 6), and Onorato and Turner's (chap. 7) self-categorical selves.

A second theme revolves around the issue of the symbolic. The chapters in Part IV differ from the other chapters in their emphasis on symbolic processes. Although clearly acknowledging the importance of the personal and social, Kashima and Foddy (chap. 8) and Kashima (chap. 9) argue that symbolic processes involving cultural meanings make a significant difference to self-processes. They make a case for an analytical separability of the symbolic despite the intrinsic inseparability of the symbolic from the personal and social in concrete human activities. The other chapters in Parts II and III do not so much ignore the symbolic as take it for granted, assuming that personal and social processes are meaningful, but that meanings are transparent and require no further explicit theorizing. In contrast, it is interesting to point out that both metatheories of the mind, the serial computer and connectionist versions, take the symbolic very seriously indeed. In fact, they both aspire to provide a necessary and sufficient theoretical framework for explaining human symbolic processes, especially those related to language, despite the difference in conceptions of the person that they imply.

Why is the issue of the unitary self versus multiple selves such a clear point of theoretical and rnetatheoretical differentiation? Why has the question of symbolic meaning come forward as a figure against the theoretical background in research on self and identity? These questions remind us of the social condition, sometimes called "Postmodern." Although it still remains to be seen whether it deserves the label of truly *Post*modern, it is the condition brought about by industrialization and technology (especially information technology). Particularly in Western European-based cultures and societies, traditional ways of legitimizing sociocultural practices have lost much of their popular appeal. Further, instead of more traditional face-to-face interactions, computers and Internet connections have made it very easy to participate in and construct ever-changing new social relationships. This is a time of flexibility and fluidity in social contexts; as we enter into social contact with anyone in any form, there are many possibilities of expressing ourselves or relating to another person. The fluidity and ever-changing character of social context may heighten the age-old question of the unitary self versus multiple selves issue.

With the "Postmodern" social condition, and the concomitant global-ization of the social sphere, psychology has expanded its horizon dramati-cally. On the one hand, cross-cultural contacts have become a common oc-currence, and multiculturalism has gained currency in the intellectual and political discourses in most industrialized societies, and hence also in so-cial psychology. On the other hand, the weakening grasp of the traditional ways of life has led to the resurfacing of a more humanities-oriented (or *Geisteswissenschaften* as opposed to *Naturwissenschaften*) approach to psy-chology, in which the main project is to gain an interpretive understand-ing of human experiences, more so than to provide a causal explanation of psychological processes. With this, the question of *meaning* became an integral question for social psychology.

The key Postmodern assumption, that there is no single truth, does not, however, lead to the conclusion that people are anarchists with respect to meaning. Much of social psychology is concerned with processes by which people use particular versions of truth to govern themselves and others, through processes of influence, conformity, exclusion, and so on. Because of social psychology's focus on the individual, however, the net result is a view of the person who is totally free to form him- or herself. Interestingly, this stance characterizes both the "received view" of the totalitarian ego, described in chap. 1, and the more Postmodern view, represented by theo-rists such as Gergen, whose emphasis on the (social) construction of narra-tive nevertheless ignores the constraints on those narratives provided by prevailing cultural and institutional practices.

What is nonetheless most intriguing is the kind of creative tension that these points of contention have created for social psychology of self and identity. In many ways, the volume may reflect the intellectual landscape of the contemporary sociohistorical context. We watch its future develop-ment with self-reflective eyes to the future while actively participating in its construction.

Author Index

Subject Index

A

abstract individual, 3, 9, 10, 13, 21, 41

affect, 5-9, 11, 14, 68, 80, 83, 84, 88, 91, 92, 102, 107, 126, 130-139, 146, 235

affect control theory, 102, 126, 131-139

assimilation, 155, 163

autonomous agent, 9, 12, 16, 190, 200

B

binding, 31, 33, 34, 39, 43, 238

biology, 21, 201

C

capitalism, 190-193, 197
   English model of, 196, 197

Cartesian dualism, 76-78

central processing unit (CPU), 1, 5, 9, 41, 55, 56, 81, 94, 102, 103, 119, 126, 138, 145, 208, 245

cognitive representation, 79, 103, 134, 145, 147-150, 157, 162

commitment, 19, 21, 129, 137, 193, 235, 240

comparative fit, 153

complexity, 4, 18, 188, 191, 195

composite memory, 27, 28, 31, 44

connectionism, 2, chap. 2, 126, 138, 139, 215, 245, 246

consensus, 126, 133, 159, 160

contrast, 73-75, 82, 95, 149, 150, 151, 155, 168, 169, 212

creativity, 39, 41, 43, 93, 109-112, 125, 158, 184, 200

criminality, 58, 133, 135, 187

culture, 10, 12, 16, 18-20, 47, 72, 75, 76, 82, 86, 87, 96, 130, 131, 133, 134, 139, 149, 163, 179, 180, 184, 185, 195, 196, chap. 9, 233-235, 237, 238, 240, 246
   cross-cultural, 6, 10, 11, 19, 162, 163, 180, 208, 209, 213, 214, 216, 219, 223, 232-236, 247
   cultural dynamics, 180, 207, 208, 210, 211, 219, 223
   as meaning system, 208
   as meaning making process, 209

cybernetic, 4, 5, 7, 9, 13, 125, 127, 130-134, 136, 140

cyberspace, 198, 202, 204

D

decentralization, 72, 94

decontextualization, 179, 199, 203, 212-215, 217, 219, 220, 222, 223

deflections, 132, 135, 139

de-moralization, 238, 240

dialogical, 55, 71-75, 77-82, 84, 85, 86, 92, 93, 94, 95, 96, 97
   relationships, 74, 75, 78, 81, 85, 86, 92, 94

dialogue, 73-75, 78, 93-97, 127

distributed representation, 27, 28

division of labor, 188-193, 195, 197

E

ego depletion, 64, 67, 68